The Trinity Alps Companion

Hiking trails and angling tales in the California wilderness

by

Wayne F. Moss

Ecopress

Corvallis, Oregon

"Books and Art that enhance environmental awareness"
1029 NE Kirsten Place
Corvallis, OR 97330
Telephone: 1-800-326-9272
Fax: 1-541-758-5380
Email: ecopress@peak.org
World Wide Web: http://www.peak.org/~ecopress
SAN:298-1238

Library of Congress Cataloging-in-Publication Data
Moss, Wayne., 1942-
The Trinity Alps Companion : hiking trails and angling tales in the California wilderness / by Wayne F. Moss -- 1st ed.
p. cm.
includes bibliographic references and index.
ISBN 0-9639705-3-4
1. Trinity Alps Wilderness (Calif.)--Guidebooks. 2. Outdoor recreation--California--Trinity Alps Wilderness--Guidebooks.
3. Hiking--California--Trinity Alps Wilderness--Guidebooks.
4. Fishing--California--Trinity Alps Wilderness--Guidebooks.
I. Title.
F868.T58M69 1997
917.94'14--dc21 97-26472
CIP

This book was printed on 100% recycled paper with at least 20% post-consumer content. It is acid free and elemental chlorine free.

First Edition Publication Date: September, 1997

Front cover photo: Bowerman Meadow by Lucille Kibbee

Printed in the United States of America

10 9 8 7 6 5 4 3 2

The years behind have a friendly
aspect, and they are warmed by
the fires we have kindled,
and all their echoes are the
the echoes of our own voices.
-Alexander Smith

For Julie, Heidi, Wayne Jr., Keziah–
who kindled the fires.

Table of Contents

Wilderness Users' Responsibility:

Wilderness users must be responsible for their own safety and welfare by using common sense and not relying on the advice of anyone else, whether it is a friend, a guidebook writer, or Forest Service official. Weather, water, snow, road and trail conditions change over time, sometimes in only a few minutes. Also, individuals vary in their ability to follow poorly marked trails, drive rough access roads, and withstand steep climbs or heat and cold. When in doubt, always make camp or turn back.

Special Thanks:

To Chris Beatty and Ecopress for publishing books and art that enhance environmental awareness. Without his direction, encouragement, and efforts, *The Trinity Alps Companion* might never have found its way into print and into your hands.

PREFACE

It's been forty years since I first hiked in the Trinity Alps and fifteen since my first book, *The Know-It-All Guide to the Trinity Alps*. Times have changed. I've changed. The 1950s are gone and never coming back, but my experiences and much of the wilderness remain the same.

1984 brought a huge change to the Trinity Alps with the designation of the Wilderness Area and the addition of over 100,000 acres to the existing wilderness. Most of this acreage came in the form of what was once called the Salmon Scott Mountains, that area generally north of Coffee Creek. Suddenly, instead of fifty some lakes in the Alps, now there are almost 100 named lakes.

Unlike other guidebooks, *The Trinity Alps Companion* does not outline or recommend predetermined hikes. This book portrays places I've visited and adventures I've had over the years in these mountains. What you do with this information is up to you. You are responsible for planning and finding your own adventures. Life is too short to be bound to someone else's idea of where you should go.

A guidebook is not a substitute for experience and common sense, but this book will give anyone in good physical condition enough information to hike confidently in the Trinity Alps. It will give the foolhardy just enough rope to hang themselves.

People return to the wilderness for a variety of reasons. No one has all the answers. Perhaps there is some danger involved. Perhaps this is good. Risk, uncertainty, challenge and responsibility; without them, it's just a trip, not an adventure. Rarely does a year pass that someone isn't seriously injured or "buys the ranch" in the Trinity Alps. Maybe you'll be frightened at night, as not everyone can hear what the wilderness has to say. Maybe you'll find Bigfoot. Maybe you'll hear the excited voices of Chinese ghosts up on Grizzly Creek near the Moliter Mine, as several other nominally sane people have reported. Maybe you'll find solitude.

In any case, if you need wilderness, go to it soon.

–WAYNE F. MOSS
September 1997

Upper Canyon Creek View

THE TRINITY ALPS

And then he thinks he knows
the hills where his life rose.
–Matthew Arnold

An Introduction:

We all have our childhood mountains. The hills we grew up in. Our hills of home. Mine were the Trinity Alps, that tangled mass of granite, trees, water and sky secreted away in the back country of Trinity County.

As a young man growing up on the fringe of these mountains in the 1950s, I saw them as a place fraught with the stuff of legends and romance where rare and exotic life forms still held sway. In my mind, golden trout finned the icy waters by day, watched only by a spotted owl. By night, shadows whispered across the silhouette of a rare weeping spruce. The romance of my life began in the Trinity Alps, a landscape old enough, as Gary Snyder says, to give you dreams.

There was, and still is, something seductive about any place reputed to be wild and unexplored. It attracts people the way big mountains attract climbers–with a tough, terrible beauty and an awesome power. Because it is there. Imagine the appeal then, of the Trinity Alps butted up against the imagination of a fifteen-year-old kid. It was an end-of-innocence time in my life as I began the struggle to find some sense in the world around me.

I would like to go back to the world inside that boy and rekindle the curiosity he found in himself, to know as that boy knew. I want to inhale the balmy fragrance of dry pine needles in the warm sun after a summer thunderstorm.

Back then, there were mornings when I would wake in the wilderness just after daybreak and watch the light work its way down the far mountainside. The air was thick and moist, laced with the pungent raw odor of alpine plants, air being processed for the first time by any human. I felt like I was full of the wilderness, breathing it into myself.

The Trinity Alps was the nursery of my imagination. I thought the world was alive like a creature. I could put my hands on the rocks and feel a warm pulse flowing through the mountains. I read maps like a hungry man reads a menu.

When all the experiences I've accumulated in my life, the things I've learned, the places I've lived, the people I've known, the friends I've had–when these have all evaporated, what will remain is the timeless memory of this wilderness sleeping in the sweetness of infinity.

A glance at the map reveals an immense ocean of mountains and canyons sprawling over northwestern California and southern Oregon. The California portion includes much of Trinity County. A sudden cluster of peaks rise up like whitecaps near the eastern county line, marking the high point of a loosely defined area dubbed the Trinity Alps by a resort entrepreneur in the 1930s.

Long before all the arguments and discussions about what should be wilderness and what should be logged, this was de facto wilderness. The wind, clouds, and seekers of solitude have long blown into these mountains to lose themselves in a wilderness of grandeur not exceeded anywhere. Streams as old as emeralds sing beneath jagged granite peaks and knife-edged ridges. They squeeze around boulders the size of houses, glide across polished glaciated surfaces, drift through dense forests, tumble over thunderous waterfalls, and end up in lakes the color of precious gems.

So wrinkled, twisted and contorted is the landscape that it has been said that if the Trinity Alps were hammered out flat, they would cover a surface area the size of Texas.

Here is the largest uncut, diversified forest in California. The crest dividing Horse Linto, Tish Tang A Tang, and Red Cap Creek is rugged, remote and waterless, with ragged rock outcroppings just begging to be named the Devil's Backbone.

Somewhere in Red Cap Creek is a lost gold mine. Mack Jones picked up what he thought was a piece of firewood to toss on his campfire, but as he glanced at the object in his hand he was horrified. Quickly he dropped it. At his feet lay a moldy, fire-blackened human skull. Kicking leaves and moss around his campsite, he soon uncovered the charred remains of a cabin and a sooty skeleton. Another lay outstretched on the flat near the cabin site. The year was 1914. Jones realized he had found the lost gold mine, but he died from pneumonia the next year and the location of the mine was buried with him.

Horse Linto Creek? The stream slashes through beautiful hard granite that narrows frequently between light-colored stone walls, dropping over small waterfalls into quiet deep pools teeming with clouds of rainbow trout. The forest along Horse Linto has the look, feel and smell of the steep canyons in the coastal redwood areas, except here you find huge Douglas-firs instead of redwoods. The names Horse Linto and Tish Tang A Tang are the result of Anglican tongues trying to say Hupa words.

The vast, trackless portion of the Trinity Alps that borders Humboldt County, called the Green Trinities, is a verdant velvet extension of thickly carpeted valleys and twisting ridges of the Coast Range, breached by few roads and even fewer trails. This is Pre-Columbian America. The seldom seen, secretive wolverine, thought long extinct outside of the Sierras, has recently been spotted in the Green Trinities.

Untouched by time and dominated by 8,000-foot peaks, the Trinity Alps offer a topography with countless mountains, valleys, and streams that can be enjoyed for a lifetime. Comparison to the Swiss Alps is superficial at best. The common name does both a disservice. Nowhere do the peaks of the Trinities approach the size and scale of those in Europe. In fact, the actual Wilderness Area would fit nicely into one Swiss valley. However, nowhere can the Swiss Alps offer the variety of wildlife, flora, or depth of wilderness available here.

You can drive completely around the Trinity Alps in one day. Travel west from

Weaverville on Highway 299 to Willow Creek, then turn north there on Highway 96 to Hoopa, Orleans, and Somes Bar. At Somes Bar, the route turns up the Salmon River along a gut-grabbing, gear-gnashing road slung casually against vertical canyon walls where sometimes the only choices for the driver are a logging truck head-on, the river 300 feet below, or the unyielding flank of the mountain. Locals refer to it as the Salmon River Freeway. Survivors of this portion of the drive arrive in the old gold mining town of Forks of Salmon. Locally just called "Forks", it's a wide spot in the canyon to catch your breath before plunging back into the canyon of the South Fork of the Salmon River to Cecilville, where the road improves considerably as it climbs over a high mountain pass to connect with Highway 3 at Callahan. The course then is south over Scott Mountain through Coffee Creek, Trinity Center and back to Weaverville. The entire circuit occupies a leisurely drive of 10 hours. Not much of what lies hidden deep in the interior of the Alps will be revealed on such a drive, but hints of mountain mysteries can be glimpsed.

The sun shines intensely and continuously throughout the summer. Clouds are so rare as to invite comment when they do appear. Occasionally, a thunderstorm with spider-like legs of lightning will move through these mountains on short notice and leave the air tinglingly alive, the vegetation scrubbed sparkling clean.

But from November to March it rains and snows in the Trinity Alps. Up to 80 inches annually is wrung from the storm clouds that swirl in from the Gulf of Alaska. This is enough to fill the dozens of lakes that dapple the back country and overflow millions of acre-feet of water tumbling down the streams into the Klamath River via the Trinity and Salmon rivers. At least that was the case prior to construction of the Trinity Dam near Lewiston. Now nearly all of the water flowing from the Alps north of Stuart Fork ends up in the rice paddies, tomato patches and hot tubs of the Sacramento Valley.

An abundance of water and a crushing annual snowpack of 15 to 18 feet provide the moisture needed to create a delightful, fragrant garden of wild azaleas with their pungent perfume. Entire valleys are often crowded with the white and pink blossoms as hummingbirds flit about. Here also are found rhododendron, tiger lilies, columbine, red monkey-flowers, orchids, dogwood, the meat-eating pitcher plant, black raspberries, huckleberries and blackberries. The pools below falls and rapids of the streams are thickly grown with large-leafed shrubs and dainty herbs and mosses. There are poisonous plants and berries to avoid. Don't eat anything you can't readily identify. In recent years people have died from eating poisonous plants in the Trinity Alps.

William J. Feratte's *A Flora of the Trinity Alps of Northern California* lists and describes more than 300 species of plants found above the 5,000 foot elevation level. There are 20 different species of cone-bearing trees alone. One, the Brewer or weeping spruce, is found nowhere else in the world. The excellent reference book *Flowers and Trees of the Trinity Alps*, by Alice Goen Jones, has 332 color photographs of plant life in this area, and yet her book represents only a fraction of the species that can be found.

The visual explosion of wildflowers starts in February in the very lowest valleys and follows the melting snow upward week by week until reaching a stunning, but short-lived, climax of riotous colors in the snow pockets of the highest basins in August. In total, spring lasts a very long time, but above 8,000 feet the growing season is quite abbreviated.

As varied and exciting as the flora is, there is poetry in the geography. The place names evoke memories of early mining days: Jim Jam Ridge, Deadman Springs, China Peak, Bake Oven Ridge, Jake's Hunting Ground, Robbers Roost, French Creek, Hobo Gulch, Alaska Mine, Election Camp.

Election Camp? Three hundred miners working this part of the Alps planned to vote in the 1864 presidential election at Lake City, but were thwarted when warring natives burned Lake City to the ground. So here, on top of a 6,200-foot windswept ridge, votes were cast for Lincoln, McClellan or Jefferson Davis. How the vote went that day has long been forgotten, the ballots lost, but a plaque on a tree still denotes Election Camp.

It was only a few months after gold was discovered by James Marshall at Sutter's Mill in 1848 that Major Pierson B. Reading discovered the same thing on a river he mistakenly thought flowed into Trinidad Bay. He called it the Trinity River. In spite of the mistake, the name stuck and set off the nomenclature on dozens of physical features, including the Trinity Alps.

Gold miners littered even the most remote places of the Alps with ditches, flumes, cabins, dams, pipes, and machinery. Backpackers are often puzzled to find the rusting hulks of mechanical monstrosities languishing abandoned in gullies miles from the nearest road. The passing of time has long obliterated the intended function. Those who foraged for gold in the Trinity Alps were not deterred in the least by the steep, inaccessible terrain. Dreams of wealth obliterated any thought of personal discomfort or the disruption of the environment around them.

Between Emerald and Sapphire lakes the remnants of equipment and machinery offer mute testimony to the energy and ingenuity required to divert water into a 20-mile-long system of ditches, tunnels and siphons to deliver water to the La Grange Mine near Weaverville. Water from the Alps was used to wash millions of dollars' worth of gold from the hills surrounding the town. Called the La Grange Ditch, this scar is still visible as it penetrates deep into the Alps like a sinuous wounded snake at the 3,800-foot contour along Stuart Fork.

The rush for gold came and went fast in the Alps. The rush is now a gold "hush." The Dorleska, Yellow Rose of Texas, Boomer, LeRoy, Uncle Sam, Bob's Farm, Alaska, Globe and many other sites are reminders of earlier searches for El Dorado. Alice Eastwood traveled up Canyon Creek in 1899 and reported occasionally passing a lonely cabin in which some old miner lived. Eastwood thought these men were the driftwood of humanity left behind on the great tide that swept over the country in the days of '49.

Even though there is a road around the Trinity Alps, it only shows a blur of wood, water and sky. Nope, that will never do. To see the Alps you've got to get out of the car and walk.

On foot, the time warp of that ancient mode of travel magnifies the simplest of experiences into impressive perspective. After paying the price of admission, a few pounds of sweat on a steep rocky trail, the payoff is a valley full of granite peaks ablaze with a golden apricot color of alpenglow. The pungent fragrance of a pitchy fir campfire twangs the nose. The evening air has a silky feel.

Waterfalls reach perfection in the Alps. The highest one flings itself outward from the granite lip of Grizzly Lake, splattering to pieces after a freefall of 70 feet to the rocks below. In Canyon Creek there are three major falls scattered between the trailhead and the lower lake, as well as a hidden beauty just above the upper lake. In August, when the heat of the Central Valley is pushing thermometers over 110 degrees, there is no better place to be than slipping under the spray of one of the falls up Canyon Creek.

On the outlet stream from Little South Fork Lake is a waterfall seldom seen by anyone. There is no trail, and those few who are fighting the brush in search of Little South Fork Lake are so exhausted that they can hardly appreciate this hidden gem.

Beyond the highest waterfall in Canyon Creek, at the mouth of the highest and most remote section of the canyon, under the somber face of Wedding Cake and Thompson Peak, another surprise awaits: golden trout.

Long before there developed a conscience about introducing exotic species, the California Department of Fish and Game planted gold nuggets in the gin-clear headwaters of Canyon Creek. The nuggets were *Oncorhynchus aguabonita*, golden trout. Although this practice works out poorly in many areas, I can't say I'm sorry they brought goldens to the Trinities. The golden didn't displace any native fish and they add to the beauty and wonder of these mountains.

This treasure of golden fish has lain buried for several decades. The Izaak Walton Argonauts of the 1990s plot and scheme for the day when the icy blue fingers of winter finally relax their grip on the high country and purple crocus punches up through the slushy snow. Sometimes it's August before they can waft a minuscule artificial fly on cobweb-weight line over a grassy overhanging bank and watch as the water explodes in a ripping frenzy of a thousand droplets of golden, scarlet, and crimson trout.

The air is so clean and the water so clear that it seems that angler and fish are suspended in the same medium, a shared world with no barrier between. The golden trout is so beautiful that even the neophyte bait caster can be persuaded to return the fish live to the stream. In autumn, the bent meadow grass becomes strands of gold under a few gilded dwarf aspen trees pointing to where the treasure lies. The campfire, the sunset, the canyon walls, all form a background as the prospecting angler returns empty-creeled knowing the experience is worth more than the kill, the quest is worth more than the conquest.

Many people need not see a golden trout. The appreciation of the fish comes from knowing that the ambiance of the Alps is favorable for the species. If this discriminating life form can exist here, it must be wilderness.

Striving for solitude rewards the Alps rambler with a feeling of oneness with the wilderness. A person becomes part of the wilderness, not just a spectator. Make no mistake: what happens in the wilderness is authentic. The thrill of nearly stepping on a rattlesnake is a real adrenaline rush. Time spent in the Trinity Alps is not an escape from the world as much as it is a coming to terms with the world you really live in. And how you fit in it.

When night creeps into Canyon Creek and the stars seem to come down into touching range, the wilderness speaks to those willing to listen. It is not always dramatic sensory delights of scenery that fill the minds of people when lying in a sleeping bag under a twinkling sky alongside an ebony lake. A rare weeping spruce casts an opaque shadow across granite rocks etched smooth by a glacier 140 million years ago. The natives called it Crazy Creek.

The indigenous people believed that anyone living near the stream we call Canyon Creek for any length of time would become demented. They wouldn't eat the fish from this creek. An account handed down among the tribes was that of an entire native village being buried in a landslide. The moaning victims can still be heard on moonlit nights. Today, there is an occasional report of babbling voices in the darkness keeping backpackers awake. Rational backpackers (perhaps an oxymoron) theorize that such stories are merely caused by the sounds of the many waterfalls in the area. Perhaps, but the sounds of nature shouldn't have fooled the natives.

Ola Sward Peterson, who died at the age of 92, lived for many years on a mining claim on Canyon Creek with her husband, Ray. She explained the name Crazy Creek by saying that up near the Canyon Creek Lakes there has always been a recurring happening. Although no roads have ever reached up there, campers have plainly heard at midnight the rumble of wagons and the beat of horses' hooves. The lack of sleep and the baffling mystery were supposed to drive a person crazy in a short time.

Ola Peterson related a number of stories of murder and suicide along the creek in early days, many under unusual circumstances. Even now, hardly a summer passes without a tragic death, most frequently from drowning in the creek. One summer it was the senseless fatal shooting of a backpacker and the wounding of his wife by a stranger.

In 1912, Charles Wilson, owner of a candy and ice cream store in Weaverville, carried a portable fishing boat made of wood and canvas into Lower Canyon Creek Lake. A few hours later his companion found the empty boat, Charlie's hat and his fishing gear. A couple of days later his body was recovered from the bottom of the lake and taken back to town by horseback.

Ola and Ray Peterson said they had heard the slow distant ringing of a large bell on several occasions, a sound Ray felt was way out of place in the mountains. Ray had an encounter with the ghost of John Hughes, who was buried in a wooden coffin near where the Petersons built their cabin on Canyon Creek. Apparently the apparition of Hughes was just checking on things, since he never appeared again.

Ola knew personally of four buried treasures in the Canyon Creek area. One story of discovery was when Arthur Kercher, a mining engineer, hired two Chinese men to hose out an old rock-lined cellar he was renovating. When Kercher returned to check on their progress, he was told the two Chinese had left for China after finding a metal can in the cellar wall. The can was full of gold nuggets.

The suspicion that the western edge of the Trinity Alps borders on prime Bigfoot habitat in the Klamath and Six Rivers national forests does little to ease the night thoughts of light sleepers. To awake in blackness, alone, fifteen miles from the nearest road with the moon and wind playing hide-and-seek in the shadows of the pines is to test the mettle of Bigfoot believers and non-believers alike. It may be just a deer making that coughing sound. Maybe.

The last reported sighting of Bigfoot in the Alps was in 1968, when a hiker claimed that he was chased by one of the creatures. The next day a man said he saw a Bigfoot drinking from a river in the same area.

It was in 1934 that Dave Zebo, who later became aviation director for Humboldt County, was on his way to the top of Weaver Bally to spend the night in the lookout. He came across and followed a set of large, human-like tracks that cut diagonally up the mountain in a very straight line. Dave was impressed enough to take photographs of the tracks.

Not seeing Bigfoot is not proof that it does not exist. Most people have never seen a mountain lion or wolverine, species known to live in these same mountains. Anyone who has traveled cross country in the Alps without benefit of trail will testify that if Bigfoot is stomping around these mountains, he is one tough critter. It has been suggested that Bigfoots are really no more than backpackers who decided to stay on in the wilderness rather than return to a 9-to-5 job.

No mechanical vehicles are allowed in the Wilderness Area. To the dismay of some, this includes bicycles. To walk or ride a horse and leave the mechanized world behind is to enter the mountains as if they were a time machine with the controls set on reverse. The footloose backpacker can walk back to a simpler, primitive world that operates on slower, more basic rhythms. Changes require thousands of years in the mountains. It only appears to us, whose lives are just a flash in the pan, that time is standing still and that the mountains are eternal and everlasting. In reality these mountains are very young, very active, shifting, sliding, constantly changing. A phonograph record played at one revolution *per century* does not make a sound we can hear, but the music is on the record just the same. Geologic time scales, like the national debt, seem a little fantastic anyway. Who can deal with 140 million years? How many days is that? How many hours? Perhaps we need not know to find pleasure in hiking, fishing, swimming, sleeping, or just hanging out in the Alps, but it is difficult to ignore the enormous primal forces that forged this magnificent mountain range. Granite is formed when molten rock cools before it reaches the surface and is exposed to oxygen. If it had reached the surface and found the atmosphere while still a liquid, it would be lava. Things like that seem to matter when you are sleeping on the rocks.

Some geologists say the Alps were once part of the Sierra Nevada range but broke away and drifted to their present location. In a few million more years they will most likely drift off to somewhere else. I have been fortunate to have a small chunk of wilderness, albeit drifting past, right on my back doorstep.

The Fires of 1999

In August 1999, thunderstorms spawned several small fires in the New River drainage of the Trinity Alps Wilderness Area. Most quickly burned out, but two smoldered for days becoming the Megram Fire and the Onion Fire. During the next 81 days, aided by mismanaged fire suppression efforts, they grew together and charred 140,000 acres, most of the Northwest Section, pages 51 to 71, in this book.

Hundreds of miles of fire lines were carved with chainsaws and bulldozers, the forest was bombarded with thousands of pounds of toxic chemical fire retardants, and dozens of ridge tops were scrapped clean for helicopter landing pads. Needless backfires and burnouts doubled the size of the fire. Backfires started along Slide Creek, when the actual fire was miles away, swept westward over the historic mining remains of Denny, Marysville, and White Rock City.

The backfiring strategy was completely ineffective and actually exacerbated and heightened fire activity and severity by preheating and drying fuels. Ultimately, the rain and snows of autumn extinguished the fire, not the $80,000,000 spent on reckless suppression efforts.

OK. That's the bad news. The good news is the New River wilderness, no stranger to fire, is recovering very nicely. Don't avoid a trip to the New River country because of the 1999 fires. In fact, it's an excellent reason to sample the untraveled environs of the Green Trinities. Major stream courses are remarkably untouched by the fire. The flames skipped over many timbered mountainsides. Grasses, wildflowers, dogwood, tanoak, and madrone are thriving in the severely burned places. Evidence of the conifers reestablishing themselves is readily apparent. These valleys and ridges have burned many times in the past and will burn many times again in the future. Fire is a critical component in the wilderness equation.

Visitors may be surprised to find the effects of wildfire enhance rather than degrade a trip into the still very much Green Trinities. Views and vistas open where once there were none. Old mining ditches, cabin foundations, mineshafts, stamp mills, abandoned trails, and here-to-fore hidden artifacts from previous centuries are exposed. Burned hillsides and gullies reveal mining relics and machinery hidden by trees and brush for decades.

All the whiskey bottles, dishes, rusty cans, knives, spoons, picks and shovels scattered about the Old Denny Mining District are protected by the Archaeological Resources Protection Act (ARPA) of 1979. Enjoy them right where they are. Take any home and you risk a $10,000 fine and up to a year in the slammer. If caught taking home artifacts a second time and it could set you back $100,000 and up to ten years.

The upside of the ARPA is if you catch someone removing historical artifacts you can report them and collect up to a $500 reward. That would pay for your gas and trip expenses to the Alps.

Part One:

Enjoying the Trinity Alps

Trinity Alps Regions

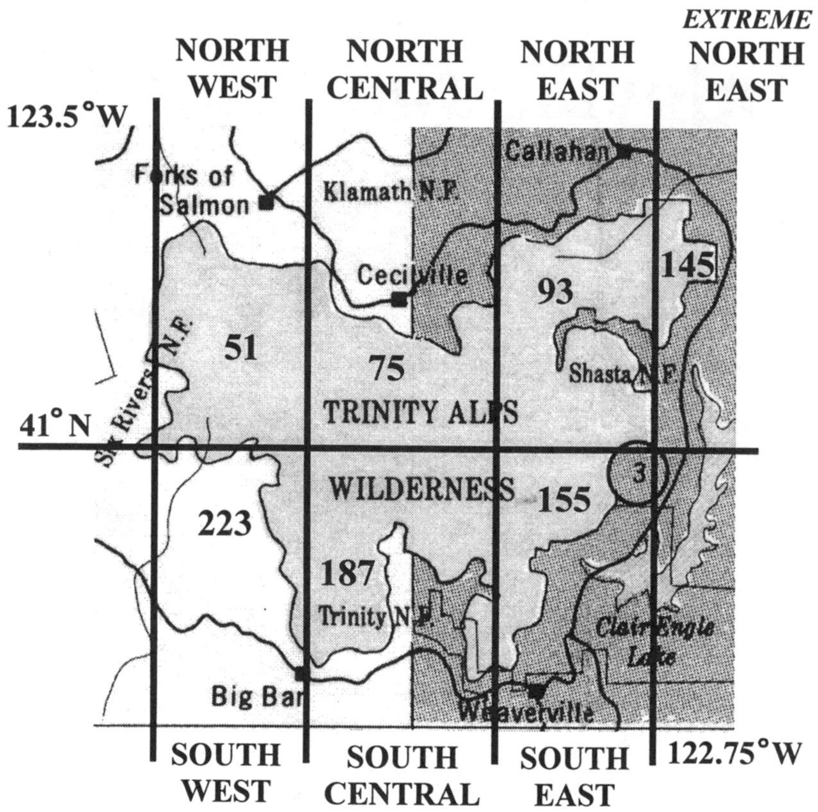

MAP PAGE NUMBER LISTED IN BOLD FOR EACH REGION

Chapter 1

FACTS AND STATS

In the mountains there is time for everything.

–anon.

The Trinity Alps Wilderness was added to the National Wilderness Preservation System on September 28, 1984. It's located in the Klamath Mountains physiographic region, which is biologically quite diverse, especially when it comes to trees. The total size of 512,005 acres includes 4,285 acres of private land, called inholdings. Elevations range from 1,360 feet, near Big Bar along the Trinity River, to 9,002 feet on the summit of Thompson Peak. It is drained by the Trinity, Scott and Salmon rivers, all of which run into the Klamath River.

There are 11 livestock grazing allotments, which allow 784 cattle to munch on more than 91,500 acres each summer. Mining is still allowed on 76 placer claims and 24 lode claims within the wilderness. The remainder of the wilderness has been withdrawn from mineral entry. Of these 100 claims, only about 25 percent are actively worked. Since the designation as a Wilderness Area, the pattern has been one of claims slowly becoming abandoned and void when claimants fail to file their annual proof of labor.

The climate of the Trinity Alps has been described as Mediterranean, in which the winters are cool, cloudy and wet, while the summers are warm, dry and sunny. At low elevations (below 3,000 feet), the precipitation occurs mostly as rain, and above 5,000 feet it falls as snow. Average annual rainfall for most areas ranges between 30 and 50 inches, although it is often more at the highest elevations. During the summer months, temperatures can reach into the 100-degree range in the lower elevations while high temperatures in the 80s are common at the higher elevations. Winter temperatures often dip below 0 °F.

The earliest known human visitors to the Trinity Alps came from the canyon of the Trinity River near Cox Bar, where projectile points have been found and dated at around 5,000 to 8,000 years old. Euro-Americans showed up in the late 1820's as fur trappers with the Hudson Bay Company. In 1848 gold was discovered near Douglas City, and the Alps quickly filled up with humankind.

It's difficult to determine how many people visit the Trinity Alps each year. The Forest Service measures human traffic in RUDs–Recreational Use Days. An RUD is recorded for each person each day they are in the wilderness. A party of 10 people spending one day would be 10 RUDs; one person staying 10 days would also be 10 RUDs.

In 1994 the Trinity Alps Wilderness had 108,400 RUDs. We also know that 90 percent traveled on foot and 10 percent on horseback. The average stay is three nights. A survey in 1991 found the average age of Alps visitors to be 39, while the average level of education was at least some college.

Central Alps from Sawtooth Ridge

For comparison of wilderness use, John Muir Wilderness had 855,000 RUDs, Ansel Adams Wilderness 542,000, Desolation Wilderness 305,000. Keep in mind that the Trinity Alps is the second largest in size of the 53 Wilderness Areas in California.

Threatened and endangered species known to be present in the Trinity Alps include the American peregrine falcon, northern spotted owl, golden eagle, northern goshawk, Pacific fisher, and the northwestern pond turtle. There are unverified reports of several other endangered species: foothill yellow-legged frog, southern torrent/steep salamander, Pacific western/Townsend's big-eared bat, spotted bat, California wolverine, Sierra Nevada red fox, Franklin's bumblebee, Siskiyou ground beetle, Trinity Alps ground beetle, and the Trinity bristle snail.

THE SEASONS OF THE ALPS

The calendar and elevation dictate the climate/weather throughout the Alps. Elevations vary from 1,300 feet, where it seldom snows, to almost 9,000 feet, where you can find snow the year around. Most of the time you will be around 6,000 feet. Summer days can be very hot, with cool nights. Sixty degree variations within a 24-hour period are common. I have seen it snow in every month in the Alps except July. Summer thunderstorms are short, but often violent. Above 5,000 feet, snow is on the ground and lakes are frozen from about November 1 to late April or early May. Some areas can be snowbound into July.

APRIL

Given some good weather, it's possible to salve your cabin fever with a trip around the fringes of the Alps and the lowest elevations. Streams are high and often dangerous and impossible to cross. Nights are still pretty nippy, but daytime temperatures can have you stripping down to shorts and short-sleeved shirts. Lakes are seldom open. Trails might be blocked by blowdown. Always bring foul-weather gear from season open through June. Some folks carry it all year.

MAY

Spring starts on the west side of the Alps and travels eastward. May is the time to visit the Green Trinities and follow the vivid redbud. Streamside hiking and camping below 5,000 feet. Some creeks and rivers are dangerous and impossible to cross.

JUNE

Most lakes up to 6,500 feet are open. Meadows are damp and boggy. Mosquitoes can be bothersome. The creeks are high and swollen with passion from winter. More than one wannabe Alpsperson has cashed in their chips and gone to that great wilderness in the sky while trying to cross a raging, frigid stream. But the waterfalls are everywhere and roaring. There is plenty of filterable drinking water from side streams along the trails lined with newly blossomed wildflowers. White dogwood and azaleas frame the still snowcapped mountains. The weather is wonderfully unpredictable. It might rain every day in June. It could snow. It could be fun.

JULY

July days are more inviting to the Alps traveler. Days are hot, nights often warm. Twilight lingers until after 9 p.m. The streams and lakes have become swimmable. There are countless days without a cloud in the sky, and wildflowers are going wild at the higher elevations. Blue and silver are your days, velvet nights allow you to touch the moon. The trails are beginning to wax dusty.

AUGUST

These are the summer days, my friend, that you think will never end. The weather is dependable. An August thunderstorm is usually a brief, zapping thing of beauty, especially if viewed from safety below timberline. Drinking water along the trails is getting scarce, but dry creek beds open up many new routes. Now you can walk watercourses, rock-hopping where the creek used to be, avoiding the trail for miles at time. The mosquitoes have all but gone. Days are hot, but the night air has a hint of autumn on its breath. Take a lesson from the leaves.

SEPTEMBER

For many people this is prime time in the Alps. The crowds have vanished. Trails and campsites are empty. A touch of color in the deciduous trees replaces the faded wildflowers of August at the high elevations. In September the wilderness is wild again. Fish are strong and ravenous. The weather remains fairly stable, but a short spell of rain is common. You might encounter deer hunters.

OCTOBER

Even during the first few weeks there are often warm, cloudless days wedged between crisp nights. You might wake up to frost on your sleeping bag. It gets dark earlier each day.

NOVEMBER TO APRIL

You're on your own in the Alps in the winter. Consult a book on snow camping and re-read the story of the Donner Party. Leave word of your where-abouts with the Forest Service or Sheriff's Department. Keep your powder dry, as any rescue attempts may take several days.

Winter travel in the Alps is still in its infancy. Not many people do it. Those folks who do are a breed unto themselves and need no advice from me.

WILDERNESS ETHICS/ NO-TRACE CAMPING

The challenge to wilderness travelers is leaving no trace. The concept is to leave no clue that you were ever there. Most wilderness abuse comes from ignorance, not premeditation.

1. Carry out all unburnable trash, including foil freeze-dried-food envelopes. Burnable items must be thoroughly burned. Aluminum foil, plastic and glass will take forever to break down into the soil. Trying to burn aluminum foil releases toxins into the soil that prevent plant growth. Take some extra trash out with you, if there is any.

2. When possible, and it usually is in the Alps, camp more than 200 feet from lake shores and streams.

3. Wash dishes in a pan away from lakes and streams and dump the wash water at least 200 feet away from the lake or stream.

4. NEVER use soap of ANY KIND to wash yourself in a lake or stream.

5. Select a little-used campsite with little or no ground cover more than 100 feet from a trail.

6. Use a backpack stove for cooking. Warming fires don't generally need a fire ring, unless there is already one there.

7. Leave standing trees standing, whether dead or alive. Gather wood that is dead and down at some distance from camp or don't build a fire at all.

8. Don't dig trenches around tents, even it says so in the Boy Scout manual.

9. For human waste, dig a hole 6 to 8 inches deep at least 200 feet from rivers, streams or lakes. Fill in the hole after use. Carefully burn toilet paper or carry it out. No one should ever know where your toilet was.

10. Camp in small groups of fewer than 8 people.

11. Never cut across switchbacks. Stay on the trail.

12. Leave dogs at home unless you are willing to clean up after them, and keep them out of the water source and away from other dogs and campsites.

13. Do not disturb historical or archeological objects. Respect the history of the wilderness and avoid a fine or jail sentence.

14. Because hikers leave less evidence of passage than horses do, travel on foot whenever possible.

15. Select the least-used area and trail, or if experienced, go cross-country. Never build rock piles to mark the trail.

SHOULD I DRINK THE WATER?

There are few pleasures of the wilderness that can beat a cool drink from a high country lake or stream. Unfortunately, that inviting sip of cold water can be hazardous to your health.

The most common problem is wild strains of the normal intestinal bacteria E. coli which is found in those areas of the Alps heavily used by humans or grazing animals. Another nasty bug you may ingest is the protozoan Giardia lamblia. The best measure to avoid both is to use a water filter. Second best is to use water purification tablets.

E. coli will hit you in a few hours with stomach pain and diarrhea (the Trinity Alps Quickstep). Giardiasis takes a little longer to make itself known. Onset of its effects can occur within several days to six weeks. You'll need professional treatment for this one. Dormant cysts can survive in lakes and streams for up to three months.

Some back-country water in the Alps is drinkable without treatment. Use your head. Freely flowing springs that lack seepage above or around their margins are often a safe bet. When in doubt, use a filter or suffer the consequences.

Packin' Light

Traveling light is more a state of mind than what goes into your pack. If the enjoyment of the outdoors, your companions, and the hike are the highest priorities on your outing, then why waste energy packing too much junk? Preserve your energy for the priority tasks, like hiking, not playing mule.

Furthering the state-of-mind philosophy, you must be willing to forgo many of the luxuries to which you are accustomed, i.e., having clean clothes, maybe hot meals , probably some of your food (most people carry too much of the wrong types of food), the wrong type of clothing, overweight equipment, and just plain luxury junk.

Pack. The pack itself is a major weight item. After many years with an external frame, I've found happiness with an internal frame pack that weighs 3½ pounds empty. Once you go light, you take less crap and need less space. Hence a smaller capacity, lighter pack. If it won't fit into the pack, don't take it. The old saying is: if you have a large pack, you will fill it up. Nature abhors a vacuum. Or an empty side pocket.

Sleeping bag. Don't fool around. Get a down bag if you can afford it. I've had the same down bag for almost 25 years. It weighs only four pounds, and with a liner it keeps me warm even when the temperature dips below freezing. If I get cold in the bag, I put on extra clothes. On summer trips with a good weather forecast, I consider not carrying a tent.

Tent. I have a cheap two-person tent that cost $39 ten years ago. It weighs about six pounds with the fly. In early or late season or with the prospect of rain, I pack it, otherwise it stays home. Only pilgrims and newlyweds feel a need for a tent in the summer Alps. A little imagination and a ground cloth will handle the unexpected shower.

Sleeping pad. Since a good night's sleep is essential in recharging your body for the upcoming hiking day, don't scrimp when it comes to a pad. I use a full-length Thermarest® LE Deluxe. "Go-light" zealots chide me about it, but they don't sleep as well as I do either.

Other Equipment. Suffice it to say, buy the lightest there is, regardless of cost. It seems that the lighter equipment is, the more it costs. However, at my age, I need all the advantages I can gain, even if I have to buy them! Sometimes my decision to buy a piece of equipment is based solely on weight. Clothing, footwear, stove, mess kit, flashlight–all purchased as light and small as I could find.

My personal checklist

*day pack or fanny pack
*rain parka
*hat
*undershirt
*running shorts
*long sleeve shirt
*hiking shorts
*down parka
*socks (3 pair)
*boots
*long pants or sweat pants
*sunglasses
*shelter
*sleeping bag
*foam pad
*pocket knife
*fork/spoon
*stove
*stove gas
*1-quart bottle (plastic)
*pot tongs
*mess kit
*sponge
*salt/pepper shaker
*matches
*paper towels
*sierra cup
*plastic water container
*maps
*towel
*50-foot nylon cord
*snakebite/first aid kit
*insect repellent
*stuff sack
*notebook/pencil
*flashlight/batteries
*personal toilet articles
*food (see discussion)
*water filter

Maybe the following:
*camera/film
*fishing gear
*reading book
*binoculars

Food. Don't take extra food. Take only what you can eat during the trip plus a day (or two at most for longer adventures). If you don't use it or eat it, don't bring it. For backpacking and climbing, you want low sugar, high carbo food (both slow and fast burning). Weigh your food. A pound per day is about right.

All food can be purchased at the supermarket, but you'll need to repackage in baggies. If you have developed a penchant for the freeze-dried foods sold at sporting goods stores, it means you are willing to pay for convenience.

In the Alps you eat what you want, when you want. Forget that three-meals-a-day, no-snacking, nonsense. Fig newtons and tea make a fine meal any time. A Grand Slam Breakfast of banana-peanut butter pancakes smothered in maple, chocolate syrup will put the lead back in your pencil. Lunch might start just after breakfast and continue into supper. Supper blends into bedtime. All meals are served one course at a time if you want them hot. Here are some of my staples:

*prepared powdered casserole-like meals
*bacon bar
*jerky
*crackers
*margarine
*candy bars/power bars
*cereals
*cheese
*nuts
*honey/jam/peanut butter
*jello
*powdered milk
*cooking oil
*instant potatoes
*puddings
*spices
*salt/pepper
*cookies
*cocoa/tea/coffee
*powdered drinks
*instant pancake mix
*tuna mix
*instant rice
*Ramen noodles

Stove. You want it lightweight and no fuss. Butane canisters are landfill fodder and it's not much trouble to carry white gas in a refillable bottle. Cooking over a campfire is a medieval mindset in today's wilderness, but some folks enjoy it for the retro feel.

Clothes. These are the other heavy items in your pack. Clothing is based strictly on whether you are usually warm or cold. If you don't use an item of clothing, eliminate it. I've spent a considerable amount of money on clothes for effective layering and light weight. Non-absorbing, wicking undergarments (such as polypropylene or Capilene®) and breathable, waterproof outerwear (like Gore-Tex®) pay back big dividends in comfort. If an item of clothing can keep you dry and warm, it's worth the money. A down coat takes little space and might even save your life sometime.

The key is to wear as little clothing as possible and still stay dry and warm. Whenever possible, I hike in shorts.

Sweatshirts with hoods and sweat pants can double for day and night wear, but beware of cotton if it might get wet. Cotton is worse than no clothes once wet and usually takes a long time to dry. I typically wear the same shirt, pants and running shorts for the duration of a trip.

If they stink, wash ‘em. Don’t carry extra clothing just so you won’t stink, because you will anyway. My exception: a couple of pair of extra socks are a luxury worth taking along.

Chapter 2

RUNNING WILD

I was born to be fast, I was born to run.

–Emmylou Harris

Running, for pleasure and sport in the mountains, like patience and common sense, came to me late in life. With the backpacking craze that swept America in the 1970s also came the jogging craze spawned by the guru of aerobics, Dr. Kenneth Cooper. It occurred to me that running would make me a stronger, fitter mountaineer and backpacker. I was in my late twenties before I ran more than a mile. Gradually I extended the length of my daily runs, and before long I found that I could find exhilaration rather than exhaustion after a five-mile jaunt.

I was hooked.

Speed has nothing to do with it. Quality has everything to do with it. Life is short. The mountains are vast. Time is relative. Experiences are individual.

Nothing is closer to the wilderness ethic than running in the Alps–running in any wilderness. No fires. Short stay. Leaving only a few tracks, and darn fewer of them than a backpacker.

Running long distances in the Alps may seem a disrespectful, even wasteful use of wilderness, there being no time to enjoy waterfalls and flowers, yet the speed of passage has value, compressing the wilderness experience; rocks, waterfalls, flowers, trees, lakes, streams, sunsets, and clouds become a unified wilderness impression. Perhaps a person comes closest to the mystical experience sought by the romantic spirit near the end of a 15-mile trail run in the Alps, the body anesthetized by fatigue, the consciousness released from the flesh, and seemingly the essence of sky, or river, or forest bombards all the senses.

There are hazards, to be sure. More than once I have had to do a mid-air twisting dance to avoid snakes suddenly appearing in the trail. Luckily, a snake is as surprised as a runner, and I find I'm well beyond striking range before the snake even realizes I'm there. I also keep in mind that far more people are killed by lightning in the United States than by rattlesnake bites. I don't spend much time worrying about getting hit by lightning, so why worry about snakebite?

A far greater hazard is sprains, especially sprains of the ankle or knee. My right ankle still has a deformed bump from an untreated sprain I suffered one afternoon deep in the Alps. I was only four miles from the car and repeatedly soaked it in a cold stream, but by the time I got home it was the size of a grapefruit and the irreparable damage had been done.

Discovering trail running is like going from horse and buggy to jet plane. Trips that used to take hours now take only minutes. What used to take days can now be covered in a few hours. There is no destination in the Alps that can't be reached and returned from in a single day if you run.

You need to be reasonably fit to savor running in the mountains. If it hurts, don't do it. Five miles per hour is a good pace where elevation gains approach 1,000 feet per mile. Drinking a lot of water is important. If you are not urinating frequently, you should increase your water intake. Carry a water bottle to tide you over the dry stretches. Some side streams are still drinkable, whereas the main watercourses are health risks from people and animal contamination.
The safe bet is to filter everything.

In a fanny pack you can carry enough food to sustain yourself for a day. Crackers, cheese, fruit, candy bars, and cookies run well. For sure, you will spend more calories than you'll consume. That's good.

Over the years, I've come to know where to go for easy runs and where to go when I need a "power run." The best runs in the Alps are those that end at a swimmable body of water and/or follow streams that invite submersion of a hot sweaty body on an August afternoon. Here are some excerpts from my running journal, illustrating a few of the myriad possibilities:

Wednesday, July 23–*at 10 a.m., Julie and Wayne Jr., let me off at the locked gate below Carter's Resort at the head of S. Fork Salmon River and I was off. In less than two hours I was at the divide between Salmon and Willow Creek. Took a side trip to look at Salmon lake, #51 on my life list of Alps lakes, and then I was down Willow Creek. But that divide between S. Fork Salmon and Willow Creek will have to go down as one of the most beautiful places in the Alps. It is a long, wide meadow that slopes up and meets the jags of Sawtooth Ridge. It is just wild, lonely, and beautiful. From this high meadow it was a long downhill run of 16 miles to where I left my truck parked at the Stuart Fork boat ramp. I stopped at Morris Meadows for a dip in the creek, and then as the day wore on and I wore down, I stopped and dipped my body in Stuart Fork several times. The stream water was cool blue in color and measured 58 degrees F. My legs were getting pretty numb by the time I got to the truck, but three cans of Pepsi awaited me. I inhaled them and it seemed to relieve the discomfort.*

Morris Meadow

Thursday, August 2–*Union Lake and Foster Lake (Bear). Union Creek is exceptionally gentle country...easy running. Before starting up last mile to Foster (Bear) Lake, take a good drink of water...no more 'til lake.*

Saturday, July 14–*Canyon Creek Boulder Lake and Forbidden Lake (first time).*

aspen trees
rare weeping spruce
two hours from car to Forbidden Lake

Tuesday, July 31–*Alpine Lake*

surface water 70 degrees F.
dirty campsites
rare weeping spruce trees
two hours five minutes from car
too steep to run last three miles before lake.

Friday, June 20–*my legs are pretty sore from running up to Granite Lake today. The azaleas were in full bloom along Swift and Granite creeks. I had the lake all to myself for a while and then worked my way up the red rocks of Seven Up Peak to Seven Up Lake. That makes lake number 50 for me; only a few more and I'll have been to every lake in the*

Alps. It was a fantastic day of sun, meadows, shaded trails and warm rocks. I wish I could do the same thing tomorrow...

Saturday, June 30–*got to Echo Lake by running up through Red Mountain Meadow, over Stonewall Pass and past Van Matre Meadow. After my visit to Echo Lake, I ran/walked over Little Stonewall Pass to Siligo Meadow and a quick visit to Summit Lake. I looked down into Deer and Diamond lakes.*

With my present running abilities, I'm able to cover ground that once took days. The day passed very rapidly, as it seemed I was constantly moving. My faith in wilderness is restored. I spent the entire day, visited four lakes, covered about 18 miles of trail and still I didn't see a single soul! Saturday–first weekend in July– and not a person did I see!

Saturday, August 4–*the hardest trip I have ever tried to make in the Alps was today–Mirror Lake via Canyon Creek. It is good running to the lower lake, then it is a scramble up to Ell lake, a bushwhacking job to the saddle, then loose, broken boulders down and over to Mirror. That is bad enough, but then I had to return over the same terrain. Mirror Lake will not be visited by many runners. I got the impression that it is not often visited by anyone. I sure love to run in Canyon Creek. Took several dips in the creek on the way back.*

Friday, August 10–*you never see any fat people running in the Alps.*

August 17–*Long Canyon to Deer Creek and out Stuart Fork to the boat ramp on Highway 3. Twenty-five miles in eight hours, of which seven were spent running/moving. What a day!*

Wednesday, July 3–*A really good hot day. I was at Canyon Creek Boulder Lake by noon. I could feel the woods heating up as I ran up the trail. The creek and falls are pretty much going full blast. It may be drought time around California, but there seems to be plenty of water in the Trinity Alps.*

I whiled away a few hours in the shade of a tree next to the lake. Jumped in and out a few times. Luckily the air was warm because the water, though not freezing numb, was pretty cool. The granite rocks were remarkably warm to lie upon. I could feel the sun starting to blister my skin, so I found some shade.

...The warm wilderness-scented air in the shaded portions of the trail is wonderful. I doubt that I'll ever get tired of the experience. Stopping by one of my favorite places, the little falls above the Lower Falls, I worked my way around on the dark, wet rocks and sat for a while, getting drenched in the misty spray from the water roaring and dashing white and dazzling in front of me.

Friday, August 17–*sometimes even this old woodsman bites off too big a chunk. Julie dropped me off at the Long Canyon Trailhead and I took off running. Seven hours later, with downright sore legs, I stopped running. It was up Long Canyon to Bee Tree Gap, Deer Lake, Summit Lake, Diamond Lake, Luella Lake, Round Lake, and then down Deer*

Creek to Morris Meadow, and eventually out to the Stuart Fork boat ramp. The hardest part, I think, was going by the dining hall at Trinity Alps Resort after six and a half hours of running. The tourists' supper smelled mighty good!

This same trip I took 21 years ago, only Bill Horstman and I spent three days doing it with packs on our backs. Now, 21 years later, I covered the same ground, alone, in eight hours total time (seven hours and fifty minutes.)

My legs feel like limp noodles after a marathon. I probably covered 25 miles today.

Wednesday July 4–*Ran for a couple of hours up North Fork. Had planned on going as far as Jorstad Cabin, but the day was warm and the creek beckoned. Excellent trail to run, as it bobs and weaves streamside, providing river views in an old-growth forest of colossal Douglas-fir.*

Tuesday, August 21–*I took a good run up Canyon Creek....It was cold, wet, in the Alps, not at all friendly. Usually when I'm in the mountains I'd like to pull the trail in behind me and stay there forever. But on a day like today I'm glad that my visit is temporary. A wilderness can be wicked and forbidding on a stormy day.*

I came upon places that hold warm day memories and find it hard to picture that it was ever real when frigid rain is beating down on the rocks while clouds rumble and gurgle overhead.

Tuesday, August 28–*Gave myself a nice workout by running to Stoddard Lake via the East Fork of Coffee Creek. Walked a couple of the steeper sections, but generally ran most of the way to Stoddard Meadow and Stoddard Cabin. Thought about zipping over to Doe Lake, but opted instead for Stoddard Lake, where I relaxed on the shoreline and made a couple of sketches of the lake with my pocket watercolor set. Returned to the truck in less than an hour, all downhill. Saw no one on the East Fork Trail. Most people come into Stoddard from the trailhead over on Ripple Creek.*

Friday, June 21–*First day of the summer of '91, astronomically speaking. Decided late in the day to mark the occasion with a run up Stuart Fork. Left the trailhead late in the afternoon and went as far as the bridge at Deep Creek. Dipped my tee shirt in the cold creek water and then wrapped it turban-like around my head and ran, hard at times, back to my truck. Passed a few backpackers who must have thought they'd stumbled onto a crazy Arab.*

SUGGESTIONS FOR ALPS RUNS

Swift Creek –Open meadows with no steep grades. Seven to eight miles each way. Cows, horses and llamas in area, so carry water or filter.

Stuart Fork–Eight miles to Morris Meadow, another five to Emerald Lake. Rolling terrain with many creek swimming opportunities along the way.

Canyon Creek–Several short, tough grades. Excellent swimming at several places above the lower falls after four miles and eight miles at Lower Canyon Creek Lake or nine miles at Canyon Creek Boulder Lake. Last mile to Canyon Creek Boulder more suited to walking than running. All downhill on return to trailhead. Carry water. Water in main canyon is suspect.

Union Creek–Six to seven miles of running with gradual increase in elevation all the way to Union Lake. Carry water or filter.

Trail Gulch and Long Gulch Lake–Two to three miles of easy running, with excellent swimming at each.

North Fork of Trinity River–From Hobo Gulch Trailhead, miles and miles of creekside running. Stream water quality is questionable.

Trans-Alps Run–Leave a car at the Stuart Fork Trailhead and shuttle to Big Flat at the end of the Coffee Creek Road. It's a relatively stiff eight-mile run to Big Caribou Lake, followed by a steep half mile to the top of Sawtooth Ridge, where the real fun begins. It's all downhill via a hundred switchbacks to Portuguese Camp on Stuart Fork and then level and downhill running to the trailhead at Bridge Camp. The twenty-five plus miles can be done in a day, and afterward you can claim to be one of the few who have run clear across the Alps. Carry water.

Pacific Crest Trail–The PCT just nicks the northern edge of the Alps for about 16 miles. The specs on this trail called for no more than a 5 percent grade anywhere on the trail. Spectacular views as the trail contours around the southern side of the Trinity/Siskiyou county line between Scott Mountain and the Cecilville/Callahan road. Along the way it flirts with several of the lakes strung like blue necklace beads on the north side of the divide, but doesn't touch any of them. Car shuttle between Scott Mountain Trailhead and the heliport parking lot on Carter Meadow Summit. Carry water.

Chapter 3

TRINITY ALPS FISHING

Angling may be said to be like the
mathematics that it can never be fully learnt.

– Izaak Walton

Piscatorial Pursuits

Hiking to experience the simple pleasures of mountain views and fresh air is probably the number one reason people come to the Trinity Alps. Catching fish is probably number two.

Interestingly, there were very few fish in the area before the 1930s. Some steelhead and resident trout thrived in the permanent creeks, but many of the lakes were barren of fish. Early settlers and now the California Department of Fish and Game have planted Eastern brook trout, rainbow trout, golden trout, and brown trout.

Can't tell what kind of fish you've caught? If your trout has white edging on its bottom fins, you've caught either a brook or a golden trout. The brookie has light, worm-like markings on a dark background, while the golden has dark spots on a lighter background. If the fins are not tipped with white, then it is a brown trout or a rainbow/steelhead. The brown trout has both dark and red spots on a body that is dark above and pale to yellow below. Rainbows have small dark spots over the body and tail and often a pinkish stripe down the body. Steelhead are genetically very similar to rainbows and are hard to distinguish, especially juvenile fish. If you catch a one of these fish in a lake, it's probably a rainbow stocked by the state. If you catch a several pound fish in one of the streams with passage to the Klamath River, it's probably a steelhead. Smaller fish in the streams may be difficult to separate, so release them and hope they come back as steelhead!

Except for the occasional steelhead, Alps trout are usually small. Most range from 8 to 12 inches and weigh under a pound. Anything bigger than 12 inches in the high country is a trophy. Other exceptions are browns and brookies that can reach 1-3 pounds in a few select lakes where fishing pressure is light and the food supply is exceptional.

Eastern brook (Salvelinus fontinalis)

Native to the Atlantic coast and a variety of char, the brook trout has been widely stocked throughout the American West. It can be recognized by dark, wormlike markings on the back, red and whitish spots on the body, and white on the leading edge of the lower fins and lower tail-fin lobe.

Brookies can reproduce in many Alps lake since they will spawn in shallow areas of lakes with underwater spring seepage. Most are less than 12 inches, but in some lakes they grow to enormous size. Fox Creek Lake has produced a number of 5 pound brookies. These voracious eaters (I've seen them attack a bare hook) are in their best condition in September and October after fattening all summer.

Rainbow trout (Oncorhynchus mykiss)

This native of Western North America requires gravel in flowing clear water to spawn, so reproduction can't occur in many of the Alps' closed lakes. However, the California Department of Fish and Game has found rainbows are well-suited to artificial propagation and every year thousands of rainbow fry are airdropped into selected Alps lakes to maintain a steady population. In streams where reproduction can occur, it is usually in the spring.

Steelhead (Oncorhynchus mykiss)

Despite their reputed wariness, many anglers have caught a steelhead and didn't even know it. Before heading out to the ocean, young fish often hang around for a few months looking just like a 6 to 14 inch bait-snatching rainbow. So, some of the rainbows caught on free-flowing Alps streams are actually juvenile downstream migrating steelhead. Catch and release is a great idea, particularly for these fish.

Once they have spent a couple of years in the ocean gorging themselves on seafood, they return a different beast. Trinity steelhead range from 3 to 14 pounds with the average about 6 pounds. Hooking one is often the easy part. Big, husky, and acrobatic, less than half of those hooked are ever landed. The saying is, "Yeah, I caught a steelhead, but I released him at 30 yards."

The Trinity Alps Wilderness Area is not a strong steelhead fishery. Most of the steelheading takes place from November to February on the main Trinity River.

Brown trout(Salmo trutta)

What kind of name is "brown" for a trout? How can it compete with "rainbow," "golden," and "steelhead?" Fact is, browns are very wily competitors in the wild and often maintain their numbers against fishing pressure better than other trout. Browns first arrived in America in 1883 via Baron Lucius von Behr of Germany. Before that, browns were being caught and written about long before the discovery of America.

This legendary member of the trout family can be found in Lower and Upper Canyon Creek Lakes, lakes in Caribou Basin, Granite Lake and Fox Creek Lake. By Alps standards these fish can grow quite large and 2 and 3 pounders have been caught. Big browns are notoriously nocturnal feeders and many are taken late in the evening or after dark.

Brown trout are fall spawners and also prefer moving water and a gravel bed to lay their eggs on. Lakes with stream inlets are a good place to look for larger browns in October.

Golden trout (Oncorhynchus aguabonita)

Nuggets of metal are not the only gold in the Trinities. The rare golden trout can be found here, too. A turn of the century zoologist, David Starr Jordan, wrote, "the most beautiful of all our western trout is the famous golden trout of Mount Whitney."

Watching a golden trout can be pure delight. One moment it blends into the amber-hued stream bottom as a camouflaged shadow in the depths. The next instant it transforms into gleaming gold and red as it turns and catches the sun–a flash of pure beauty and joy! Scientist aren't sure why these fish exhibit such remarkable colors. Perhaps it's a form of communication.

It has been called the "Fish from Heaven." Small and beautiful, distinctive and spectacular, the typical golden trout with its vibrant colors evolved over thousands of years adapting to the high country meadows of the Kern Plateau in the southern Sierras. This is the state fish of California.

Introduced to the Trinity Alps in the 1960's, they can still be found in the headwaters of Canyon Creek above Upper Lake. Only motivated anglers will ever encounter this splendid trout.

As small and rare as they are in the Alps, I can think of no reason to kill a golden trout. Catch and release this little fish from heaven.

Fighting a crowd is a rarity for Trinity Alps fishermen

Lakes

There are 93 named lakes within the Trinity Alps Wilderness Area. Almost all of them provide suitable habitat for trout.

With the geographic expansion of the Alps in 1984 came a number of name duplications for lakes. There's a Mill Creek Lake at the western edge of the wilderness, another on the eastern edge. There used to be a Mill Creek Lake in the middle, but most people call it Lois Lake now. We have Rush Creek *Lakes* and Rush Creek *Lake* in two different places. The South Fork Lakes on the north side of the Scott Mountain Divide are way different than Little South Fork Lake over by Sawtooth Ridge. There's two different Granite Lakes, and God only knows how many Boulder Lakes there are!

Understanding lake structure can pay off big time in the Alps. Sometimes fish seem to be spread all over the lake and other times they are schooled up in some hidden hole. Upon arrival at a lake, put your human brain on hold and start thinking like a trout.

Fish the inlet first. Trout, just like people, want to get the most food for the least effort. They do this by hanging out next to the food-bearing flow of water into the lake, quietly finning in the current like so many patrons at a lunch counter. They wait until something resembling food floats by, then dart out to snap it up.

With a swim mask and snorkel I've drifted face down from inlet streams into Alps lakes and been amazed by the density of fish lingering along the invisible edge where the current slacks into the stillness of the lake. When they see me coming, looking like a

170 pound caddis larvae, the trout scatter in all directions, but soon return to wait for more food to wash down.

If the inlet fails to produce, read the lake. Fish will hang below sharp underwater dropoffs, over underwater springs (look for bubbles), and in the shade of submerged logs. They often follow the morning and afternoon shade line as it moves across the water. In early morning and late evening they will move warily into the shallows to feed.

A rainstorm can actually improve lake fishing. The gray sky and rain dappled water makes it difficult for the fish see your shadow and the fish seem to know that a good rainstorm brings in a lot of new food for them.

For lake fly-fishing in the Alps, I prefer a five or six weight rod with a floating weight forward line. You don't need this much rod for the fish, but this kind of system allows for longer casts to reach out into the lake or to fight off a stiff breeze. Sinking or sinking tip lines are great, but in the spirit of packing light, I only take one line and there's no way you want to miss out on possible surface activity that is common in the mornings and evenings.

Leaders can and should be pretty light unless the lake is notorious for larger fish. Two to four pound tippets are fine.

It doesn't take a lot of flies to fish many situations successfully. On the surface, various caddis and midge imitations are a basic need. A lot of fish have been fooled with #14 elk hair caddis in these mountains. Callibaetis mayflies are also present in some waters. In the late summer, terrestrials such as grass hoppers and beetles round out the menu. Your wet fly/nymph collection should include the early life stages of the caddis, midge, and mayfly already mentioned. In addition, damsel nymphs and attractors such as buggers and zonkers will often produce. Stripping these bigger patterns over shoals in the evening can create exciting results.

Fly-fishing purists cringe at the thought of it, but a proven method of catching fish in Alps lakes is with spinning gear using a fly and bubble. Snap a bubble about 3 or 4 feet up the line from your fly and loft it out into the lake. Let it sit for awhile until things calm down from the bubble's impact and then start twitching it around like a live insect. Many a fish has been duped by this technique.

Other spinning techniques include spinners, spoons, and plugs. Lures are only effective if they are moving, but a slow spin or wobble is often best. An erratic motion will usually entice more strikes than a steady pull. Quality spinners with a few different finishes may be all you need. A selection of Mepps or Blue Fox spinners in sizes 1, 2, and 3 with silver, gold, chartreuse, and black blades are a good start. During low light or in turbid water, try flashier offerings. On a bright day, try a variety, but don't forget black.

My father was a dedicated "spoon man". He consistently hooked huge trout with a red & white Daredevil. His theory was big aggressive fish strike lures out of anger rather than looking for a meal. The only thing better than a hungry fish is an angry fish.

Fishing with plugs can be an effective method for anglers looking for trophy-sized trout. Rapalas, Flatfish and other plugs can be cast or trolled from a float tube. Use sizes that are one to three inches in patterns such as frog, trout fry, silver and gold. Try a variety of depths and retrieves. Typically, a few less fish are caught, but the size will be larger. Fishing early and late is especially important with this method.

Streams

All the water, whether it be from rainfall, snowmelt, or streams, that flow from the Trinity Alps eventually ends up in the Klamath River. Well, actually, it used to. Now, ninety-five percent of the Trinity River is shunted through the Clear Creek Tunnel, near Lewiston, to the Sacramento River.

At Weitchpec, the Trinity River dumps in all the water it has gathered from a wide arching sweep around the south and east sides of the wilderness. The South Fork of the Salmon shares duty with the Scott River in draining the north-flowing streams. These three rivers all empty into the Klamath. Red Cap Creek on the western edge of the wilderness has a direct connection to the Big K.

There are two streams within the Wilderness Area designated as Wild and Scenic Rivers: New River, and the North Fork of the Trinity River. The purpose of this designation is to preserve the river in a free-flowing condition; to maintain the quality of the water; to protect the river and its environment for the benefit and enjoyment of future generations. Actually, all the streams that flow within the wilderness enjoy the same protection.

Approximately 4.7 miles of New River and 12.7 miles of the North Fork of the Trinity within the wilderness are classified as wild river. Both of these streams are home to summer steelhead.

The streams of the Trinity Alps are not blue-ribbon trout waters. Big fish are not typically found in these waters. If you catch a trout of more than 12 inches in these wilderness waters, it's something of a trophy. There are exceptions; the North Fork of the Trinity and the South Fork of the Salmon both have summer steelhead seasonally. Several particularly remote and/or fertile lakes also produce some large trout.

Stream fishing in the Alps is a little different from the lakes. The biggest is that you have to keep moving to cover a lot of water. Some call it fish hunting, since much of your time is spent looking for fish rather than casting.

Value-added benefits of stream fishing include wading up to your crotch in icy water, face swatting overhanging branches, snot-slick rocks, tangled lines in brush thickets, and usually small fish, to name a few. Some people just can't stay away from the sound of the babbling brook.

Stream trout eat much of the same stuff as their lake buddies, but they do it a little differently. The stream trout does not have to move around much to feed. The flow of the stream supplies a constant piscatorial smorgasbord. Read the hydraulics. Where will the flow carry your offering? How does that rock midstream affect the flow? What's the depth? The speed? The trout underwater is constantly monitoring these things in anticipation of grabbing a quick bite to eat. Stream trout spend most of their lives holding in quiet water next to a steady current. This holding water can be under an overhanging bank, behind rocks, or below submerged logs and roots.

It wasn't until I spent some time floating downstream with a swim mask and snorkel that I understood where fish hang out in relation to the water flow. Watching fish in their wild habitat can be as enjoyable as catching them. Obviously, the fish are all facing upstream from whence comes dinner. This means you should work your way and cast upstream as you go. This accomplishes two things: 1) fish are less likely so see you coming, and 2) your bait offering will drift naturally with the current like real trout food does.

To figure out what the trout might be interested in, watch the bushes near the creek. Look for hatching mayflies, caddisflies, or stoneflies. You can also pick up a few rocks from the streambed and look at the nymphs on the bottom. This will probably tip you off on the bug du jour.

Don't throw your fly or lure directly into the holding water. Flip it upstream and let the current naturally carry it down to where the trout await. Luckily stream trout have learned to grab food quickly as it passes without a lot of hesitation. You have to be ready to give a quick tug to set the hook because you'll only get the one chance.

Lures are tough to work directly upstream, unless the current is slow. It can be done as long as you can crank it in faster than the stream flow. A better way is to work from the sides, casting slightly upstream and across, then retrieve as the lure drifts downstream. Often fish will hold at the tail of a pool just where the water begins to pick up speed. Casting downstream, you can toss a lure into the smooth part at the tail of the pool and slowly bring it up against the current into the pool. You won't have to reel in very quickly because water motion will keep the lure dancing.

To fish a stream you have to keep moving, upstream if possible. After a few casts into good-looking holding water, be looking for the next hideout. Moving smoothly and quietly is essential as stream trout are easily spooked. They can hear the rocks you clank together, see your shadow, even see you against the sky. Spook a stream trout and it'll go into hiding for hours. Many Alps streams have to be waded right up the middle. On a meadow stream you may have to crawl on hands and knees to avoid detection.

Casting from an almost prone position can be challenging, but may be necessary.

The conditions found on Trinity Alps streams are such that I prefer a three weight fly rod that is fairly short. The fly collection does not change a whole lot, but add a few stonefly nymphs and egg patterns to the box. Spinning gear should be ultralight. Two to four pound test on a four and a half to six foot rod will give you opportunity for great sport with a minimum amount of distraction from the surrounding foliage.

Other notes and gear

Ultralight and portable is key to Alps fishing gear. Your rod needs to either break down to fit into your backpack or you will constantly be untangling yourself from the brush. Well, at least that's my experience! Reels are a matter of personal preference. Transparent back country water demands the lightest lines and leaders possible. Two-pound test is common, four-pound test is maximum.

All of your fishing supplies can fit into a small nylon bag if you take what you need, not what you might you need. Here are a few other items that are useful:

Polarized glasses are critical for spotting fish and structure, especially in streams.

One package of split shot for distance and getting deep in lakes.

Take a dozen snap swivels, as small as possible. Advised for using lures and to attach a bubble when using spinning gear.

Spin fishermen should take three or four bubbles of various sizes. You can heave a fly a long ways out into a lake with a large bubble.

A hemostat or narrow-nose pliers for unhooking fish.

Nippers for trimming line and knots.

Extra line: Take a spool of 2 or 4 pound test. Sometimes you'll get in such a mess that it is easier to replace the line rather than spend the rest of your life untangling a mass of curls and knots. Extra leaders and tippet for fly-fishing.

Flotation: While some anglers pack in inflatable rafts to cover the larger lakes, a more practical solution is a float tube.

Insect repellent and sunscreen if you aren't camping or don't have it in your other gear.

License: Not likely you'll see a game warden in the Alps, but you still need a license. It's worth the cost. The money goes to a good cause, the management of fish and game all over California, including maintaining the trout in the Trinity Alps. It's the price of admission to hours and hours of entertainment. A real bargain. Don't leave home without a fishing license.

Fishing regulations are complicated and change annually, sometimes more often. Always check with the California Fish and Game or a local sporting goods store about what's legal and what's not in Alps waters. Bradys Sport Shop (916) 623-3121 on Main Street in Weaverville is a reliable source for fishing information and regulations.

Fishing Calendar

May is about the earliest fishing begins in the Alps. The lower elevation lakes, those below 6,000 feet, are beginning to melt and swell the streams. Fish can be taken with flashy spinners in the streams and from open water as lakes unfreeze. The lake fish are often not in good condition from the long winter. Sometimes you'll think you've caught an eel, but it's a brookie or rainbow with a big head and a skinny little body.

By late June or early July, almost all lakes are ice free and the browns and brookies are on a feeding frenzy making up for lost meals during the long winter. Fly-fishing can be exceptional during this time. Trout cruise the shallows looking for an easy meal, including trout fry or fingerlings. Evenings and mornings seem to precipitate hatches which bring fish up to feed.

Late July and August can be a little slow on Alps lakes as the water warms and the fish go deep to cool off. To reach them, you may have to sink your offering deep. Evenings and early mornings can yield fish in shallow areas as they cruise for insects.

When crimson and gold splashes the maple and dogwood covered hillsides, the best fishing conditions to the Alps arrive, September and October. The crowds have gone, the days warm, the nights crisp, and the fish fat from a summer of feasting. This time of year you'll probably catch fewer fish, but they'll be larger, the survivors of another fishing season. Remember, many of the dumb fish have already been caught. The biggest and smartest brookies and browns are all that remain in the high mountain lakes after mid-September. If you release everything you catch, the fish will be even bigger next year.

Catch and Release

One of the significant redeeming values of fishing is the fact that you don't have to kill to enjoy the sport. The challenge, the pursuit, the beauty of where trout live can all be experienced without killing a living creature. Trout are too precious to kill without forethought and far too valuable to waste if you do kill them.

An angler should keep only an occasional fish to eat and return the rest unharmed. To release fish successfully, don't fish with live bait. You don't need it to catch fish and it tends to get swallowed, which seriously reduces the possibility of a live release. Crushing or filing the barbs off your hooks goes a long way in preventing damage to fish intended to be released. Single, barbless hooks make it possible to release a fish without removing it from the water. Slide your fingers down the line to the hook and quickly slip it out.

Handle fish as little as possible. The thin mucus-like covering on fish protects them from fungus and other aquatic diseases. Excessive and careless handling leaves them vulnerable to disease. If you do take the fish from the water, minimize the trauma by gently placing it back, head upstream to get water flowing through the gills. Tired fish should not be released until it can keep itself upright and swim without wobbling. Grip the wrist of its tail and cradle the belly, moving it back and forth to stimulate gill action. When it's ready, it will swim forcefully out of your hands.

PART TWO:

Regions of the Trinity Alps

Trinity Alps Regions

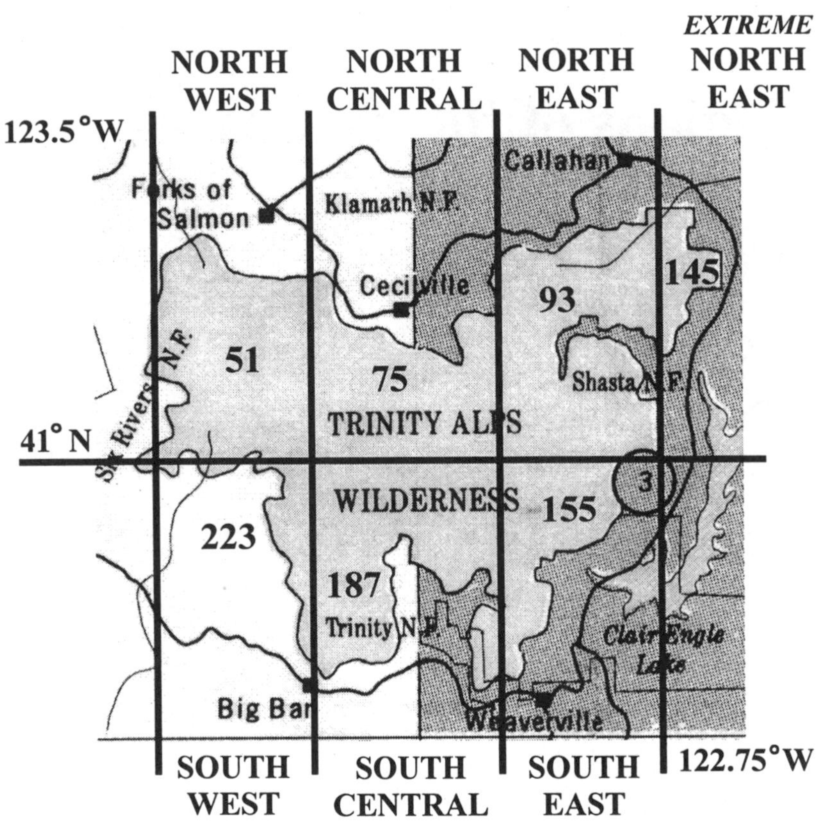

MAP PAGE NUMBER LISTED IN BOLD FOR EACH REGION

Organization of this guide

The Trinity Alps are a half million acres of wilderness. That's a lot to grasp. The strategy is to divide it up into more fathomable pieces. In this guide, we have chosen six regions (well, actually seven including the extreme northeast region). An organic entity such as this does not lend itself well to straight lines, but trying to shape the book to the landscape would make for some rather odd-sized pages! In any case, our seven regions are divided into north and south by the forty-first parallel (41 degrees north latitude). Along an east-west traverse, the regions are divided into quarter degree increments corresponding to the quadrangles of the U.S. Geological Survey. Use the "page-finder" feature in the lower right-hand corner to navigate between maps.

Northwest- From the western boundary of the wilderness at approximately 123.5 degrees west longitude to just west of the Limestone Ridge (123.25 degrees). This region includes the Red Cap and New River drainages, part of the Salmon Mountains ridgeline, and the Devil's Backbone.

North Central- The Salmon ridgeline continues into this zone which also covers the headwaters of Grizzly Creek and the Salmon River. Limestone Ridge is a prominent north-south feature. Thompson Peak, the highest mountain in the Alps, is near the border with the South Central region.

Northeast- Much of the Salmon Mountains (added to the wilderness in 1984) are in this region. Most of the Coffee Creek drainage is here along with portions of the headwaters of adjacent creeks. This region has the most lakes, including the many "Boulder" lakes (Middle Boulder, East Boulder, etc.).

Extreme Northeast-As with any man-made, arbitrary lines, they don't fit the landscape perfectly. This area "fell off" our nice grid, but includes some popular features in the Tangle Blue and Eagle Creek drainages.

Southeast-This area includes the popular Stuart Fork and Swift Creek trailheads. This is the quarter degree square bounded by 41 degrees latitude on the north and 123 degrees longitude on the west.

South Central- The North Fork of the Trinity River and Canyon Creek are enclosed by this region. Limestone Ridge and the Thurston Peaks dominate the western edge of the area.

Southwest- Much of this area is outside of the wilderness boundary, but several trailheads including Devil's Canyon, Waldorff Ranch, and Jim Jam Ridge are included. Big French Creek is primarily in this area.

Features such as lakes, peaks, streams and trails are listed alphabetically within a section. A pair of maps at the front of each section will help you understand the area. The left-hand map is a surface map which has a three dimensional feel that is more intuitive than conventional topographic maps. The right-hand map shows the detailed features useful for hiking in the Wilderness Area.

In addition to the maps included here, you may want to stop by and pick up a Forest Service map of the Shasta-Trinity National Forest along with your *required* wilderness permit. The wilderness permit is free. The map costs $5.

Truthfully, the very best map of the Alps is a gigantic 1930s relief map hanging on the wall in the lobby of the Weaverville Ranger Station. Check it out. A similar map in the Forest Supervisor's Office in Yreka is worth a visit, too.

Scott River Ranger District
11263 N. Hwy. 3
Ft. Jones, CA 96032
(916) 468-5351

Salmon River Ranger District
P.O. Box 280
Etna, CA 96027
(916) 467-5757

Big Bar Ranger District
Star Rt.1, Box 10
Big Bar, CA 96010
(916) 623-6106

Weaverville Ranger District
P.O. Box T
Weaverville, CA 96093
(916) 623-2121

Lower Trinity Ranger District
P.O. Box 668
Willow Creek, CA 95573
(916) 629-2118

Orleans Ranger District
Drawer B
Orleans, CA 95556
(916) 627-3291

This chapter describes how to get to each of the campgrounds and trailheads in each section, as well as the peaks, lakes, creeks, and other features of interest. Don't overlook the possibility of finding a stream crossing or side canyon and plunging off into the wilderness and following it to its physical limit, assuming it is within your physical limits. There are numerous opportunities for freelance exploration, sans trail and trailhead, in the Trinity Alps.

With the addition of the Salmon Scott area lakes in 1984, some confusion of names is possible. The original namers of geographical features in both the Alps and the Salmon Scott Mountains were not overflowing with originality. Their repertoire ran from "Deer" to "Bear" with a few variations now and then, and a "North Fork" or "South Fork" thrown in for good measure. What we have now in the Trinity Alps are several Boulder, Rush Creek, Bear, South Fork, Granite, and Twin lakes. Everywhere there is a dearth of imaginative nomenclature. Instead, we get such features as the East Fork of the North Fork, West Branch of the South Fork, and the East Branch of the East Fork of the North Fork of (insert the name of any stream here).

Difficulty of trails in the descriptions below is based on the following criteria:

EASY: less than 7 miles round trip, less than 1,000 feet elevation gain, no cross-country travel. Sometimes called a cakewalk. Example: Long Gulch Lake.

MODERATE: 7-10 miles round trip, 1,000- 2,000 feet elevation gain, no cross-country. Sometimes called enjoyable. Example: Lower Canyon Creek Lake.

DIFFICULT: 10-12 miles round trip, up to 4,000 feet elevation gain, some cross-country required. Sometimes called challenging. Example: Lake Anna.

STRENUOUS: Over 12 miles round trip, over 4,000 feet elevation, cross-country with treacherous footing, dangerous terrain, and route-finding problems. Sometimes called a gut-buster. Example: Smith Lake.

Notes on Trinity Alps Peaks

Standing on a Trinity Alps summit is as close to flying as you can get without leaving the ground. Your eyes soar like a bird for miles in all directions over razorback ridges and velvet valleys covering a landscape impossible to ever walk upon. The shadows of clouds pour across the hillsides, flowing like flat silken ships over the tops of distant peaks, and then disappear; ghosts from days gone by. Witness a mountaintop sunrise or a sunset and you'll never again question why people climb mountains.

A 7,000-foot mountain is a big mountain in the Trinity Alps. An 8,000-foot peak is major. Only one, Thompson Peak, exceeds 9,000 feet, but only by a mere two feet. Any of the peaks can be climbed in one day from the trailhead, although some require a very long day. A bona fide peak bagger will establish a base camp in the midst of many peaks and then knock them off over a period of days. There are opportunities to bag two or more summits in a single day.

Safety is critical on any back country expedition, especially climbing. Always leave your plan with someone you trust and don't climb alone. While most of the Trinity Alps have a non-technical route, don't assume that you are on it! Training , experience, and your own judgment are the tools to count on. If you think the route you are on requires more technique or equipment than you have, you are probably right. Don't go beyond your limits.

What follows is a description of the *named* peaks within the Wilderness Area. There are many unnamed peaks of equal stature, both esthetically and geologically, deserving attention by peak baggers. Some of these unnamed mountains have picked up unofficial names from whimsical mapmakers over the years: Mount Daisy, Mount Caesar, Trinity Journal Mountain, King Mo Peak, Matterhorn, and Mount Izaak, to name a few.

One naming problem I haven't been able to resolve is the two Deadman Peaks. Same name on two different peaks about two miles apart. I climbed what I thought was Deadman Peak above Trail Gulch only to find out later that the real Deadman Peak may be the one above Poison Lake to the west. Just to be sure, I climbed that one too. And old forest ranger told me that if it felt like I was on the real Deadman Peak, then I was.

The naming of geological features is an enigmatic endeavor flowing from the hands of the cartographer to the final judgment of common usage.

What makes a name *official* or *unofficial* is tied to the cartographic source. Over the years a number of maps of the Trinity Alps have been produced by several different sources, any of which could be quoted as *official.* You have maps from the United States Forest Service, the United States Geological Survey, the California Department of Mines and Minerals, and the California Department of Fish and Game, along with a couple of private mapmaking companies. There's no disagreement over the names of the major peaks and mountains, but on each map you'll find a couple of names attached to previously unnamed summits.

Some peak baggers like to play arithmetic games. Common is the challenge to climb all of the sixty-some-odd peaks in the U.S. over 14,000 feet. Another is to climb the highest point in every state, or the highest point in every county in the state of your choice (which is not much of a challenge if your choice is Florida). There was a time when I set out to climb every peak in the Alps over 7,000 feet. It turned out there were a lot that fell into that category, plus I got tangled up in the name/no-name dilemma.

I then decided to climb every peak over 8,000 feet. This made the number of candidates to be climbed much smaller, but there was still the dilemma of what to do about the unnamed peaks. In the end I decided mountain climbing is not arithmetic and that each mountain, named or unnamed, is a worthy challenge on its own terms.

There are many beautiful peaks in the Trinity Alps waiting to be named, waiting to be climbed.

Chapter Four

NORTHWESTERN ALPS

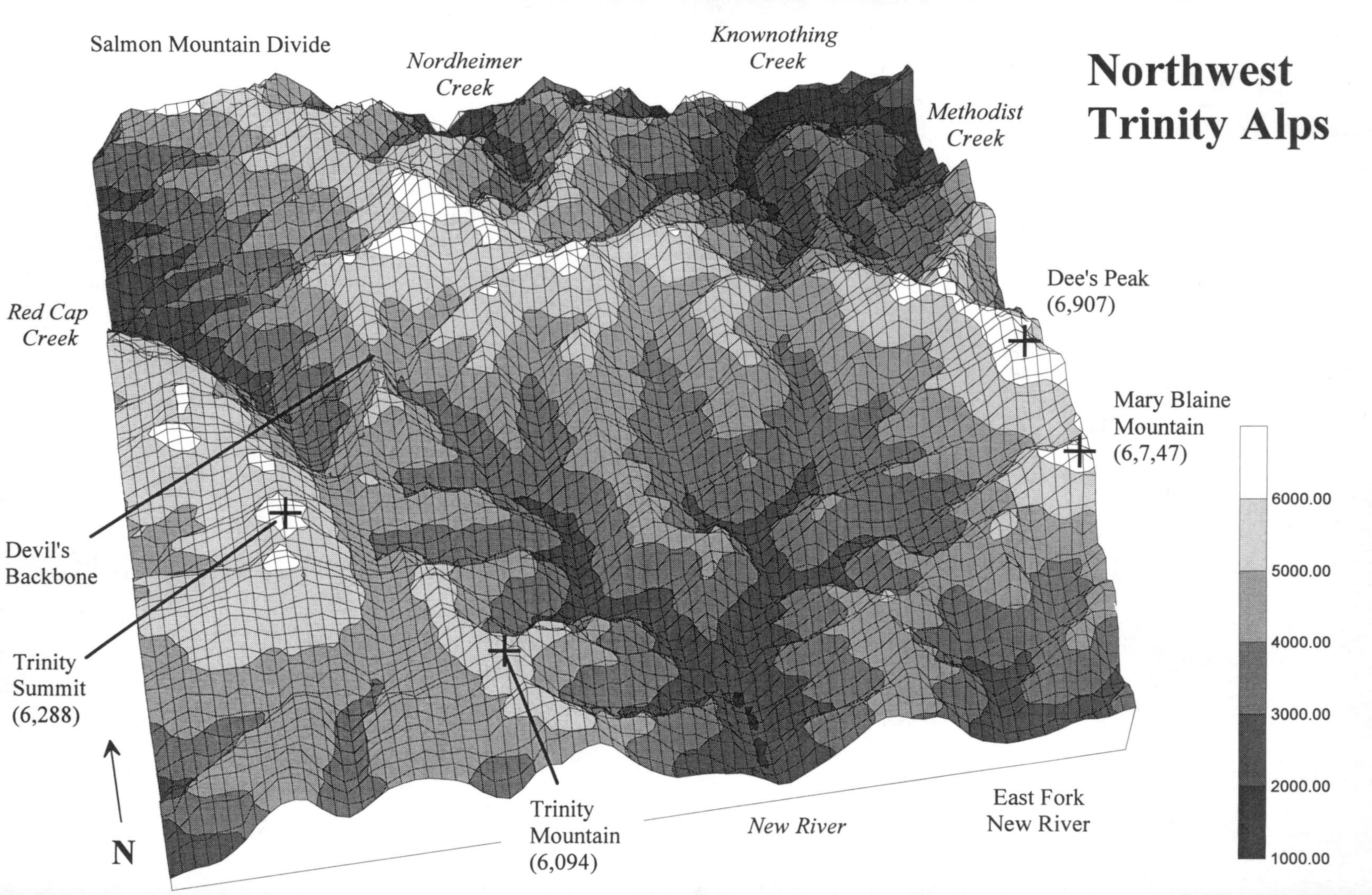

Northwest Trinity Alps
Salmon Mountain Divide
Nordheimer Creek
Knownothing Creek
Methodist Creek
Red Cap Creek
Dee's Peak (6,907)
Mary Blaine Mountain (6,7,47)
Devil's Backbone
Trinity Summit (6,288)
Trinity Mountain (6,094)
New River
East Fork New River
N
6000.00
5000.00
4000.00
3000.00
2000.00
1000.00

Northwest Trinity Alps

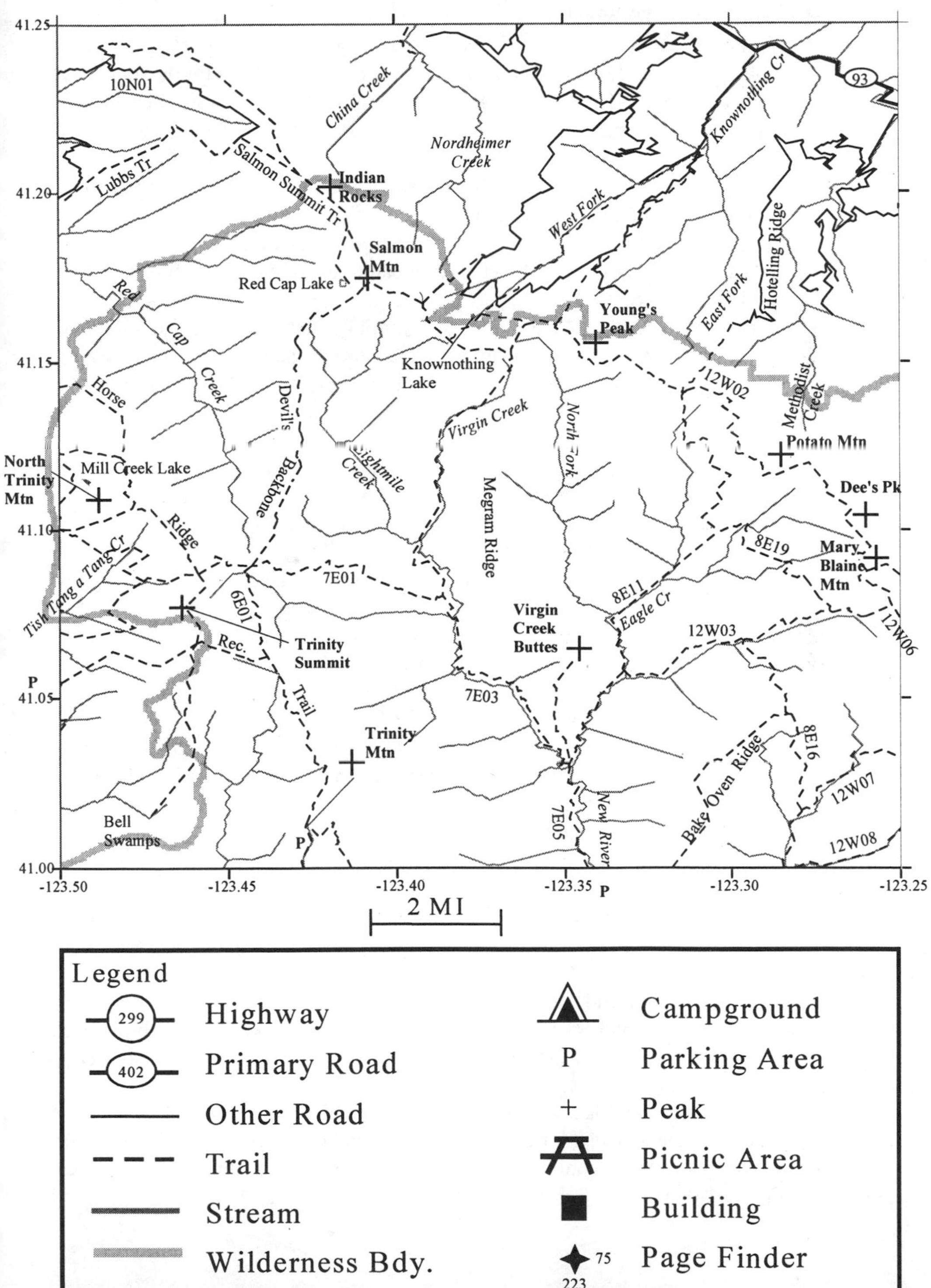

BEAR HOLE TRAILHEAD

Access: From Hoopa on Highway 96, take Big Hill Road and stay with what looks like the major road at all intersections for 8 miles. Watch for the sometimes unsigned Road 8N15. Six miles farther on 8N15, at a four-way intersection, go right two more miles to the trailhead at road's end. Campsites and corral at trailhead.

Trails: Trail 6E16 joins 6E74 at Crogan Hole and Trinity Summit via Horse Ridge National Recreation Trail (6E08).

Destinations: Trinity Summit, Devil's Backbone, Crogan Hole.

Elevation/Difficulty: 4,700 feet at trailhead to 6,288 on Trinity Summit. Easy to Moderate hiking.

Summary: Nice day hiking to Trinity Summit through meadows and tall timber to old Forest Service cabin on top. Superb panorama view of the high Alps to the east. Best in springtime before the summer cows and fall hunters arrive.

BLACKS LAKE

Elevation 5,200 feet; 1.5 acres; 7 feet deep. Can be found on the west side of Horse Trail Ridge and Red Cap Prairie in the Red Cap Creek drainage. Eastern brook trout and possibly rainbow trout present. **Tish Tang A Tang, Horse Trail Ridge Recreation Trail, or Grizzly Camp Trailhead.**

The Yurok tribe, when traveling in unfamiliar mountains, would find two pine knots, readily available from decaying trees. Placing the two ends together, tip to tip, they would set them afire. While they burned, the Yuroks would tell the spirits of the unfamiliar mountains that they brought no harm and didn't want any trouble.

Not a bad idea, but be careful not to start a forest fire if you try it.

Finding Blacks Lake will test your route-finding and navigation skills. Don't even try to find this lake unless you know what you are doing. It's a good two hours of steady walking from the Horse Trail Ridge Recreation Trail Trailhead to the point on Red Cap Prairie where you can begin looking for the way *down* to the lake. Resist the temptation to start down too soon. Miss the lake and you run the risk of being lost and/or trapped in the one of the most rugged and inaccessible canyons in the Alps. The Red Cap drainage is nothing to trifle with.

Stay on the trail (old jeep road) going south through the prairie until it starts to drop in elevation. Check the eastern horizon and see if you can see the far high Alps in the distance. Then find the bare ridge that heads off down into Red Cap Creek. This is your ticket to Blacks Lake. Descend the ridge and keep an eye to the left for an icy cold spring (you'll want that on the way back up) and an open hollow. The lake is down through the trees and brush below the hollow. Big Eastern brook trout have been reported, as well as "nice-sized" rainbows.

Most people day-hike to Blacks Lake. It would probably would get just too lonesome there to spend the night. Besides, who wants to lug a sleeping bag and stuff that far downhill only to pack it uphill later? There are a zillion good camping spots in Red Cap Prairie nearby.

DEES PEAK

(6,907 feet) Plummer Creek Trailhead. New River Trailhead. Dees Peak appears to be the twin sister of nearby Mary Blaine Mountain. The nearest parking is at the Plummer Creek Trailhead on the South Fork of the Salmon, but most people prefer the longer route (and I do mean longer) from either New River or East Fork New River trailheads.

It's nearly 5,000 vertical feet in seven miles if you use the Plummer Creek route.

About the same vertical-mile elevation gain from the New River trailheads, but stretched out over fourteen to seventeen miles, depending on which way you choose, makes for less work. Plus there's fishing streams and old mining towns to help pass the long miles.

DEVIL'S BACKBONE TRAILHEAD see Tish Tang A Tang Trailhead

HORSE LINTO CREEK

Grizzly Camp Trailhead and Tish Tang A Tang Trailhead. Here, on the left-hand side of the Trinity Alps, is found a landscape dramatically dissimilar from any in the Wilderness Area. The ridgetops are wide, flat, gentle plateaus, while streams trench steep canyons resembling a coastal rain forest. Horse Linto Creek is the feature stream although very little of it is actually within the Wilderness Area.

The intriguing name comes from a Hoopa village once located on the Trinity River at the creek's mouth. Euro-Americans had trouble pronouncing the Hupa word. Has-Lintah or As-Lin-Ta or Xaslindin or Haslinding or Hoss Linten–take your pick. It was the mapmakers who worked it into Horse Linto. The Yuroks called it Yati.

Trails flirt with the headwaters of Horse Linto Creek, but none follow the stream bed. Off-trail opportunities abound.

Grizzly Camp is on the East Fork of Horse Linto Creek. Surrounded by massive trees, both Douglas-fir and white fir, it's the place to begin exploring this terra incognita of the Alps. The trail contours along the west side of the divide and just nips the top of Horse Linto Creek near Lipps Camp. Look for several different species of orchids in early summer. The section of Horse Linto Creek flowing south and then west from here is trailess and uncharted. Explore at your own risk if you go downstream.

Staying on the trail from Lipps Camp will take you along the Soldier Creek/Horse Linto Divide to an exquisite meadow, lush and inviting, with incense cedar trees and glacier-polished boulders, an idyllic setting called Devil's Hole. Just a mile over the ridge is another "hole," Bret Hole, larger and perhaps even more beautiful than Devil's Hole. And beyond Bret Hole is yet another called Crogan Hole on yet another branch of Tish Tang A Tang Creek.

The trail south from Devil's Hole follows a dead-end plateau-like ridge between two branches of Horse Linto Creek into a maze of meadows and streams guarded by magnificent incense cedars, called Bell Swamps. There are campsites galore.

For the physically and mentally prepared, this is the place to drop in to Horse Linto Creek and enjoy a genuine wilderness waterway sans trail. Late in the summer you'll think you're in a coastal rain forest among Douglas-firs the size of redwoods, fern-lined nooks, and banana slugs. A downstream scramble offers waterfalls falling into cool green pools teeming with trout, deep watery pockets for swimming, and eventually sandy beaches and driftwood fires. Throw a few sticks on the fire, lean back against a rock and identify the species from the essence of the smoke. It might be Pacific yew, Douglas-fir, western hemlock, cedar, or alder.

Make no mistake about it, this kind of beauty exacts a price. It is difficult. At times the stream bed narrows, forcing a climb up and around or a neck-deep swim in order to proceed. Once committed to Horse Linto Creek, there is no easy way out on either side of the canyon. Travel in Horse Linto Creek is serious business, but abundantly rewarding.

HORSE MOUNTAIN TRAILHEAD

Access: Drive 7 miles east of the town Forks of Salmon on the Salmon River Freeway. Cross the South Fork of Salmon River on road 39N34, which goes up Methodist Creek. Go left up Johnson Creek, left again and then right to road's end.

Trails: Trail 12W26, if you can find it, climbs steeply up the north ridge of Horse Mountain a mile or so before cutting around the east side. Eventually meets the Salmon Summit trail near Potato Mountain.

Destinations: Headwaters of Plummer Creek, Potato Mountain, Upper New River historic mining district, Mary Blaine Mountain.

Elevation/Difficulty: 3,600 feet at trailhead to 6,600 feet on Salmon Divide. Difficult and strenuous.

Summary: Difficult to find trailhead. Trail may be overgrown from lack of use and/or maintenance. Incomparable wilderness in the West Fork of Plummer Creek.

HORSE TRAIL RIDGE RECREATION TRAIL TRAILHEAD

Access: From Hoopa on Highway 96, take Big Hill Road to 10N02 for a total of 20 miles. From Orleans on Highway 96 take Red Cap Road (Forest Road 10) six miles, right on 10N02 to Mill Creek Gap, continuing to trailhead another 10 miles. Watch for sign. Large flat for camping and horse corral across road from trail start.

Trails: Horse Ridge National Recreation Trail 6E08 begins here and passes through Red Cap Prairie on the Horse Trail Ridge to Trinity Summit Station and eventually to Grizzly Camp Trailhead and other destinations.

Destinations: Red Cap Prairie, Blacks Lake, Lost Lake, Mill Creek Lakes, Water Dog Lakes, North Trinity Mountain, Trinity Summit, Devil's Backbone.

Elevations/Difficulty: 4,800 feet at trailhead to 6,362 on North Trinity Summit. Easy to moderate trails depending on how far you go.

Summary: Car shuttle possible for through hiking of Red Cap Prairie, Horse Ridge National Recreation Trail and surrounding ridge top.

GRANITE GULCH TRAILHEAD

Access: On the Salmon River Freeway 1.5 miles upstream from Forks of Salmon, watch for a road up Knownothing Creek. Drive two miles to the forks of Knownothing Creek and road's end.

Trails: Trail 8E09 jumps on the long north ridge of Bowerman Peak and follows it almost to the summit before cutting around and up into Slate Gap on the Salmon Divide.

Destinations: Salmon Divide and points east and west from there or down into Virgin Creek.

Elevation/Difficulty: 1,800 feet at trailhead to 6,000 feet at the divide. Very difficult and strenuous.

Summary: Interesting mines along the trail early on, but soon turns into a steep climb with no water. There are easier ways to get on the Salmon Divide.

GRIZZLY CAMP TRAILHEAD

Access: Take the Denny Road north from Highway 299 at Hawkins Bar, left after 7 miles on 7N26 to 8N02, then right on 8N02 14.5 miles to a locked gate, a bombproof, wheelchair-accessible pit toilet, and trailhead at wilderness boundary. Road is paved except for last five miles. Three campsites at trailhead. Note: some road signs are spelled "Grizzley."

Trails: The trail, the southern terminus of the Horse Trail Ridge National Scenic Trail (6E08), is a actually a road for several miles, wandering around the headwaters of Horse Linto Creek to the divide at Lipps Camp and junction with trails to Trinity Summit and Devil's Backbone. Short, steep, brushy spur trail leads to summit of Trinity Mountain.

Destinations: Trinity Mountain, Trinity Summit, Devil's Hole and Devil's Backbone.

Elevation/Difficulty: 4,400 feet at trailhead to 6,000 feet on Trinity Mountain. Moderate to difficult, depending how far you go.

Summary: Seldom-used trail offering access to ridgetop adventures in remote old growth forest.

INDIAN ROCKS

Salmon Mountain Trailhead. Standing like Easter Island sentinels, these rock formations are just inside the wilderness boundary on the Salmon Mountain Trail. Whiteys Peak and Salmon Mountain are sacred places with ancient spiritual significance for tribes in the area. The Karuks found Indian Rocks to be a power point for enhancing their hunting prowess. The semi-circles of rocks stacked all over the ground date back many years, as many generations of hunters considered it good luck to set a rock in place.

KNOWNOTHING LAKE

Elevation 5,200 feet; 1 acre; 5 feet deep. **Knownothing Trailhead.**

An idyllic meadow with a pond is called Knownothing Lake. This is a good place to test your route-finding skills, whether you come by trail or cross-country. First you have to get to the town of Forks of Salmon, no easy task even in the 1990s. Just south of town, take USFS Road 10N04 and follow it for about eight miles past High Point. Keep on going past the sign that says *Mullens Camp* another three miles to a point south of Bowerman Peak. Now you can start looking for the trail. It doesn't matter if you don't find the trail. It's less than a mile to the divide, and only about 500 feet of elevation gain through big timber. Once on the divide you'll have no trouble finding the Salmon Summit Trail which runs roughly east and west along the northern spine of the Trinity Alps for 30 miles. You will want to head west until you come to what's left of the Summit Mine. Somewhere around here there is a faint trail going down to Knownothing Lake, if you can find it.

If you are not up to plunging down into the canyon to look for the lake, stay on the trail until you hit the trail coming up out of Virgin Creek. Climbing up through another little pass, the trail then drops down into swimmable Rock Lake. Now you can follow the drainage a little farther down and find Knownothing Lake.

Described above is about a four-mile hike. Trust your route-finding abilities and you might want to watch for the outlet stream on the road between the *Mullens Camp* sign and Bowerman Peak. Make certain the stream you pick is the West Fork of Knownothing Creek and strike out upstream. The lake is less than a mile away. This is big timber country with few visual clues. You may miss the lake and end up on the Salmon Divide. If you come to the trail on the divide, obviously you've gone too far and will have to readjust your direction accordingly.

KNOWNOTHING LAKE TRAILHEAD

Access: Find road 10N04 just south (upstream) from the town of Forks of Salmon. There are many forks, but the main road is obvious to High Point. Turn up road 10N07 for a mile to the wilderness boundary. **Nordheimer Flat Campground** is five miles downstream.

Trails: Trail 08E11 starts out as an old jeep road and soon reaches the Salmon Divide Trail (12W02).

Destinations: Knownothing Lake, Rock Lake, Salmon Mountain, Summit Mine, Youngs Peak

Elevation/Difficulty: 4,800 feet. Moderate to ridge top, moderate with difficult stretches afterward.

Summary: Quickest route to get on the Salmon Summit which is pretty low-key compared to the high peaks in the eastern Alps, but gives access to some delightful, quiet, wooded wilderness niches.

LOST LAKE

Elevation 5,800 feet; 1 acre; 5 feet deep. Located on the east side of Horse Trail Ridge on a tributary of Red Cap Creek. No fish. **Bear Hole, Red Cap or Mill Creek Lake Trailhead.**

So you want to be alone. You could spend the summer here and collect a dollar from every person who showed up and you wouldn't make gas money. The Western section of the Alps receives very little human traffic, and Lost Lake even less.

Trying to find Blacks Lake is a good warmup for this one. Along the Horse Trail Ridge Trail through Red Cap Prairie, find your way south from the open meadow (prairie) to a low, timbered gap between the headwaters of Domingo Creek and the gully containing Lost Lake. Use your map and your head. It's steep, brushy, frustrating, and challenging to say the least. It's one of those challenges you'll take on while camped in Red Cap Prairie: to while away a day just so you can say you found Lost Lake.

There's yet another unnamed lake south of Lost Lake on another branch of Red Cap Creek; it's a little easier to find because the country is more open and there's better visibility. Spend a night there and you are entitled to name it whatever you like.

MARY BLAINE MOUNTAIN

(6,747 feet) New River Trailhead or Plummer Creek Trailhead. Nearby Dees Peak's twin sister. The closest trailhead is almost a vertical mile below and seven miles away at Plummer Creek on the South Fork of the Salmon River. Most traffic (using the term "traffic" very loosely) comes from the longer but less strenuous trails up the New River drainages.

Mary Blaine Meadow on the southwest side of the mountain is the lush green pasture that can be seen from miles around. The Mary Blaine Mine was located in 1884 near the summit.

The meadows and mountain are surrounded by deep evergreen forest and resplendent with ravishing wildflowers. There's a cold spring at the top of the meadow and a fenced stock area in the middle.

Who was this Mary Blaine? She operated a saloon and stopping place about 100 yards below the meadow. A prostitute, well regarded and respected by the miners for her kindness and willingness to listen, she often gave money and merchandise to those whose luck was bad. It is not known where she came from or where she went, but she remains a legend, the madam with a heart of gold, in Trinity County history.

During the last years of the 19th century, when new discoveries of gold resulted in the establishment of three mining communities near Mary Blaine Mountain, this area provided summer pasture for the many saddle and pack animals. Today there's plenty of pasture for everyone.

MILL CREEK LAKES

Elevation 5,200 feet; 2.5 acres; 12 feet deep. Small lake on the north side of North Trinity Mountain. **Mill Creek Trailhead.**

The Green Trinities are not known for mountain lakes. This westernmost lake of the Alps is a surprise to find. North Trinity Mountain crouches behind the cool green of the lake forming a dark granite headwall surrounded by Brewer spruce, noble fir, and the low Kalmia bush resplendent with pink flowers in springtime. The shoreline is mostly brush, making it difficult to fish from shore. Bring flotation devices.

The name should be singular, Mill Creek Lake. There's really only one lake. Maybe there's some ponds in the thick brush nearby, but the effort to find them would not be worth the effort.

It's an easy walk of a couple of miles from the trailhead on an old logging road. The turnoff to the lake is easy to miss, so pay attention. Use is light and fishing for rainbows can be good at times.

MILL CREEK LAKE TRAILHEAD

Access: From Hoopa on Highway 96, take Big Hill Road (8N01) 16 miles to 10N02, then 8N10 to locked gate at wilderness boundary. From Orleans take Red Cap Road (Forest Road 10), right on 10N02 past Mill Creek Gap to 8N10. **Box Camp Campground** two miles away.

Trails: Trail quickly forks three ways: left on 6E14 to Mill Creek Lakes, right on 6E74 to Crogan Hole and Trinity Summit via Horse Ridge National Recreation Trail (6E08), and straight ahead (no trail#) up and around the south side of North Trinity Mountain to Water Dog Lakes.

Destinations: North Trinity Mountain, Water Dog Lakes, Mill Creek Lakes, Crogan Hole, Trinity Summit Station, Devil's Backbone.

Elevation/Difficulty: 5,100 feet at trailhead to 6,362 feet on North Trinity Mountain. Moderate hiking, but trails sometimes faint and unmarked.

Summary: Car shuttle possible for through hiking of Horse Ridge National Recreation Trail and small lakes along ridge crest. Several easy loop hikes available. Closest approach to southern end of Devil's Backbone.

NEW RIVER

New River Trailhead. A river as beguiling and splendid as this deserves a better name, but New River it is. A major tributary of the Trinity, it drains the vast western portion of the Alps known as the Green Trinities. By 1851 mining operations were spreading up the river. By 1855 it's estimated that 300 Europeans, Anglo-Americans and Chinese were mining on New River. Interest in mining dwindled for a few years, but location of rich gold deposits fired things back up again in the 1880s. Several towns sprang up: White Rock City, Marysville, Denny (now referred to as Old Denny), Lake City, and Francis. This brought stores, saloons, post offices, hotels, sawmills, and stamp mills into the tributary canyons of New River.

Today, travelers in the New River country will stumble across the rusting, rotting remnants of the buildings and machinery once assembled to extract gold from the wilderness. There are only a couple of miles of New River within the actual Wilderness Area. Two miles from the New River Trailhead, the New River splits into Virgin Creek and Slide Creek. Seventeen miles from the trailhead puts you in the heart of the upper New River mining area.

Although this country was mined as early as the 1850s, gold deposits discovered between 1882 and 1884 really got things hopping. By the time the dust cleared and everyone went home in the 1920s, 4,000 ounces of gold and 1,500 ounces of silver had been found and shipped of to the rest of the world. The riches flowed from mines named Boomer, Hunter, Toughnut, Hardtack, Sherwood, Uncle Sam, Lucky Strike, Ridgeway, Mary Blaine, Cinnabar, and Gun Barrel.

Old Denny or New River City was the first of three rival townsites established, the other two being White Rock City and Marysville. In 1890 New River City was renamed Denny to honor A.H. Denny, a prominent businessman the miners liked. For a few years the post office used both names. In 1920, Frank Ladd closed up the New River City store and hotel and moved everything downriver 20 miles to a place then called Quimby. He set up a store and hotel, renaming the place Denny.

New River City is slowly sinking back into the ground and vegetation of the wilderness. Pieces of metal, broken glass, wood stoves, timbers, nails, foundation rocks, parts of machinery mark the site.

A short distance from the New River City site is what remains of Marysville. Here Peter Larcine, a Frenchman from Humboldt County, built a hotel in 1883. The town was named after his only daughter, who died at age eighteen. There are still a few scattered boards and bits of pottery where the hotel once stood.

A half mile north of Marysville was White Rock City. It had a post office from 1885 to 1896, but by 1904 it was all over and was abandoned. It was actually bigger than Old Denny for a while, boasting many Chinese residents. Considerable evidence of the place still remains, including a cemetery to the south of the site.

NEW RIVER TRAILHEAD

Access: Take Denny Road north from Highway 299 at Hawkins Bar, 19 miles to town of Denny. Continue another 4 miles, then left on 7N15 for 6 miles to the trailhead.

Trails: The trail (7E05) works its way down to New River, clinging to the steep side slope to Virgin Creek, forking into the Slide Creek Trail and the Virgin Creek Trail at 2.9 miles.

Destinations: This is the gateway to the historic Denny mining district. Old town sites and abandoned mining machinery galore can be found up the Slide Creek Trail (12W03). This 10.1 mile trail follows the creek to the junction with the Eagle Creek Trail, crosses Eagle Creek and continues past Robbers Roost Mine, Emmons Cabin, the Old Denny site, and into Mary Blaine Meadow. The Virgin Creek Trail (7E03) follows Virgin Creek northward, occasionally climbing high bluffs to avoid cliffs, past the Soldier Creek Junction and Jumbo Mine, and makes a steep finish at the Salmon Summit Trail. Total miles 13.2. The Eagle Creek Trail (8E11) crosses Eagle Creek several times for 4.9 miles, where it forks right to the Battle Creek Trail and left to Salmon Divide Trail. Battle Creek Trail (8E19) winds for 8.2 miles through Marysville and Old Denny town site. Soldier Creek Trail (7E01) is a steep 4.0 miles from Virgin Creek to the Devil's Backbone offering dramatic views of deep forests and distant peaks.

Elevation/Difficulty: 2,200 feet at trailhead. Trails in the canyons are easy to moderate, but become difficult when they leave the canyon and climb up to the 6,000-foot ridgetops.

Summary: One of the best places to visit historic mining ruins and enjoy cool river canyon camps with fishing opportunities. Low-use area, offering solitude in high doses.

NORDHEIMER LAKE

Elevation 5,550 feet; .75 acres; 6 feet deep. Small pond at the headwaters of Nordheimer Creek. **Salmon Summit Trailhead.**

Talk about close. A slip of the survey's pencil and Nordheimer Lake would have not been included in the Alps. Just over the divide and the county line, with Indian Rocks towering in the background, is this tiny frog pond with the distinguished German name. It's a short cross-country, but a cliffy and dangerous drop down from the Salmon Summit National Scenic Trail of less than half a mile if you care to visit. I talked to a man who told me he once killed a 158-pound deer "down on Nordheimer," as he put it, and he spent six hours packing the dead animal back up to the trail.

Or, from Forks of Salmon there is a long, often indistinct, nine-mile trail up Nordheimer Creek. Either way, Nordheimer Lake is a stretch of the definition for lake.

NORDHEIMER LAKE TRAILHEAD

Access: 13 miles from Somes Bar on the Salmon River Freeway. **Nordheimer Flat Campground** is where you take road 10N10 to trailhead at end of road.

Trails: Trail 7E18 follows creek 3.5 miles where it climbs up a small ridge, where it becomes trail 7E18A and eventually returns to the creek bottom and climbs steadily and steeply to Nordheimer Lake 9miles from the trailhead. Trail 7E16 goes all the way to 6,192-foot Orleans Mountain Lookout, which is not in the Trinity Alps.

Destination: Nordheimer Lake.

Elevation/Difficulty: 1,800 feet at trailhead to 5,500 feet at the lake.Strenuous due to distance and elevation gain.

Summary: Long and scenic route to a minor lake. Much closer and easier to hit Nordheimer from the Salmon Summit Trailhead.

NORTH TRINITY MOUNTAIN

(6,362 feet) Mill Creek Lake Trailhead This is the highest point south of the Devil's Backbone, but it's really a granitic hump surrounded by deep green valleys and the largest ancient forest of Brewer spruce and Noble fir south of the Klamath River. Views are limited by large trees that grow all the way to the summit.

The easiest approach is from the Mill Creek Trailhead en route to Water Dog Lakes. About 50 minutes of steady climbing through dense forest and angled meadows brings you to the open divide where the trail descends to Water Dog Lakes. Instead of descending, stroll northward to the summit. It's only a few hundred vertical feet from the divide.

A campsite at the upper Water Dog Lake faces the granite slabs and boulders of North Trinity Mountain and might entice you to spend a couple of hours boulder-hopping to the top.

PONY BUTTES

(6,606 feet) Plummer Creek or East Fork New River trailheads. Butte is not a geographic term we find commonly used in the Alps.

Butte (būt), n. [French, *but*, mound behind targets] A conspicuous isolated hill or mountain rising abruptly with sloping sides and a flat top.

Pony Buttes fit the description. Rising abruptly south of the Salmon Divide and Mary Blaine Mountain, we have a pair of flattened, six-thousand- foot mounds right smack dab in the middle of the Alps.

The most reasonable approach to these remote summits is from the East Fork of New River Trailhead, called Pony Buttes Trailhead on some maps. It's 10 miles up the East Fork and then Pony Creek to Pony Lake at the base of the south butte. A shorter, steeper way would be from up Plummer Creek on the South Fork of the Salmon. If you happened to be camped in the Mary Blaine Mountain/Meadow area, there is a faint trail, no longer maintained, to the Boomer Mine and then up over the top of the south Butte. The only drawback is the elevation you have to lose and then gain getting to the Boomer Mine.

The highest point is the southernmost butte. The northernmost one is called "Stud" on some maps. In between are three other distinct points nearly equal in height. It's brush free, so you can move with ease from one point to another, spending a day romping about the buttes. There's water and campsites just to the north at Election Gap/Camp.

Election Camp? See the introduction to this book.

PONY LAKE

Elevation 5,495 feet; 1 acre; 7 feet deep. Small fishless pond on a tributary of the East Fork of New River at the base of Pony Buttes. **East Fork of New River Trailhead.**

It's usually said that there are no lakes in the Alps of the vast New River drainage. Almost true, but not yet. In a few more hundred years, Pony Lake will become a meadow, as many alpine lakes eventually do. Until then, yes, there is a lake in this immense mountainous wilderness. Lonely and small, this pond half a mile off the Pony Creek/ Election Gap trail two miles from the Salmon Divide Trail awaits its fate.

Lacking an outlet stream much of the year, it will test your route-finding skills. The point where you need to leave the trail is in heavy timber. The visual clue is the stream crossing about three-quarters of a mile below Mullane Corral. (Mullane Corral is a sign on a tree locating where there once was Mullane Corral). The stream you cross *is not* the Pony Lake outlet stream. Follow it and you'll end up on top of one of the Pony Buttes. What you want to do is start up the stream, but very soon start working your way to the left (west) toward the mountain you can see through the trees. The land levels somewhat, and soon enough you'll break into the small meadow partly wrapped around the lake.

There is a fire ring, evidence that at least a hunter or two each year casts his lot with Pony Lake.

POTATO MOUNTAIN

(6,708 feet) Plummer Creek Trailhead, Hotelling Ridge Trailhead, Horse Mountain or New River Trailhead. The very few people who knock off this remote summit do so while traveling the Salmon Summit Trail. Potato Mountain is one of several humps along the county line. Superb views down wild and remote Plummer Creek and out across the South Fork of the Salmon River. That's the Cecilville/Callahan Road you can see hugging the river bottom a vertical mile below.

The Salmon Summit Trail is reportedly almost overgrown in places from disuse. A couple of men in the summer of 1991 were riding east on the trail and only got as far as Potato Mountain before the brush became so thick it knocked them off their horses. They turned back.

RED CAP CREEK

Salmon Summit or Red Cap Trailhead. This is the major stream draining the western side of the high and dry Devil's Backbone. It's been logged, mined, and burned by forest fires, but still remains a very wild waterway. There are no trails. Either you are going to fight your way downstream from Devil's Backbone or take off upstream from the road 10N02 crossing. Only the upper third of the canyon is actually inside the wilderness boundary, but all of it might as well be.

Devil's Backbone is as rough as a dragon's spine. Sun-blasted rock is sparsely shaded by scattered manzanita brush and digger pine. The slopes fall sharply into the steep boulder-strewn canyon of Red Cap Creek. The perfect setting for a lost gold mine.

The Devil's Backbone was an important link between the Salmon River and Trinity River mines in the 1880s. The pack trains that plied the trail along the ridge not only transported supplies for the mines; they also functioned as perambulating general stores.

The packmaster of the mule train crossing the Devil's Backbone on a summer day in the early 1880s was not surprised when two old sourdoughs appeared and wanted to shop for some groceries. The men were pretty haggard-looking. Reports say one of them had fiery red whiskers and the other "resembled a bear looking out of a brush patch."

The size of the miner's poke was a jolt. "The heft of those bags made a man's arm ache" was the report in a Somes Bar saloon over at the mouth of the Salmon River. In succeeding months the men reappeared periodically to meet the pack train. They always displayed plenty of gold to pay for their supplies. A few fruitless attempts were made to follow them.

"Them boys just seemed to disappear," one old-timer recalled nearly fifty years later. "They split up a whole mule load of supplies into two packs, slip them onto their shoulders and fade off down into the Red Cap side of the Backbone. They never traced them more than a couple of hundred yards."

There came a day when the two sourdoughs failed to meet the pack train. The gold-laden miners never appeared again. During the 1890s people around Willow Creek noticed that an native with no obvious means of support was gradually becoming wealthy. Each fall, he and his wife vanished into the Red Cap Creek country for two or three weeks. When they returned, they had enough gold nuggets and dust to last the rest of the year.

For years a Willow Creek merchant tried to buy the directions to the secret bonanza from the native. Finally, in his old age, he agreed to tell in return for a herd of horses and some land. On the day he was going to lead the merchant to the mine, the man swung up into his saddle, his horse spooked at something and bucked him off. He was impaled on a picket fence.

His wife, horrified and frightened speechless by the accident, evidently felt a punishment had been visited upon her husband for attempting to reveal the secret of the mine. She clamped her mouth shut and carried the secret to her grave.

It remained a secret until Mack Jones showed up in the summer of 1914 and camped on Red Cap Creek. He found the bones of the two miners, evidence that the mine had been worked after their deaths, and plenty of gold. Winter snows forced him out of the mountains and down to Blue Lake for the winter.

In January 1915, Jones caught pneumonia. In the hospital, his two sons listened as he gasped and wheezed directions to the gold mine. They spent five summers after their father's death combing the ridges and valleys. No luck. The location of the mine was buried with Mack Jones.

It's still there. A good place to start looking would be along Red Cap Creek and its tributaries west of Devil's Backbone.

RED CAP LAKE

Elevation 5,200 feet, 3 acres, 12 feet deep. It's a fairly easy 4-mile hike from the trailhead, the last mile downhill to the lake. Eastern brook trout allegedly present. **Salmon Summit Trailhead.**

There's Red Cap Creek, Red Cap Mine, Red Cap Prairie. Makes sense to have a Red Cap Lake. The name has nothing to do with a porter in a railway station. It's a result of an 1854 California law which made it illegal for white people to trade or sell guns to the natives. It also prohibited natives from possessing guns. Near Orleans some miners took the law into their own hands and enforced the law, killing two natives in the process.

One group of natives, Karok men, organized their own army, known as Red Caps. The Red Caps took to the high mountains around Orleans and worried white settlers for awhile. Eventually things escalated in the Red Cap War of 1855, which had puttered along for years. Lake City in the New River country was burned by natives during this time. Once the hostilities were settled, the Hoopa Indian Reservation was established in 1864.

Lonesome is probably the best word to describe Red Cap Lake. A rock- slide tumbles down to the lake like a broken petrified waterfall. Intense green meadows splattered with wildflowers, verdant hillsides, somber cliffs ring the lake. Black bears and deer are typically the only companions available to those who venture into this region of the Alps.

You can have your pick of campsites any time of year, except maybe during deer hunting season, and stay as long as you can stand the silence.

The lake is a bit mucky for swimming, but there are rumors that large Eastern brook trout find it an agreeable place to swim.

RED CAP PRAIRIE

Horse Trail Ridge Recreation Trail Trailhead. Trail 8E06 climbs steadily until it finds an old logging road and follows it to the ridgetop an hour away. Along the way, somewhere in the middle of Section 29, some maps have marked "Red Cap Tree." I've never known which tree was so designated, but I have a nominee. Just before the trail breaks out of the tall timber there is a mammoth Douglas-fir that once had a three-spiked top. The main spike broke off a couple of years ago and partly blocks the trail. I like to think this may have been the Red Cap Tree.

Many people are not prepared for what an old-growth forest looks like. Douglas-fir and cedar achieve stunning size in the Western Alps. Thick of trunk, soaring to the sky like columns in a Gothic cathedral, they give a sense of timelessness not possible in so-called managed forests. Old-growth forests harbor a palpable silence.

Many people are surprised to find miles of open meadow on top of a mountain. The trail (actually an old jeep road) undulates along the broad ridgetop through open country, with long distant vistas in all directions. Bears seem to especially love this meadow highland.

RED CAP TRAILHEAD (see Horse Ridge Recreation Trail Trailhead)

ROCK LAKE

Elevation 6,250 feet; 2 acres; 6 feet deep. **Knownothing Trailhead.**

Looking for a private place to take a swim? A place where you will not see another human being? Look no farther. This little round lake, just inside the wilderness boundary, is tucked up in a two-acre stone cup near the top of the Salmon Divide, waiting for visitors who seldom come.

Those who do come find their way to the top of the Salmon Divide from the Knownothing Trailhead and follow the roller-coaster ridgetop south, often through myriad wildflowers, to the lake. Those who stay have a secluded camp on the shady side of the Alps where an evening stroll to the ridgetop might be rewarded with a westerly view of endless dark mountains sinking into a dazzling golden-pink sunset. The topography, with the right combination of fog and lighting, is reminiscent of East Asian landscape painting.

SALMON MOUNTAIN

(6,957 feet) Salmon Summit or Knownothing Lake Trailhead. This could have been called Tri-County Mountain, since the Humboldt, Siskiyou, and Trinity County boundary lines intersect on its summit, the highest point in Humboldt County. You can stand in three counties at the same time.

In the 19th century this summit touched four counties: Humboldt, Siskiyou, Trinity, and the now defunct Klamath met here. It was a custom back then for all men who passed by to stand and, in a sweeping 360-degree turn, urinate in all four counties.

Easily climbed now that roads have been pushed in from logging on all sides, Salmon Mountain gives some fine views of the upper left-hand corner of the Alps. On a clear day you can see west to the Pacific, northeast to the Marble Mountains, and south along the Devil's Backbone. The interesting gray rock formation to the north, standing like sentinels, is called Indian Rocks and marks the edge of the Trinity Alps Wilderness on the Salmon Mountain Divide.

It's a long trip from anywhere in the world to the town of Forks of Salmon and another eight miles from there to where you can start looking for the trail. But then it's a relatively short hike to the top. You can navigate with a current Forest Service map through the labyrinth of logging roads to the jumpoff point on the road that climbs into the West Fork of Knownothing Creek, or save time by asking locally where the trailhead currently is located.

From the town of Forks of Salmon, take USFS 10N04 eight miles south and look for a sign, *Mullens Camp,* pointing to the right. This spur road goes to the wilderness boundary, where it turns to trail and climbs up to the skyline, the Salmon Mountain Divide.

Once on the Salmon Mountain Divide on the Trinity/Siskiyou County line, you'll pick up the trail that follows its 30-mile length. Turn west and follow it around the headwaters of Eightmile Creek to the intersection with the Devil's Backbone Trail arriving at this point from the south. The summit of Salmon Mountain, with the biggest rock cairn in the Alps, is just to the north over what looks like an old jeep road, but is really a leftover firebreak from the early '60s. Slightly greater in length, but more genial vertically than the Knownothing Creek route, is a route from road's end beyond Le Perron Peak. From the town of Orleans on Highway 96, at the east end of the bridge over the Klamath River, turn southwest on the Red Cap Road, then follow USFS Road 10N02 to 10N01 to Le Perron Peak and beyond. It's a total of about 20 miles from the highway to the clearcut where the trail marked *Salmon Summit Trail* takes off.

Salmon Mountain is a spiritual place for the Karuk. It was a place to come in winter and get silver fox skins to use in sacred dances. The numerous quartz ledges in the headwaters of Red Cap Creek provided sharp tools used in ceremonies involving self-mutilation. The singing and dancing often went on all night long.

SALMON SUMMIT TRAILHEAD

Access: From Orleans, at the east end of the Highway 96 bridge over the Klamath River, turn southwest on the Red Cap Road. At 6 miles turn left on 10N01, signed to Le Perron Flat and other points. After 2 miles, go left again at a Le Perron Peak sign on 10N01 for 13 miles to where the road ends at the trailhead in a clearcut.

Trails: Trail 6E03 picks up where the road leaves off until it becomes trail 12W02. For 36.5 miles it travels the crest of the Green Trinities all the way to Cecil Point before it abandons the ridge line. This is the high road of the lonesome Western Alps, but now overgrown from low use in many places. A spur trail forks to Red Cap Lake at 3.5 miles.

Destinations: Red Cap Lake, Salmon Mountain, Rock Lake, Devil's Backbone, Potato Mountain, Dees Peak, Youngs Peak Mary Blaine Mountain, Election Camp.

Elevation/Difficulty: 5,500 feet at trailhead. Trail grades are moderate.

Summary: Trail stays on the crest of the Salmon Mountains, offering few sources for water or campsites. Overgrown with brush in several places. Access to several trails descending south into the Trinity Alps and north into the Klamath National Forest.

TISH TANG A TANG TRAILHEAD (DEVIL'S BACKBONE)

Access: 16 miles from Willow Creek on State Highway 299. Take road past the golf course and watch for road 8N03 to the left at 5 miles. **Horse Linto Campground** at 7 miles from town of Willow Creek. Called **Devil's Backbone Trailhead** on some maps.

Trails: Trail 6E31 climbs past Ladder Rock to Ferguson Meadow to where it joins 6E20 and dead-ends in Bell Swamps. 6E18, with a spur to 4,963-foot Tish Tang Point, goes to the ridgetop and hooks up with Horse Trail Ridge Recreation Trail (6E08) and then north to Trinity Summit. There are two forks from 6E18: 6E35 leads to McKay Meadow, across Tish Tang A Tang Creek to Bear Hole Trailhead, while 6E29 climbs up and down to Bret Hole and to Crogan Hole.

Destinations: Crogan Hole, the glaciated basin headwaters of Tish Tang A Tang Creek, Bret Hole, Devil's Hole, Bell Swamps, Trinity Summit, and North Trinity Mountain.

Elevation/Difficulty: 3,600 feet at trailhead. Trails in the area are moderate, but route-finding can be difficult.

Summary: This area is interesting for the lover of virgin forests. The dense stands of Douglas-fir, noble fir, and Brewer spruce were slated to be logged, but to the surprise of many, the new wilderness boundary was drawn to include the undisturbed western slopes between the ridgetop and the roads inching in from the west. Well preserved cabin on Trinity Summit. Pronounced Tish-ton-a-ting, the curious name, from the Hupa language meaning "neck of land projecting into the river," was spelled either Djectanadin or Djishtangading.

TRINITY MOUNTAIN

(6,094 feet) This mountain, easily bagged from the **Grizzly Camp Trailhead**, straddles the Humboldt/Trinity County line. Find the steep, brush-overgrown trail about a mile from the trailhead and hack your way another mile to the summit.

TRINITY SUMMIT

(6,288 feet) Tish Tang A Tang or Bear Hole or Mill Creek Trailhead. This mountain is often confused with North Trinity Mountain up by the Water Dog Lakes a couple of miles to the north and Trinity Mountain several miles to the south. If you find an empty-eyed cabin staring at the wide expanse of the Alps to the east as it has since the 1930s, then you'll know for sure you are on Trinity Summit.

The most direct route is from Bear Hole Trailhead on trail 6E16, which starts out gently enough until it crosses Tish Tang A Tang Creek and starts up for the divide through Crogan Hole. You'll see some outstanding specimens of the cedar family along the way.

Once on the divide and the Horse Trail Ridge Recreation Trail (6E08), it's a stroll to the summit and the cabin. Along this divide stretch of the trail you'll find what has to be, for sheer size and scale alone, the most beautiful and panoramic view of the high Alps available.

Sit along the trail just below the summit with the deep gash of Soldier Creek at your feet and drink in the 180-degree sweep of the Alps. Gazing slowly from left to right, note the sun-beaten, black volcanic-looking Devil's Backbone leading your eye up to Salmon Mountain. Moving to the right is Youngs Peak, Potato Mountain, Dees Peak, and Mary Blaine Mountain with its famous meadows. Then the highest of the Alps fall into place: Mt. Caesar, Thompson Peak, Wedding Cake (looking like a hat on the ridge), three or four nameless peaks, and Mount Hilton. Swinging your eyes back to the left and to the middle ground you see Pony Buttes, Cabin Peak, Pony Mountain, and the Thurston Peaks. A sharp eye can pick out Monument Peak on the farthest horizon.

Mount Shasta dominates the background, almost twice as high as any of the peaks you can see.

The cabin on the summit has begun to fall apart in recent years. Locals think it is only a matter of time before the Forest Service burns it down. Too bad. It's an intriguing structure in a unique place gaining in historical value as the years pass by. The interior of the cabin has served as a summit register for decades. You can spend some time reading the entries written on the walls and ceiling and get a sense of the place and the people who have spent time here.

Mostly, people have come to Trinity Summit to kill things. Mainly deer and bear. The writing on the cabin walls documents the failures and successes. Here are some that caught my eye:

"Sept. 25, 1960 – James Jackson killed a fifth here."

"Kilt nothing but time" – Sept. 17, 1953.

"Stuart Ethingerton – 8/2/82 – killed 5 deer flies with his bare hands."

A campsite in the meadow below the cabin affords long dreamy views of the ragged peaks of the Alps to the east. Time it right and you'll see a full moon rise over distant Mount Shasta. To the west, you may witness a world- class sunset into the Pacific Ocean. The flat orb of orange sinks into the ocean haze, sending horizontal streaks of flaming crimson and gold upward to blend into greens and deep blues. Stunning!

VIRGIN CREEK

New River, Salmon Summit or Knownothing Lake Trailhead. Virgin Creek, pristine and primeval, joins Slide Creek three miles from the New River Trailhead to form New River. But before reaching this point, it has meandered its way through thirteen miles of dense old-growth forest. Ponderosa pine, sugar pine, Jeffrey pine, Douglas-fir, white fir, maple, madrone, and oak create an intimate hiking and camping environment unmatched in the Alps.

The confluence of Slide Creek and Virgin Creek forms an emerald swimming pool. Nearby is the perfect streamside campsite. The newly formed New River cascades down through walls wrinkled with ribs of solid rock, creating enticing pools and waterfalls.

Days are spent dozing and reading in the deep cool shadows of ancient trees. Twilight lingers for hours, allowing time to dangle a fly behind the boulders in the creek before firing up the stove and fixing supper. Anglers are sometimes startled when hooking up with a native rainbow trout or even a steelhead summering over. Darkness softly steals through the pine-needled ceiling, wrapping an umbral cloak around those who stayed up late to stare into the campfire. Moonlight beats down upon the anvil of evening. Here comes the night. Silent stars glide over the clustered mummy bags where visions of Bigfoot stir restless dreams.

The Virgin Creek traveler will see evidence of gold mining, old roads and old shacks, even an abandoned truck where Soldier Creek comes in. Activity has diminished since the area was included in the wilderness boundaries drawn in 1984. Now it's possible to spend several days without seeing anyone along the creek.

My first look at Virgin Creek was from the back seat of a helicopter. Summer of 1973 found me on a fire-fighting crew for the U.S. Forest Service. In a grassy field near Denny we packed ourselves into a Bell 210 helicopter and were whisked away up the New River to a fire ripping out of control between Fawn Creek and Twomile Creek. Tongues of fire licked the edges of a smoke pillar mushrooming thousands of feet into the sky. A full 8,500 acres of forest turned to ashes in a few hours. We spent days containing the fire and mopping up smoldering stumpholes. The fire was later determined to be caused by an escaped campfire.

There's still plenty of firewood along Virgin Creek, but be careful.

VIRGIN CREEK BUTTES

(4,709 feet) New River Trailhead. Here's a peculiar island in the middle of the New River country. Slide and Eagle Creek pass by on the east, while Virgin Creek is on the west side. There used to be a fire lookout on the highest point.

These are probably the lowest named mountains in the Alps. Nonetheless, if you decide to climb them, you'll work every bit as hard as you would on an 8,000-foot mountain. Steep. The key to success is to find the old trail to the former lookout. It used to take off at the forks of Slide and Eagle Creek and follow the spine of the ridge to the summit. On old maps it was trail 7E04.

You'd think any summit once used as a fire lookout would yield good views, but in this case they seem to have made a mistake. Vision is limited by heavy timber, giving only brief peeks at the surrounding countryside.

WATER DOG LAKES

Elevation 5,500 feet; .25 acre; 3 feet deep. Boggy ponds on the Red Cap Prairie Trail near the west side of North Trinity Mountain. **Tish Tang A Tang, Mill Creek Lake, or Grizzly Camp Trailhead.**

Definitely not a destination unless you happen to be enamored with trailside puddles. However, connoisseurs of meadowy plateaus will be delighted to find acres of low bushes of mountain heath with pink flowers called kalmia, which only grows above 4,000 feet and is often called American laurel. The white flowers of the marsh marigold and lavender-purple shooting stars splash the open areas like an impressionist painting.

A campsite at the upper end of the granite-boulder-strewn basin offers large wooden benches and a lake (pond) reflecting the rocky face of North Trinity Mountain.

The pungency of a cedar fire on the evening air and distant Mount Shasta glowing amber in the sunset more than make up for the lack of a real lake.

It was sublime one late spring day at the Water Dog Lakes. So soft and quiet that you could hear the movement of a lizard nearby scurrying through the rock pile. Birds piped in the underbrush. My attention was captured by a dozen damselflies having group sex a few inches above the surface of the water. The late afternoon sun shining through the wildflowers made them glow like stained glass. I gazed through half-closed eyes at the meadow pond and realized that unfulfilled dreams last longer than the wilderness itself.

This is a place of good loneliness, a place to spend an afternoon with a giant cedar tree watching the sky unfurling skirts of grizzled virga over the far mountains with the smell of impending rain on the wind

"I saw the lightning's gleaming rod
reach forth and write on heaven's scrolls
the awful autograph of God."

–Joaquin Miller

YOUNGS PEAK

(6,236 feet) Knownothing or Hotelling Ridge Trailheads. A brushy bump on the Siskiyou/Trinity county line where you can sit and gaze at a myriad of clearcuts, visible to the horizon, cutting holes in the dark carpet of the forest.

The Salmon Summit Trail contours around the peak at the 5,300-foot level. At some point along the trail you have to find an opening in the brush and make your way to the top.

Chapter Five

THE NORTH CENTRAL ALPS

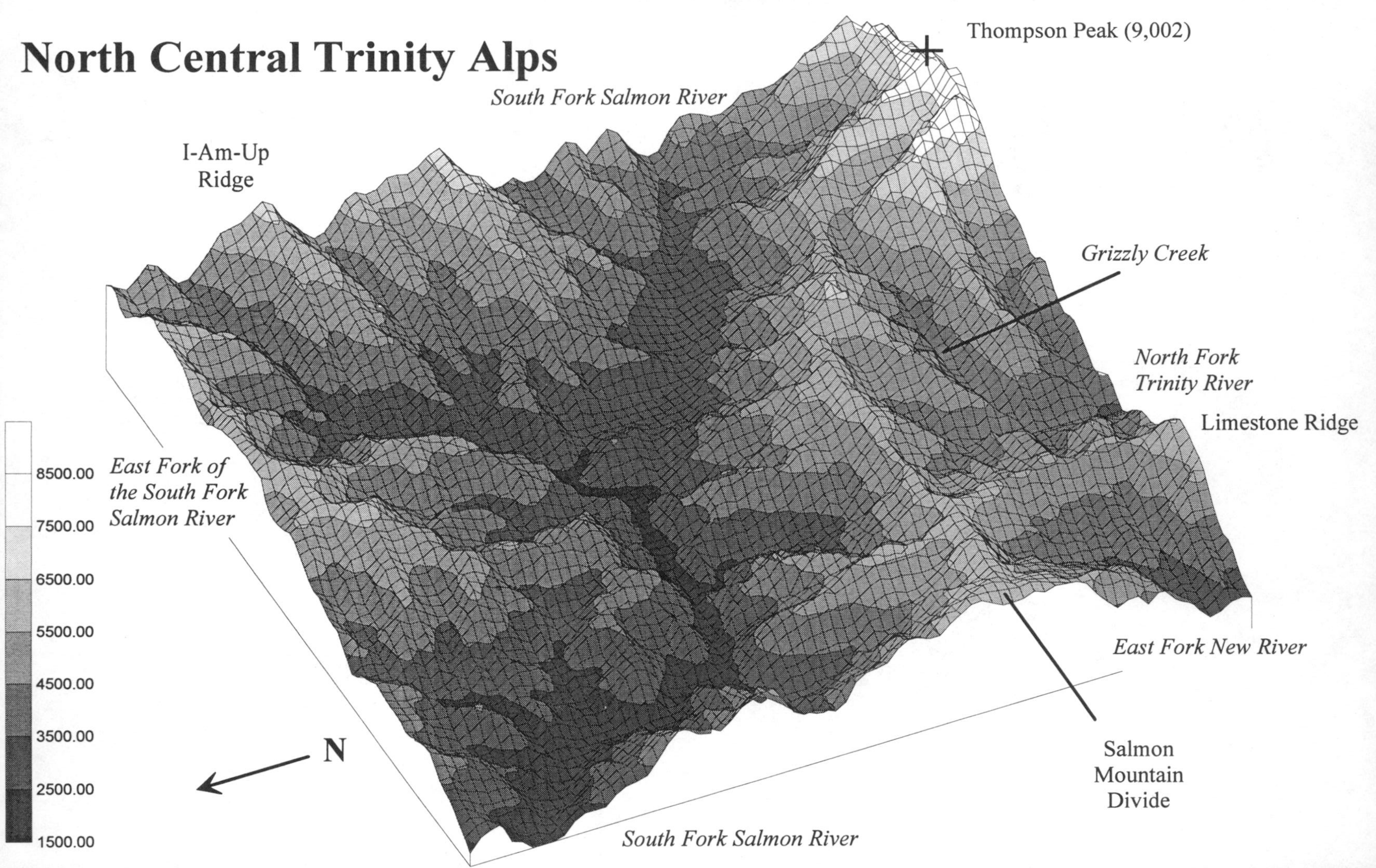
North Central Trinity Alps
Thompson Peak (9,002)
South Fork Salmon River
I-Am-Up Ridge
Grizzly Creek
North Fork Trinity River
Limestone Ridge
East Fork of the South Fork Salmon River
East Fork New River
Salmon Mountain Divide
South Fork Salmon River
N
8500.00
7500.00
6500.00
5500.00
4500.00
3500.00
2500.00
1500.00

North Central Trinity Alps

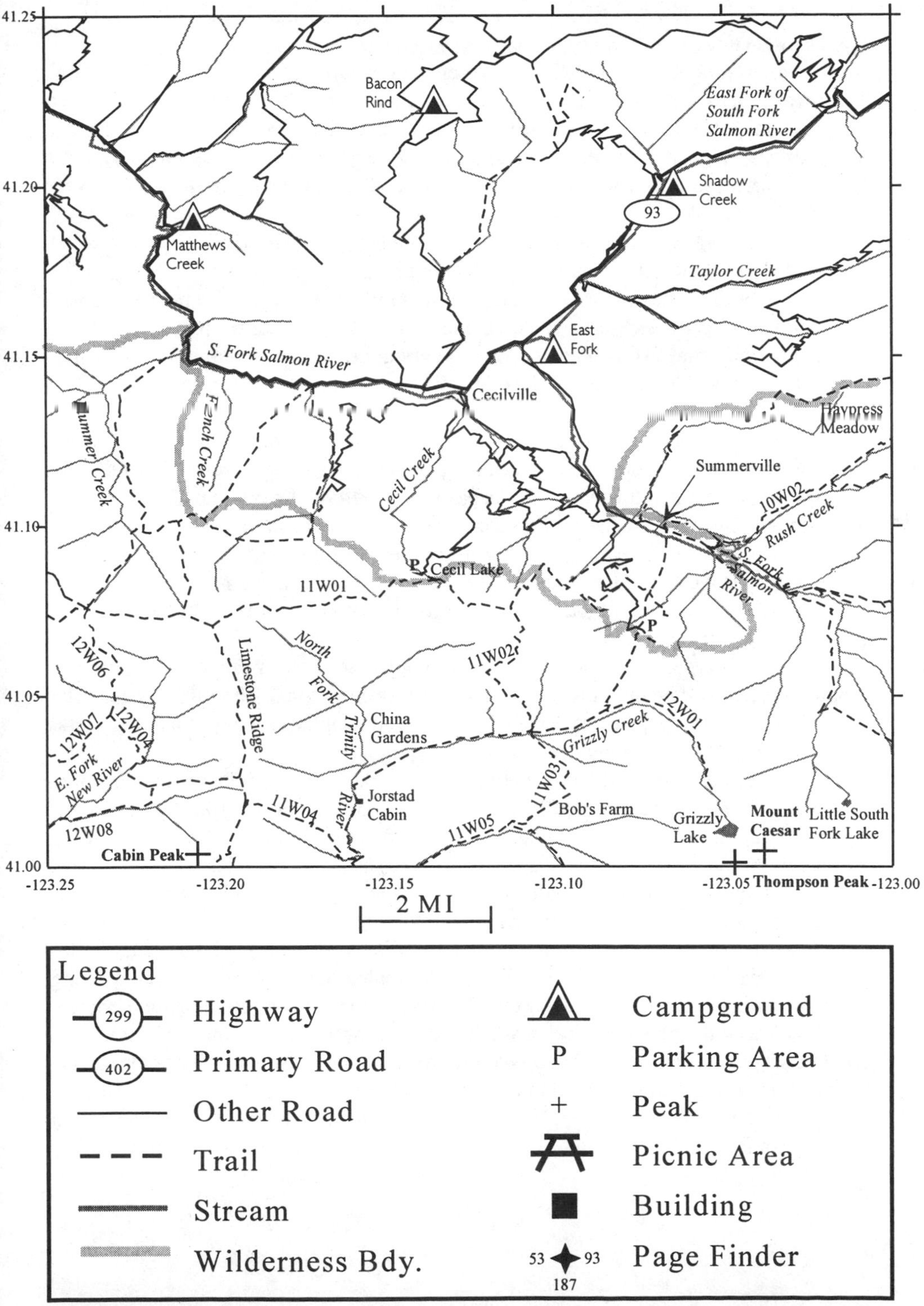

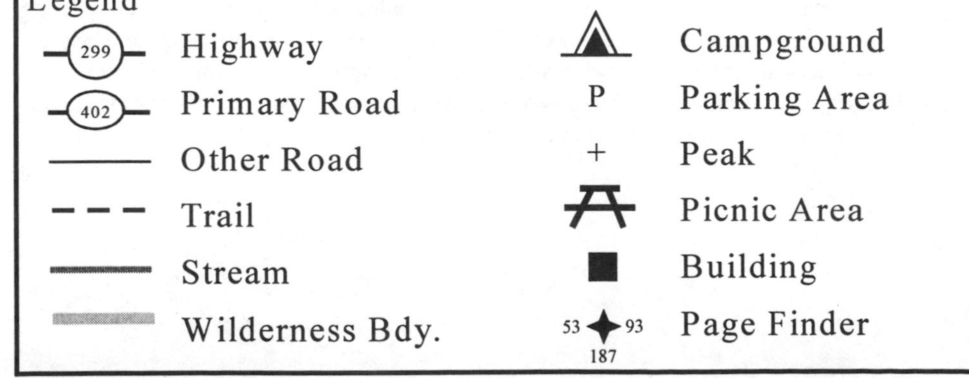

CABIN PEAK

(6,870 feet) Hobo Gulch Trailhead, Green Mountain Trailhead, Jim Jam Ridge Trailhead, East Fork New River Trailhead. High and lonesome, this conical-shaped peak resembles a volcano when viewed from the west. Rising abruptly at the southern end of Limestone Ridge, it offers first-class solitude. Once hosting a fire lookout many years ago, now there's just the wind, silence, green valleys, and blue hazy mountains in every direction.

There are two ways to get there from the Hobo Gulch Trailhead on the North Fork of the Trinity River, or combine both into a loop.

You can follow the North Fork trail to a mile and half past Rattlesnake Creek. A trail to the west crosses Morrison Gulch and climbs steeply, real steep in places, to the Limestone Ridge trail. At the intersection, you are going to turn south on the trail which circles the west and south sides of the mountain. At any point you can break away from the trail and start zigzagging to the summit.

The more direct way is to leave the North Fork of the Trinity River on the Whites Creek/Bear Wallow Meadow Trail and gain the ridgetop at Hunter's Camp. The trail north follows the ridge, then dips down at Marble Spring before climbing up and contouring around the peak. Head for the summit about the time the trail starts to contour.

The 360-degree panoramic view from the summit makes it obvious why a fire lookout once stood here. It was classic lookout architecture: a cabin with windows for walls, perched on stilts. The lack of water and lack of easy access are clues to why a lookout no longer stands here.

You'll probably spend an hour on top of Cabin Peak. A few people spent four months at a time during the summers the lookout was operational. The workday consisted of scanning the landscape every half hour, ten to fourteen hours a day. And after work? Well, scan the horizon, but not get paid for it.

A former Cabin Peak lookout (a person, not the building) told me thunderstorms were the highlight of the summer. It was his job to watch for downstrikes (places where lightning appeared to hit the ground), and mark them on the map. After a storm had passed, he would carefully check each location for smoke. Sometimes it would be days after the storm before smoke would appear. Then he'd grab the radio and shout, "Fire Flash on the Shasta-T," and give the coordinates for the fire.

One evening a lightning storm moved across Cabin Peak and lingered until after dark. Total darkness punctuated with blinding flashbulbs simultaneous with ear-splitting, window-rattling thunder livened things up. Between explosions and flashes, my friend was fascinated with the blue electrical sparks dancing from the stove to the bed frame. The stool he sat on had glass insulators on the legs for protection from the thousands of volts flowing between ground and cloud through the cabin.

But most days on Cabin Peak are just like they are the day you are there: high and lonesome.

CECIL LAKE

Elevation 5,700 feet; 1 acre; 12 feet deep. The lake is just inside the wilderness boundary near the Siskiyou/Trinity county line. **Cecil Lake Trailhead. East Fork Campground** eight miles away.

A short hike to a small lake. Cecil Lake is not the kind of place where you would want to spend a lot of time, perhaps overnight, before or after you hike up to the county line to look things over.

The steep trail on the east side of the lake climbs around the shoulder of the 6,440-foot mountain (called "Divide" on older maps) and intersects that long, long winding trail running the spine of the Salmon Summit for more than 20 miles. Recent reports are that the trail is almost overgrown by brush in places due to lack of use and/or maintenance.

Hike west seven miles to Election Gap/Election Camp and rummage around the historic mining ruins of the upper New River country. If someone dropped you off at the Cecil Lake Trailhead or you arranged a car shuttle (a *real long* car shuttle), you could work your way downstream to the New River Trailhead and enjoy mostly downhill walking all the way.

Maybe you car-shuttled, or someone is going to meet you at the Salmon Summit Trailhead. Then beyond Election Gap it's around Mary Blaine Mountain, on the trail that stays pretty much on the Trinity County side as it contours Dees Peak, Potato Mountain, and Youngs Peak on the way to Slate Gap and eventually Salmon Mountain.

Meanwhile, back at the intersection above Cecil Lake, you may choose to go east. In which case you'll plunge off down into Grizzly Creek and hit the creek at the site of the Moliter Mine, creating a four-way intersection: down Grizzly Creek to the Hobo Gulch Trailhead; up Grizzly Creek to Grizzly Lake; or straight ahead and up to Bobs Farm on the other side of the ridge. (See entry under Grizzly and Papoose Lake for information on this area).

Or, finally, you might just scramble up on "Divide" and let your eyes do the hiking. Gorgeous wilderness views in all directions.

CECIL LAKE TRAILHEAD

Access: 1 mile southeast of Cecilville watch for a bridge across the South Fork to road 38N27 and follow it beyond Cecil Point to the edge of the wilderness boundary, also known as the Harry Hull Trailhead. **East Fork Campground** is near Cecilville at the junction of East Fork and South Fork of the Salmon River. Cecilville is 37 miles from Somes Bar on Highway 96 (the Salmon River Freeway) or 34 miles from Callahan on Highway 3.

Trails: Trail 11W09 makes a short, moderate, .09-mile hike to Cecil Lake and then connects to Trail 11W01 on the Salmon Divide.

Destinations: Cecil Lake, Salmon Divide, New River, N. Fork Trinity River.

Elevation/Difficulty: 5,700 feet at trailhead. Short, moderate trail to the lake and divide.

Summary: Offers a short, quick way to reach the headwaters of New River drainage and North Fork of Trinity River.

CHINA CREEK TRAILHEAD

Access: From Callahan on Highway 3 go west 28 miles on paved road, turn left to East Fork Campground. Three miles later, watch for road 37N07 to the right. Miss it and you'll come to a dead-end and have to backtrack. Once you get on the dirt road there are ample signs to guide you to the trailhead. **East Fork Campground** is near Cecilville near the junction of East Fork and South Fork of the Salmon River.

Trails: Trail 11W33 climbs steeply with switchbacks to top of ridge and drops just as steeply down to Grizzly Creek Trail (12W01).

Destinations: Grizzly Lake, Thompson Peak, Mill Creek Lake, (Lois Lake).

Elevations/Difficulty: 4,850 feet at trailhead. Difficult. Big elevation loss and gain both coming and going.

Summary: Shortest way to reach Grizzly Lake and Thompson Peak.

Emerald and Sapphire lakes

EMERALD LAKE

Elevation 5,500 feet; 21 acres; 68 feet deep. Emerald Lake is 16 miles by trail up Stuart Fork from the end of the road. Has both brook and rainbow trout. Stream fishing up the Stuart Fork is tops. **Stuart Fork Trailhead.**

Isaac Cox, *Annals of Trinity County (1858),* said:

"Among the hills where Steward's (now Stuart) Fork takes its rise, is perpetual snow, and its course singularly characterized by its wildness and stupendous scenery, perhaps outstripping Trinity ruggedness itself."

In the 1920s, James W. Bartlett added this footnote to Cox's observation:

"The tribute paid to the wilderness and stupendous scenery of the mountains among which the stream known as Stewart's Fork rises and wends its way into the Trinity River is well merited. The hills and peaks are mainly of granite: scattered through them are a number of beautiful lakes, some of these being near the tops of mountains; at some points are to be found perpetual snows; the streams are well stocked with mountain trout; the woods are inhabited by bear, black and brown, by deer, foxes, coyotes, and at some places the mountain lion."

Couldn't have said it better myself.

There are people who consider a trip to Emerald the only trip worthy of being called a trip in the Alps. To them this *is* the Alps.

They have a point. The lake is large, geographically centered in the Wilderness Area, on the largest stream, at the end of the longest hike, and has a name denoting the jewel it is.

Unfortunately for the seeker of solitude, the place attracts a crowd all summer long. Better you push on to Sapphire Lake or beyond.

The remnants of the dam on the outlet were used at the turn of the century to control the water level for mining operations near Weaverville.

Hand-built, the rock dam was constructed in 1898 by men from the LaGrange Hydraulic Mining Company, which was named after its president, a French nobleman, Baron De LaGrange.

The dam was the first step in the mining company's attempt to keep a steady supply of water flowing to its hydraulic mine more than 30 miles away on Oregon Mountain west of Weaverville. Using a 29-mile-long ditch, with flumes, tunnels and siphons, water was delivered to the mine site, where it was used to hose the hillsides with powerful streams of water and remove the soil to locate the hidden gold.

The ditch started at the mouth of Deer Creek and extended along the east side of Stuart Fork drainage. For many miles nearly parallel to the present-day trail. A large part of this section was flume. At many points you can walk up the hillside to the east of the trail and view this piece of 19th century engineering. It crossed Deep Creek on a high trestle where it also picked up more water from a smaller extension of the flume. The water was siphoned across Stuart Fork at Bridge Camp using a 30-inch steel pipe with a drop of more than 1,000 feet. After that it went through a two-mile-long tunnel into Rush Creek, where it picked even more water, and eventually to a reservoir at the 3,500-foot level on Oregon Mountain.

Gold worth millions of dollars was recovered during the few years it operated, but the damage and debris is still evident.

Miner's dam at Emerald Lake

GARDEN GULCH TRAILHEAD

Access: Turn off the Callahan/Cecilville Road at **East Fork Campground** 35 miles from Cecilville and watch sign on left about 2 miles from the Petersburg Work Center.

Trails: Trail 10W240 skirts a private ranch and irrigated meadow before it crosses Garden Gulch several times. A couple of steep switchbacks get you up on the ridge. It then continues on past Haypress and Onion Meadow and Rush Creek Lake.

Destinations: Rush Creek Lake, South Fork of Coffee Creek, Poison Lake, Trail Gulch on South Fork of the Salmon.

Elevation/Difficulty: 2,350 feet at trailhead. Moderate to difficult.

Summary: Little-used trail along the wilderness boundary, faint and hard to follow in places. Long stretches with no water.

Grizzly Lake

GRIZZLY LAKE

Elevation 7,100 feet; 42 acres; 173 feet deep. From Hobo Gulch it's a beautiful hike up the North Fork of the Trinity River and Grizzly Creek through virgin stands of Douglas-fir and Ponderosa pine. The trail winds on through the granite into Grizzly Meadow, where there's a magnificent view of a high peak with a waterfall at its base. This is Thompson Peak, 9,002 feet high. The waterfall drops 70 feet from the lip of Grizzly Lake. Grizzly Meadow is 19 miles from Hobo Gulch, or about nine miles from the South Fork of the Salmon River via Hunter's Camp trail. From the meadow one has to climb rocks for about 45 minutes to reach the lake. This seldom-visited lake produces fat, red-meated rainbow trout, 12 inches and longer. Grizzly Creek is a good trout stream. **China Creek or Hobo Gulch Trailhead.**

And where is Nirvana in the Alps? When all desire for existence is extinguished and your soul becomes one with the Creator, open your eyes and you'll be at Grizzly Lake. Unfortunately, belying the words in the above description, you'll find Nirvana a rather crowded place.

Grizzly Lake became accessible when the route from China Creek over by Cecilville was developed. Prior to that, it was a long, lovely trek of 18 miles from Hobo Gulch. Some folks still make that hike, but they are few. Hordes of people thunder over the ridge from the China Creek trailhead. There is an apocryphal story of Dixon Jones making it in three and a half hours from trailhead to lake. He probably did. During the 1970s, Dixon had friends from the University of British Columbia who spent summers doing research on the hummingbirds around Grizzly Lake. He would take a few days off and visit them, bringing with him a few party favors not readily available at the lake.

But even with the crowds, doing Grizzly is a must (I do recommend the early or late season to avoid the crowds). An elegant waterfall at the outlet slips over the rock lip while sunsets colored golden, apricot and tangerine glow silently to the west over the tumbled mass of hills. Campers at the lake drop whatever they are doing and turn as one, staring slack-jawed until the last tinge of color is squeezed out by darkness. There is barely time to recover from the experience before the cobalt sky is assaulted by an immense full moon, a silver orb changing the night back into day.

The north face of Thompson Peak (9,002 feet) broods and sulks behind never-melting snow banks south of the lake.

If you should die after visiting Grizzly Lake, well, at least you've seen the best the Alps has to offer. This is as good as it gets. You couldn't pick a better place to take your last mountain trip. It may explain why it attracts so many people.

From Grizzly Meadow to the lake there is the opportunity to test your route-finding skills and clean up the rock ducks (rock piles to mark the trail) that often sprout on this steep stretch.

While Grizzly Lake may be your destination, traveling there can be half the fun. You may spend several days out and back from Hobo Gulch or arrange a car shuttle from the China Creek trailhead and end up at Hobo Gulch. Either way, you'll see a lot of the historic country along Grizzly Creek and the North Fork of the Trinity River.

On the North Fork, where Specimen Creek branches off, there's the remains of the Molitor Mine. Frederick (Fritz) Molitor, born in Alsace in 1862, was typical of the back-country, small-scale miners who operated either by themselves or with a partner. He extracted gold from this area between 1910 and 1920. He packed in all his supplies by burro and on his back from Helena and Junction City. His final days were spent working on a gold dredge near Junction City. Despondent over the loss of his dredging job and the state of his health, he ended his life with a bullet on a bluff top overlooking the Trinity River near Helena. He was 65 years old.

The Molitor Mine was a small operation, but five monitors have been found on the property, one a five-incher. There was also a blacksmith shop, a sawmill, and a few other scattered buildings. No one knows how much gold was recovered, but Vernon Ryan, Weaverville merchant, said the biggest nugget he ever saw mined in Trinity County came from Fritz's mine.

The trail from the Molitor Mine that goes up Specimen Creek takes you to another mine, Bob's Farm. Located on the headwaters of a branch of Mill Creek, there are a series of outcroppings of quartz rock and evidence of mining activity. As recently as the 1980s a man died from asphyxiation because of a faulty air supply to the breathing apparatus he was using deep inside a mine shaft.

Old-timers can't explain the name of Bob's Farm. Small sections of the land may have been used for early summer gardening by the prospectors and miners, but you can't escape the conjecture that the word "farm", for this locality, arose out of the same wry pioneer humor that attached the name "Baghdad" to a town at the mouth of the North Fork.

In the early part of the 20th century, especially between 1900 and 1904, Bob's Farm was very much in the local news. The Bob's Farm Mining Company hauled in stamping equipment, built a sawmill, staked out sixteen claims and planned to build a wagon road. The twenty men working there reported the snow being eighteen feet deep one winter.

It was a problem for the mining company to feed a crew of miners at a location so far from roads and at such a high elevation. They hired Bert Gilzean to hunt the herd of elk that grazed at that time in the vicinity of Papoose Lake. He was able, for a time at least, to keep the miners at Bob's Farm supplied with meat.

About a mile and half downstream from the Molitor Mine was the Lorenz hydraulic works. The Lorenzes were the same family that once owned the well-known Lorenz Hotel in Redding. This mine was much like the Molitor. On the south side of the canyon was the Stribling Mine. Most of this area was ground sluiced with water coming from the gulch on the south side where water was run through races to cut to bedrock where the gold was. It was tough work. It killed Stribling. Huge boulders were lifted out of the water races with awkward riggings and ropes. One of the rigs gave way and dropped a boulder on him.

Stribling's death ended his mining operation, but Chinese continued to work the area. What they got in the way of gold wasn't reported.

A few miles further down Grizzly Creek is a campsite known as Chinese Gardens. Here, large chunks of land were ground-sluiced by Chinese miners. How many Chinese worked here there is no way of knowing. More than one backpacker has reported hearing Chinese voices during the night.

The trail along the North Fork was at one time the principal thoroughfare between Trinity County and the Klamath country. The mining camps at Somes Bar and Forks of Salmon were supplied from Red Bluff, the end of navigation on the Sacramento River. There is record of a party on horses using this canyon in 1849, and trappers from the Oregon country may have pushed through here even earlier than that.

Just above Pfeiffer Flat, Grizzly Creek joins the North Fork. The North Fork above its confluence with Grizzly Creek never produced any gold. For some reason no gold has ever been found in the streams flowing from the west side. Getting water to Pfeiffer Flat for mining was a problem never solved. The first few miners came through and picked up the easy, big pieces, leaving the bulk of this flat virgin and unmined.

For over sixty years the most prominent landmark on the North Fork has been Jorstad's Cabin.

George (W.O.) Jorstad arrived on Pfeiffer Flat in 1937. The flat had long been a stopping place for travelers along this trail. A Dutchman named Pfeiffer had a store here in the 1890s. The place once sported a blacksmith shop, a butcher shop and a number of cabins. Jorstad found only two buildings when he arrived.

The logs of Jorstad Cabin are Douglas-fir that came from the west side of the river and were floated downstream to a dam and then skidded to the building site with block and tackle. The block flooring is cedar 10 inches thick. Jorstad said “the floor will last forever.”

George and his wife spent a couple of summers in the cabin and did some mining. They were able to stay until Thanksgiving and then left for the winter. In 1941 his wife decided that “as much as she loved wilderness, and all the creatures in it, nature in the raw was hard to take year on year.” She took a job in San Diego and George returned to the cabin on Pfeiffer Flat alone.

That year he closed up the cabin and headed back to the world to join the Army, but he ran into a friend and ended up taking a job on a sailing ship, an old windjammer carrying lumber.

He was gone five years, but when he came back to the cabin in 1946, everything was as he had left it. He spent every summer there until 1985 making friends with the hundreds of backpackers passing by.

Jorstad had this to say about the way he laid out the cabin:

“From very early I had heard that it was proper to build houses foursquare with the world. Also the human, like birds and animals, are direction-oriented, more or less. For whatever reason, the human seems to do better or feel better in four-square layouts. I do anyhow. Tangled sheets in bed, for instance, I think, are confusing.

Before laying the first logs, I stretched a long rope at the building site, polar north-south, from the North Star directly on the meridian (if possible). It was not laid out by the compass, and so is not magnetic north-south, but sidereal north-south, thus the cabin itself is a clock and a calendar. From a few simple calculations you can determine the hour of the day and the month of the year from the shadows inside–useful information in the far backwoods.”

HOTELLING RIDGE TRAILHEAD

Access: Drive 7 miles east of the town of Forks of Salmon on the Salmon River Freeway. Cross the South Fork of the Salmon River on road 39N34, which goes up Methodist Creek. Where the trailhead begins depends on how far you can drive up the ridge. Road conditions vary. **Mathews Creek Campground** is 3 miles up the South Fork of the Salmon River.

Trails: Trail 08E10 goes steeply up the spine of the ridge to the Salmon Summit Trail, where you can go east to Potato Mountain and the Mary Blaine country, west to Youngs Peak and the Salmon Mountain country, or south down into Eagle Creek and the New River country.

Destinations: Youngs Peak, Potato Mountain, Upper New River gold mining country.

Elevation/Difficulty: Elevation varies depending on where you start walking on the ridge road. Hiking is difficult to strenuous due to the long distances involved to get anywhere.

Summary: Good trailhead to gain quick entry onto Salmon Summit. Get someone to drop you off here and you can tour the historic New River gold country and 90 percent of your hike will be downhill to the New River Trailheads. Shady, big timber cover on most trails.

Lois (Mill Creek) Lake

LOIS LAKE (Mill Creek Lake)

Elevation 7,500 feet; 2.5 acres; 40 feet deep. This is the most inaccessible lake in the Trinity Alps. A stiff two-hour climb up the chimney on the south side of the upper portion of Grizzly Meadow is required to reach it. Grizzly Meadow is about 19 miles up from Hobo Gulch on the North Fork of the Trinity River, or about nine miles from the road on the South Fork of the Salmon River. This very beautiful lake was supposedly planted with Eastern brook trout in 1953. **China Gulch or Hobo Gulch Trailhead.**

Lois Lake is the most *looked at* lake in the Alps. The usual practice is to hike up from Grizzly, look down at the lake, and then proceed with the day.

Well, I walked down to it one August day because I had to touch it. All my life this two and a half acres had been perceived as the most difficult, inaccessible lake in the Alps. That's what the old *Know-It-All Guide* said. Savor the thought. Most inaccessible. It fired my imagination for years. Who can rest easy when they haven't been to the most inaccessible lake in the Alps? No matter how tough other hikes in the Alps may have been, there was one tougher: Lois Lake.

Sometimes I'd wake up in the night and wonder what it was like up there at that moment. On snowy days, while walking around town, I'd think of what it must be like at Lois Lake. A white lonesome world.

It may have been the most inaccessible lake back in the days when you had to start at Hobo Gulch trailhead. Then it was a long, long way up North Fork and Grizzly Creek to Lois. Now you can come in from Cecilville via China Creek trailhead. Figure five hours to Grizzly Lake and then another hour up to Lois and it's not a whole lot harder than many other Alps trips.

Should the crowds at Grizzly Lake get on your nerves, Lois Lake is a good escape. It faces west to guarantee spine-tingling, breathtaking, butt- kicking sunsets. If you go to Lois, you'd be crazy not to loop on up to Thompson Peak (9, 002 feet), highest point in the Alps.

Of course the notion of calling a lake the most inaccessible is relative and pointless. There are a lot of variables involved; weather conditions, time of year, fitness of the hiker, and varied approaches, to name a few. Think of it this way: Lake Eleanor is, by any standard, an easy hike. Under most conditions it's little more than a 15-minute stroll from the car. However, if you were to do it in the middle of winter, in the middle of the night, naked and walking backwards, you might think it was a pretty inaccessible lake.

If backpackers were polled, there would probably be three or four lakes that would rise to the top of the "most inaccessible" list. My personal choice would be Little South Fork. Now there's a nasty place to get into and out of any time of year, from any direction.

I'm not sure why the old *Know-It-All Guide* recommended doing a two-hour climb of the chimney on the south side of Grizzly Meadow. It always seemed to me that anyone reaching Grizzly Meadow is going to go on up to Grizzly Lake. From Grizzly Lake, the climb to the saddle west of the lake puts Lois Lake beneath your feet.

From that same saddle, it's a relatively easy climb to the top of Thompson Peak. Work your way along the south side of the ridge to the summit. You'll find fire rings along the ridge–a reminder of what an excellent place this is to camp and catch the Perseid meteor shower in August or a full moon any time. From the summit, you'll look around and know that you can go no higher in the Alps.

MORAINE LAKE

Elevation 6,000 feet; .5 acres; 8 feet deep. This small lake sits behind a glacial moraine above Little South Fork Lake. No stocking plans at this time. **Big Flat or Stuart Fork Trailhead.**

No one would ever go to Moraine Lake except that it is a close neighbor of Little South Fork Lake and you can't miss it while you are visiting there. It may have been a mistake to name it, but someone did, so we have to deal with it as a legitimate Alps lake.

Rivers, creeks, and streams that run northward generate a mystery of their own. What a north face is to a mountain climber, a north-flowing stream is to a backpacker.

When you're on a north-flowing stream the country seems foreign. It leads away from places familiar. The sun shines less, it rains and snows more, and the nights last longer at a north side lake like Moraine Lake.

The potential for adventure increases as we push onto north faces.

To reach Moraine Lake, heed the instructions outlined under Little South Fork Lake. Moraine offers a place to test this theory:

"The number of people in a Wilderness Area diminishes in proportion to the square of the distance and the cube of the elevation from the nearest road."

MOUNT CAESAR

(8,966 feet) Canyon Creek Trailhead, China Gulch Trailhead, Stuart Fork Trailhead. This peak actually has no *official* name, so Caesar is as good as any. One map calls it T2 Peak. It's the second highest mountain in the Alps. You'd think it would have some kind of official name.

Located next to Thompson Peak, Mount Caesar is approached by much the same routes. It sits at the head of Canyon Creek and can be climbed by following the creek above the lakes to the headwaters and on up to the summit.

From Grizzly Lake, go around the east side of the lake and work the ridge all the way to the top. Deep snow coats both sides of the ridge year around. These never-melting snowbanks are as close to glaciers you'll find in the Alps. The north side of the peak resembles a glacier. One of the ranches you can see far down in the valley of the South Fork of the Salmon River is called Glacierview Ranch. When you are on this part of Mount Caesar, you are part of the view.

PLUMMER CREEK

Plummer Creek Trailhead. Ever wonder what a watershed would look like it had never been logged or even had a road built in it? Note how the wilderness boundary on your map encloses the entire Plummer Creek drainage all the way to the South Fork of the Salmon River. For a mile, between Butcher Gulch and Limestone Bluffs, the south side of the South Fork of the Salmon River *is* the wilderness boundary. From the Salmon River Freeway across the canyon, a strong arm can throw a rock into the wilderness on the far side of the river. It is one of the few creeks in the Alps that managed to avoid the road builders. There's not even much of a trail. Hike up the creek a mile or two and you'll understand why.

Too many of us are interested in big, spectacular places. For the little, special places that dot the Alps, we have a blindness. We throng the established trails, hurrying past many a special place on the way to the next lake or designated campsite. We don't leave much time to wander at random. Plummer Creek is discovered by backpackers unexpectedly, like opening an ordinary door and stepping suddenly into a wilderness cathedral.

The entrance is certainly not ordinary. Once the crossing of the South Fork of the Salmon is solved and the trail located, the adventure begins. Within a mile, the trail crosses to the left side of the creek and struggles up a ridge above the unnamed (south) fork of the creek. No trail penetrates the West Fork of Plummer Creek, enticing to those seekers of untrammeled wilderness. Ancient smooth gray-trunked alders line the stream bed, and incense cedars with cinnamon-colored bark and bright green foliage add to the color scheme. A fresh down-canyon breeze carries the aroma of melting snow thousands of feet upstream, mixing with the flowering vegetation along the creek. Most of the creek is canopied by trees, like a green cave, but not gloomy and dark. Enough direct sunlight works its way through the overstory to highlight the moss and ferns on the ground, and sparkle the water tumbling over the limestone rocks in the creek bed.

There is no "place to go" up Plummer Creek. No lakes, no peaks, no meadows, only wilderness, which is not a place, but a state of mind, metaphor, and geography.

Plummer Creek is serious wilderness, not the weekend-warrior kind found in places like Canyon Creek and Stuart Fork. This is prime bear, Bigfoot, and rattlesnake habitat, and if there were still grizzly bears in California, here's where they'd be. It's a remote and difficult piece of real estate.

PLUMMER CREEK TRAILHEAD

Access: Drive the Salmon River Freeway 14.5 miles east from Forks. Or 5 miles downstream from downtown Cecilville. Watch for an old road on a sharp corner heading down to the river. Four-wheel drive advised for the 100 yards down to the trailhead, where there is barely room for two cars. You might look for a wide spot farther down the main road to park and hike back to the trailhead. Crossing of the South Fork of the Salmon is impossible during high water. Don't even try.
Trails: Trail 12W29 is steep, rugged, and demanding all the way up a remote canyon. Joins trail 12W30 from Sainte Claire Ridge and hits the Salmon Divide at Election Gap. Trails are not often maintained and may be overgrown.
Destinations: Salmon Divide, New River country.
Elevation/Difficulty: 1,800 feet at river to over 6,000 feet on the divide. Strenuous hiking of the highest degree.
Summary: The entire Plummer Creek drainage is a "challenging" piece of real estate.

RATTLESNAKE LAKE

Elevation 5,600 feet; .5 acres; 2 feet deep. A shallow brushy pond on the divide between North Fork of the Trinity River and East Fork of New River. No fish. **Hobo Gulch Trailhead or East Fork of New River Trailhead.**

This lake, located anywhere else, would not have received a name. Dozens of such shallow ponds, nameless, dot the Alps. But this one lies a few hundred yards north of the main trail between North Fork of the Trinity and East Fork of the New River. Also, nearby is a favorite camping spot of the hunting crowd, Rattlesnake Camp. There's not much traffic on the trail over the divide and not many hunters spend much time here, but enough to have named the boggy pond.

RAYS GULCH TRAILHEAD

Access: On the South Fork of the Salmon River on the road to China Gulch Trailhead. Turn off the Callahan/Cecilville road at **East Fork Campground** 3.5 miles from Cecilville and drive 3 miles. Watch for road 37N07 and turn right as if going to China Gulch Trailhead. In about a mile, look for road crossing of Rays Gulch. Roadside parking.
Trails: Trail 11W32 goes straight forward and steep 2 miles to the county line

on the divide. Go right on the divide to Cecil Lake or down to Grizzly Creek at the Moliter Mine site.
Destinations: Salmon Summit trail to points west or Grizzly Creek and North Fork of the Trinity River.
Elevation/Difficulty: 3,000 feet at trailhead.
Summary: Trail is seldom used, hard to find, difficult to hike.

RUSH CREEK/SALMON RIVER TRAILHEAD

Access: On the South Fork of the Salmon River at road's end. Turn off the Callahan/Cecilville road at **East Fork Campground** 3.5 miles from Cecilville and drive beyond Schoolhouse Flat to marked trailhead.
Trails: Trail 10W020 takes off up Rush Creek, where it forks left on a steady 9-mile climb to Rush Creek Lake and right up McNeil Creek Trail (10W250) to the Coffee Creek Divide. Trail 11W34 is the connection along the South Fork of the Salmon River to Big Flat at the head of Coffee Creek. Trail 10W26 branches off near Glacierview Ranch, crosses the South Fork of the Salmon and climbs steeply to the Caribou Basin. This is the trail from which to begin a cross-country bushwhack to Little South Fork Lake.
Destinations: Rush Creek Lake, Coffee Creek, Big Flat, Caribou Lakes, Little South Fork Lake.
Elevation/Difficulty: 2,400 feet at trailhead. Easy up South Fork of Salmon River. All other trails difficult. Strenuous to Little South Fork Lake sans trail.
Summary: Access to several private ranches. Stream fishing in South Fork of Salmon River. Little South Fork Lake possible, but tough.

SAINTE CLAIRE CREEK TRAILHEAD

Access: 16.5 miles east of Forks of Salmon on the Salmon River Freeway. Watch for good camping flat next to river at mouth of Sainte Claire Creek. **East Fork Campground** nearby.
Trails: Trail 12W30 makes a steep direct ascent to Salmon/New River Divide after climbing high on the ridge and dropping down to join trail 12W29 from Plummer Creek. Trail forks to 12W31, which leads to northern end of Limestone Ridge. **Destinations:** New River country and abandoned mines, Mary Blaine Mountain, Pony Buttes, Limestone Ridge.
Elevation/Difficulty: 2,100 feet at trailhead to over 6,000 feet on Salmon Divide. Strenuous elevation gain and faint trail. Crossing of South Fork at trailhead may not be possible during high-water conditions.
Summary: Rugged trail in a rugged land. Steep zigzags with little or no water.

TAYLOR CREEK TRAILHEAD

Access: Take the Cecilville/Callahan road 25.5 miles from Callahan, then road 38N04 eight miles east up Taylor Creek.
Trails: Trail 10W23 climbs over south shoulder of high, unnamed peak into South Fork of Coffee Creek. Poison Lake is a cross-country bushwhacking

scramble up the outlet stream.

Destinations: Poison Lake, Rush Creek Lake, Deadman Peak, South Fork of Coffee Creek.

Elevation/Difficulty: 5,100 feet to over 7,000 feet on Coffee Creek Divide. Strenuous hiking due faint trail or no trail at all.

Summary: You can bushwhack the outlet stream to Poison Lake or take the trail to the divide and work back northward over the mountain and drop down to the lake. Consider loop hike returning via the outlet stream. Shortest approach to Deadman Peak.

Chapter Six

THE NORTHEASTERN ALPS

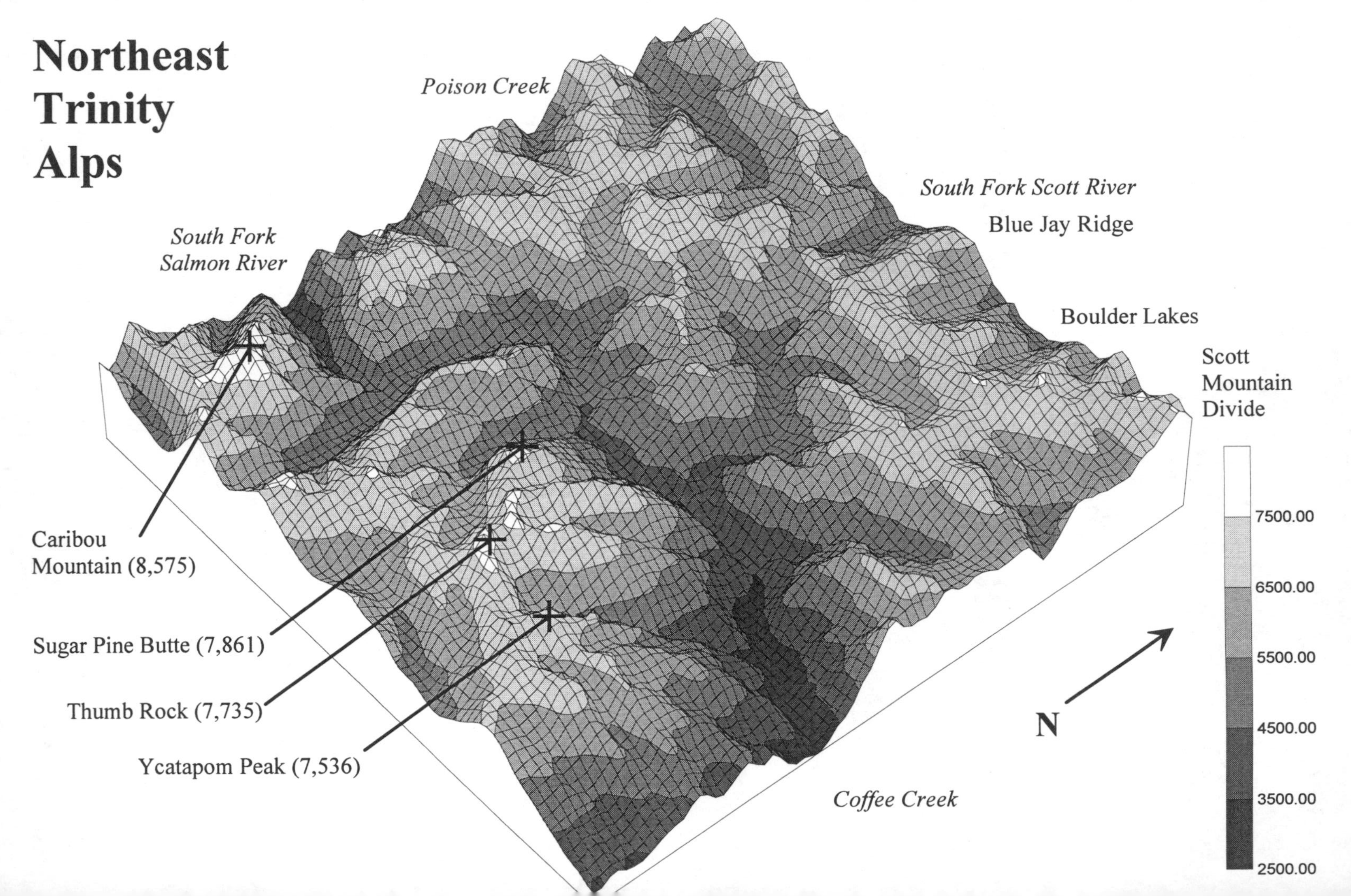
Northeast
Trinity
Alps
Poison Creek
South Fork Scott River
Blue Jay Ridge
South Fork
Salmon River
Boulder Lakes
Scott
Mountain
Divide
Caribou
Mountain (8,575)
Sugar Pine Butte (7,861)
Thumb Rock (7,735)
Ycatapom Peak (7,536)
Coffee Creek
N
7500.00
6500.00
5500.00
4500.00
3500.00
2500.00

Northeast Trinity Alps

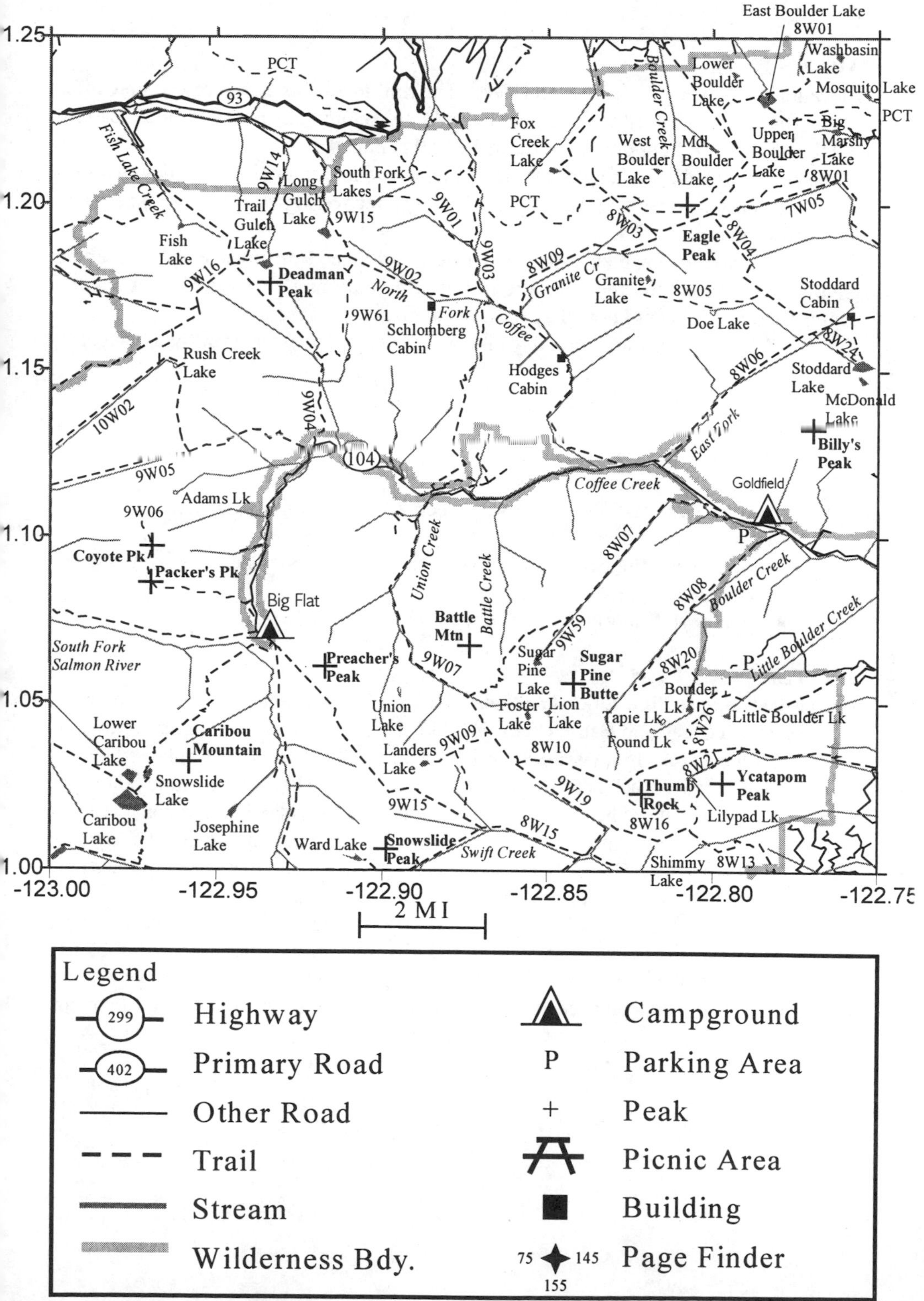

ADAMS LAKE

Elevation 6,200 feet; 1 acre; 16 feet deep. The trail to Adams Lake leaves the Coffee Creek road in the vicinity of the Upper Nash Mine. Hiking time about an hour. Eastern brook and rainbow trout present. **Adams Lake Trailhead.**

Adams Lake used to get hammered pretty hard in its pre-wilderness days by four-wheelers and horse-packing parties, but it's now recovering rather well since being included within the Alps in 1984.

It's a one-shot hike to a small frog pond lake. Not much chance of going anyplace else once you are there. The trail is still pretty much a road. Give it another century and you'll never know that you used to be able to drive to the lake.

Adams makes for a good day hike where you might catch a few bait-snatchers.

ADAMS LAKE TRAILHEAD

Access: On Coffee Creek Road (county road 104) 15.5 miles from Highway 3. Watch for sign on right.

Trails: Trail 9W73 climbs a very steep 2.5 miles to Adams Lake.

Destination: Adams Lake.

Elevations/Difficulty:4,100 feet at trailhead. Short, but steep most of the way. Moderate overall.

Summary: A short hike to a solitary lake few people visit.

BATTLE MOUNTAIN

(7,919 feet) Sugar Pine Lake Trailhead, Union Creek Trailhead. Battle Mountain, between Union Creek and Battle Creek, juts like the prow of a ship pointing northwards toward Coffee Creek. Its massive bulk is best appreciated from an airplane. Heavily timbered, the best approach is from the trail to Sugar Pine Lake. About a mile before the lake, watch for a trail on the right that cuts steeply over the ridge into the upper reaches of Battle Creek. Contour around the headwaters of the creek aiming for the low gap between you and Union Creek. No need to hit the gap right at the low spot, because the plan is to follow the ridge to the summit.

It's a bit longer, but this same summit ridge can be reached by hiking up Union Creek to about a mile below Foster (Bear) Lake. At that point, a faint, steep trail climbs over the ridge into the headwaters of Battle Creek. The downside of this approach is that more altitude is gained than needed, and has to given it up to get over to Battle Mountain.

BEAR LAKE(see Foster Lake)

BIG FLAT TRAILHEAD (COFFEE CREEK)

Access: Drive north on Highway 3 to Coffee Creek and then west for 19 miles to road's end at **Big Flat Campground**.

Trails: Trail 09W20 angles up the ridge past the Yellow Rose of Texas Mine and over the ridge to the Dorleska Mine and Union Creek. Trail 09W18 is the main route to the Caribou Lakes Basin. Trail 11W34 heads off down the South Fork of the Salmon River to the South Fork Trailhead. Trail 09W19 goes all the way to the divide at the headwaters of the South Fork of the Salmon River. Trail 09W19A uses a steep climb up Kidd Creek to reach Ward and Horseshoe Lakes.

Destinations: All the lakes in the Caribou Basin, old mining ruins, Josephine Lake (private), South Fork of Salmon River both upstream and downstream.

Elevation/Difficulty: 4,200 feet at trailhead. Gentle, flat trails in the valley, moderate to Caribou Basin, difficult up Kidd Creek and at headwaters of South Fork of the Salmon.

Summary: Some of the finest country the Alps has to offer is accessible from this trailhead: mountain streams and lakes for fishing, high granite alpine peaks, old mining ruins, and lots of room to roam.

BIG MARSHY LAKE

Elevation 6,300 feet; 5.5 acres; 15 feet deep. Drive up the Tangle Blue Creek access road to the Wilderness Area boundary. Follow the trail to the meadow just below Messner Cabin. The lake is about a one-mile, 45-minute hike from the cabin by trail. Brook trout to 10 inches. **Tangle Blue Lake Trailhead.**

Here's a case where an Alps lake is well named. It is, indeed, a marshy uninviting shoreline. Eventually all Alps lakes will become meadows over time. Big Marshy Lake is well on its way.

BLACK MOUNTAIN

(8,019 feet) Big Flat Trailhead, Swift Creek Trailhead. This is one of the more accessible 8,000-foot mountains in the Alps. If you're camped at Ward or Horseshoe Lakes, you can take the trail from Ward Lake to the Kidd Creek gap and then scramble up the ridgeline to the summit. It can also be bagged by picking your way right up the front from Ward Lake.

But it's nine miles by trail up Swift Creek to Ward Lake. A shorter approach, a nice day hike, is from Big Flat Campground at the head of Coffee Creek. It's even shorter if you are lucky enough to be a guest at the private lodge below Josephine Lake. But most of us must stop at the locked gate and walk the two miles of road to the Kidd Creek Trail. The Kidd Creek Trail means business from the git-go, climbing almost 3,000 feet in less than two miles. It'll make a mouth-breather out of you. But the view of Sawtooth Ridge and Caribou Mountain to the west is superb alpine scenery, reinforcing the notion of naming this area "Alps."

Sawtooth Ridge

BOULDER CREEK TRAILHEAD (COFFEE CREEK)

Access: About five miles west on the Coffee Creek Road from Highway 3 out of the town of Coffee Creek, just past the Coffee Creek Ranch. **Goldfield Campground** is on road 38N75 to the trailhead just across the Coffee Creek Bridge. Trailhead is a couple of hundred yards up the road from the campground.

Trails: Trail 8W08 follows Boulder Creek, passes a delightful waterfall after a mile and a half, joins the Lion Lake Trail (8W12), which trudges past Lion Lake, goes over the ridge to Foster Lake and ends with a steep descent to the Union Creek Trail (9W07).

Destinations: Conway Lake, Lion Lake, Foster Lake, Sugar Pine Butte, Cub Wallow.

Elevation/Difficulty: 3,100 feet at trailhead. Steep at times even with switchbacks. Moderate overall.

Summary: Area is only moderately used, offering a chance for solitude. Stream fishing for feisty small trout possible in Boulder Creek.

BOULDER LAKE

Elevation 6,100 feet; 8 acres; 27 feet deep. A three-hour, seven-mile trip to the lake from Coffee Creek. This is a fine lake to which a family may pack in for a vacation. Has fair-sized brook trout and rainbow. **Boulder Lakes Trailhead.**

Well, it *used to be* a seven-mile trip, but times have changed. Logging activity has pushed the trailhead right up next to the wilderness boundary to within two miles of Boulder Lake. It's an easy day hike for a picnic or a good base camp for forays to Little Boulder Lake, Found Lake, Tapie (Lost) Lake, and even a quick hike over to Lion Lake and Mud Lake (not to be confused with Carter's Little Mud Lake).

Mosquitoes! We took our ground cloths and tried to build bug-proof forts with rock walls for protection, but to no avail. Clouds of mosquitoes shrouded our heads by day and dive-bombed our ears with their high-pitched whine at night. We inhaled the bugs and ate the ones that littered our food. Nights were to be dreaded for the want of bug repellant.

Back in the 1950's it was a long haul from Coffee Creek and Goldfield Campground up to Boulder. I guess a person could still walk in from Goldfield Campground on the old trail, but it would be like visiting an old friend with a terminal disease. The area has been heavily logged; you might say stripped. Timber companies have used these hillsides to sharpen their clear-cut skills.

In the summer of 1958 we were high school kids on the trail to Boulder Lake in August with some homemade pack frames loaded down with camping gear from army surplus stores and food still in the cans and packages off the grocery shelves. We were state-of-the-art backpackers. There was still heavy timber along Boulder Creek then, and heavy fantasies. Across the canyon, on Billy's Peak, was a woman staffing the lookout and she was in *college*. Ann Sargent, where are you now? We would pant up the trail, out across the brush fields, and collapse in a pile of sweat against our packs as we gazed across the canyon to the lookout. Nothing but empty space between us and the place where Ann must be sitting in a cool breeze near the window.

Our fantasies fueled us up the seven miles of trail through the big trees. Now you can drive within 35 minutes of the lake.

BOULDER LAKES TRAILHEAD

Access: North on State Highway 3, 36.5 miles from Weaverville. Watch for sign and turn west about one-fourth mile south of Coffee Creek Bridge. Follow road 37N53 11 miles to trailhead. When in doubt as to which road to follow when confronted with a choice, always take the road that looks most traveled. Nearest campground is **Trinity River Campground** 1.5 miles north on Highway 3.

Trails: Trail 8W20 climbs easily 1.5 miles through big trees to junction with Little Boulder Lake Trail(8W11) and 0.5 miles later drops down to Big Boulder Lake. At the lake, Trail 8W20 heads downstream and around to the Boulder Creek Trail (8W08) and Trail 8W26 goes up over the ridge to meet the Poison Canyon Trail (8W10).

Destinations: Little Boulder Lake Big Boulder Lake, Tapie Lake, Found Lake, Lost Lake.

Elevation/Difficulty: 5,800 feet at trailhead. Short, easy to moderate trails.

Summary: Popular lakes heavily overused. Easy day hiking for families.

BUCKS LAKE

Elevation 6,800 feet; .8 acres; 9 feet deep. This small lake is at the head of Saloon Creek, tributary to the North Fork of Coffee Creek. Lies just over the ridge from the South Fork Lakes. Good population of brookies to 8 inches. **North Fork Coffee Creek or Long Gulch Trailhead.**

This little speck of water, off by itself with no trail, can be a lot of fun, either as a day hike from Upper South Fork Lake or as a station on your cross-country trek between Trail Gulch Lake and the North Fork of Coffee Creek. Not likely you'll see any people here, and with some luck you may ding a couple of brookies.

Big Caribou Lake

CARIBOU LAKE (BIG)

Elevation 6,850 feet; 72 acres; 72 feet deep. This, the largest glacial lake in the Trinity Alps, is located in a beautiful setting at the head of the Caribou Basin. This basin probably attracts more people than any other section of the back country. Many people make the trip just for the spectacular scenery, although the fishing is good. A four-hour ride from Big Flat at the head of Coffee Creek. Brook trout are abundant, along with fair-sized rainbow and a few brown trout. **Big Flat Trailhead.**

La madre grande! This is the big mutha. Not only is it the biggest lake in the Trinities, it is big enough to hold Emerald and Sapphire lakes and still have room left over to throw in a couple others. Caribou has a couple of islands, and–who knows–maybe even surf or its own tide!

Years ago it was said that this place was very crowded, but that has faded of late. Canyon Creek likely gets more traffic these days. Still, crowds gather at times. Thankfully, Caribou is a big enough lake that there's room for people to spread out.

It's a short stroll from the lake up to the Stuart Fork divide. A glance down the other side and you'll see Morris Meadow to the south, Emerald and Sapphire to the west. The big hunk of mountain to the southwest is Sawtooth Peak, poking an 8,886-foot hole in the sky. Zigzagging down into Stuart Fork is the trail known as KT-87. Someone counted 87 kick-turns, or switch backs, from the divide down to Portuguese camp. I think they underestimated the number.

I've never climbed *up* KT-87, but have gone *down* it several times. South-facing, the climb up can be brutal on a summer afternoon. No water. No shade. Not long ago, a young man lost his life from heat exhaustion during a scorching climb up the trail. His companions left him along the trail and continued on to Caribou Lake. When his condition was reported to a wilderness patrol person in the area, there was confusion between Big Flat and another Big Flat located miles away on the Trinity River, which further delayed rescue efforts. He died long before rescuers reached the site. Carry water on KT-87 and stick together. Good advice for most adventures.

The Caribou Basin is a fairly easy eight miles from the trailhead at Big Flat now that the trail skirts around the mountain via Brown's Meadow. The old trail, which you can still find if you know where to look, went right up over the shoulder of Caribou Mountain, 8,118 feet. It is shorter, but way tougher.

Pick a campsite on the west side of the lake and be rewarded with alpenglow on Caribou Mountain in the evening, and fantastic reflections of the moon on the water as it rises over the mountain.

CARIBOU LAKE (LITTLE)

Elevation 7,150 feet; 3 acres; 16 feet deep. This lake, which is not situated in the Caribou Basin, is a two-hour ride from Big Flat, the last mile being more suited to mule than horse travel. Contains brook trout. **Big Flat Trailhead.**

There was a time when people at least *saw* Little Caribou Lake as they ascended the old gut-busting ridge trail to Big Caribou. Now the new trail gives no hint that up at the head of Conrad Gulch is a nice little lake.

Follow the new trail until you're pretty sure you're in Conrad Gulch. Check your map. Up above the trail will be slabs of white granite. It isn't too difficult to pick and bounce up the granite to the lake. Should you find that some thoughtless person has left rock ducks (cairns) to mark the way, kindly destroy them. People coming after you deserve the wilderness enjoyment of route-finding that you were denied by the rock-duck builder. Rock ducks really are an unsightly nuisance in any Wilderness Area, and the Trinity Alps are no exception. Think about it. Wilderness implies an individual experience devoid of signs of human intrusion.

"...A wilderness, in contrast with those areas where man and his works dominate the landscape, is hereby recognized as an area where the Earth and its community of life are untrammeled by man, where man himself is a visitor who does not remain...." (The

Wilderness Act, 1964) Although not politically correct, the message is clear. A visitor to a Wilderness Area ought not be building rock ducks.

Off-trail route-finding is a satisfying and rewarding skill that all wilderness travelers need to use and perfect. Those who want a well-marked pathway in the mountains should darn well stay on the trail. The really aggravating rock ducks are those along well-established trails. What point is there is in building a rock duck on an obvious trail? It's a free country–so go ahead and build rock ducks if you feel the need. I, for one, will never build one and, this being a free country, will destroy any I find in the wilderness when I have the energy. Same goes for fire rings. Heed the admonition of the 1964 Wilderness Act, and don't be trammeling up the wilderness.

A stay at Little Caribou Lake will please the angler, sunbather, reader, and seeker of nothing to do. It's a lot like a small town bypassed by the new Interstate highway. It makes a nice destination for a day hike from Big Flat.

Any time someone tells you they have been to *every* lake in the Alps, hit'em with Little Caribou. Chances are they'll have to lie to say they've been there.

CARIBOU LAKE (LOWER)

Elevation 6,500 feet; 22 acres; 83 feet deep. Located at the lower end of Caribou Basin. A beautiful deep lake surrounded by high steep mountains and sheer granite cliffs. Has rainbow and brook trout, some of large size. **Big Flat Trailhead.**

Caribou country is Steele country–Ethel Steele Pettis. Her family has had a presence in this area for nearly 150 years. It was Ethel's great-grandfather, James Abrams, who built the cabin at Big Flat in 1850. It is still standing. They got into the horse-packing business early and have been up and down the mountains of this part of the Alps ever since.

It was the Steeles who helped pack fish to the Caribou Basin in the 1930s.

Ethel Steele was way ahead of women's lib and the ERA. She was doing it herself for more than 40 years. She was training young women in the horse-packing game before anyone figured it might be contrary to traditional gender roles.

Ethel once said, "Really living is sleeping out in the wilderness under the stars."

"I've never been lost, and I've never lost a guest," she says of herself and her horse-packing services.

Lower Caribou Lake can be a sanctuary when the crowds build up in the basin. Set your camp over on the far north side of the lake, opposite where the trail passes. The lake is big enough to make a good buffer from traffic passing through on the way to the big lake. Besides, over there, your back door opens out onto a huge chunk of wilderness. No one will be coming up Caribou Creek.

Middle Caribou Lake

CARIBOU LAKE (MIDDLE)

Elevation 6,500 feet; .5 acres; 10 feet deep. This little lake is in the center of Caribou Basin. It has a few small brook trout and an occasional brown or rainbow that has dropped down from Big Caribou Lake. **Big Flat Trailhead.**

A typical reaction to Middle Caribou is, "What! Where's the lake?"

But sure enough, there it is, tucked away under the base of a nice bunch of granite, a little waterfall at the outlet, with someone always camped on the shoreline.

You can see the diminutive brook trout with white-tipped fins cruising the clear water. If you could comprehend and understand all that is contained in this half-acre lake, the secrets of the Alps would be yours. A day at Middle Caribou Lake is likely to enrich your life. The place saturates every part of your body with its beauty. If it doesn't, the term "brain-dead" comes to mind.

Watch the expressions that appear across the lake. A passing cloud, a flash of sun, even the dab of a dragonfly touching the surface. Maybe this is what John Muir had in mind when describing lakes that lie nestled in glacier wombs:

"How boundless the day seems as we revel in the storm-beaten sky gardens amid so vast a congregation of onlooklng mountains."

Old John never made it to Middle Caribou Lake, but it's just as well. In the Alps you can be your own John Muir. Write your own book! Sing your own songs.

Caribou Mountain from Big Caribou Lake

CARIBOU MOUNTAIN

(8,575 feet) **Big Flat Trailhead.** Prior to the 1950s anyone going to the Caribou Basin from Big Flat on Coffee Creek practically climbed Caribou Mountain, since the trail went right up over the shoulder of the mountain. The high point of the trail was only about 500 vertical feet lower than the summit. That trail still exists, although it's seldom used. It's still the best approach. Where the trail reaches the top of the ridge, it's a matter of staying on the north side just below the nasty ridgeline and working your way to the summit.

Snow hangs late into the summer on this north side, requiring caution. A slip on the snow could result in a long, fast glissade that you might never recover from.

The bare granite slabs skirting Caribou Mountain offer myriad boulder-hopping and scrambling opportunities to reach the summit. Both Snowslide and Josephine lakes make excellent bases camps to work from.

CARTER'S LITTLE MUD LAKE

Elevation 6,300 feet; 1 acre; 8 feet deep. This small lake can be reached by taking the trail from Caribou Basin to the Middle Fork of South Fork of Salmon River and working up to the lake from that trail. It is doubtful that this little lake would sustain a trout population, and at present no plans have been made to stock it. **Big Flat Trailhead.**

Here is an example of the unintentional humor to be found in the original *Know-It-All Guide*. Carter's Little Mud Lake. Not many people are laughing, especially the ones fortunate enough to find it. Not many have found it. Even fewer people want to go back.

Now, where is it? Not named on the topographic map, or any other map that I've ever seen, it appears as a small circle at the headwaters of the Middle Fork of the South Fork of Salmon River. The small circle marks the frog pond called Carter's Little Mud Lake. Does the name make you think of pills, too?

This is fine, wild country. No trails. Just you and your wits on a north-flowing stream. Perhaps if you were to spend the night here you'd be able to see a glow in the sky from the campfires over the ridge at Big Caribou Lake.

The easiest way (but it ain't all that easy) is over the ridge from Big Caribou. Aim directly for the low spot to the west of the lake. Once in this gap it's straight down through the timber to the lake. You won't see it until you're there.

You could use the trail from Caribou Basin to the South Fork of Salmon River and catch the outlet stream and follow it to the lake. Then too, I suppose, you could tackle the montane chaparral slope to the north of Emerald Lake in Stuart Fork and come in over Sawtooth Ridge. That would be rough, but possible.

Only a highly motivated hiker with private reasons will visit Carter's Little Mud Lake. No one ends up at this lake by mistake.

CARTER MEADOWS TRAILHEAD

Access: Twelve miles from Callahan on the Callahan/Cecilville road. Trailhead at the summit on short spur road to the heliport. **Trail Creek Campground** nearby.

Trails: Pacific Crest Trail crosses road at this point leading north to Canada and South to Mexico. Trail 9W160 is a short, easy one mile trail to Hidden Lake.

Destinations: Hidden Lake, South Fork Lakes, Pacific Crest Trail.

Elevations/Difficulty: 6,500 feet at trailhead. Short, fairly easy. Difficult to South Fork Lakes.

Summary: Quick day hike to a small lake. Most direct route to South Fork Lakes.

DEADMAN PEAK

(7,741 feet) or (7,650 feet) Two peaks with the same moribund name straddle the Trinity/Siskiyou county line; one above Trail Gulch Lake (7,650 feet), the other overlooking Poison Lake (7,741 feet).

What gives? A surveyor for the Forest Service once told me that it appears that a lot of the surveying of Trinity County had been done in local bars. On early Klamath Forest maps the higher peak is labeled Deadman Peak, while on Shasta-Trinity Forest maps Deadman Peak is located on the lower peak above Trail Gulch Lake. Most recreation and guidebook maps are copied from the Shasta-Trinity maps and go with the lower peak. A search of early topographic maps reveals Deadman Peak to be the higher one.

You'll have to decide. Maybe climb them both just to be sure.

The 7,741-foot Deadman Peak is easiest approached from the **Trail Gulch Trailhead** on trail 9W14 to the divide and then south on trail 9W16 to the ridge south of the peak. It's a steep scramble from there.

The 7,650-foot Deadman Peak can be climbed from **Trail Gulch Trailhead** (the most direct), Deadman Gulch on the South Fork of Coffee Creek, or from the pass along the Trail Gulch/South Fork of Coffee Creek trails.

The peak, whichever it is, takes its name from an incident in January 1857 when the Rev. J.A. Brooks died in a snowstorm in the area. Rev. Brooks was from Orleans Bar on the Klamath River. He was returning from a visit to Placer County, packing 57 pounds of books for his church, when he lost his way trying to get over the ridge between Coffee Creek and the South Fork of the Salmon River. His body was never found.

DOE LAKE

Elevation 7,000 feet; 4.5 acres; 15 feet deep. A 10-mile, five- to six-hour ride up the East Fork of Coffee Creek to the lake. Eastern brook to 10 inches abundant. Campsites and feed for stock. **Stoddard Lake or East Fork of Coffee Creek Trailhead.**

It's amazing that more people don't spend more time at Doe Lake. Deep in the wilderness, at the base of a granite slope, fishing and swimming possible, all the ingredients are there. As it is, Granite Lake and Stoddard Lake get most of the action in this part of the Alps.

The trail from Granite yields stunning views of Sawtooth Peak, Thompson Peak and Caribou Mountain, the monster mountains of the Trinity Alps. Doe Lake can be reached from either the North Fork of Coffee Creek Trailhead or the East Fork of Coffee Creek Trailhead. The two trailheads are only a mile apart, so a loop trip is natural. Choose your direction, clockwise or counter-clockwise.

Counter-clockwise takes you up the East Fork of Coffee Creek to what's left of Stoddard Cabin and then through Doe Flat to Doe Lake. Past Doe Lake, you'll drop into Granite Lake and roll down Granite Creek and on down the North Fork of Coffee Creek past Hodges Cabin to the North Fork of Coffee Creek Trailhead. Clockwise, obviously, is just the opposite.

Waterfall on Granite Creek

EAGLE PEAK

(7,789 feet) West Boulder Creek, East Boulder Creek, Eagle Creek Trailheads. An Interstate highway in the form of the Pacific Crest Trail runs all along one side of Eagle Peak. At any point along the PCT you can make a trip to the summit. The most direct approach would be from the West Boulder Creek Trailhead, hiking past Telephone Lake to the gap leading to the PCT. From the gap, follow the ridge to the top.

Near the Shasta View Mine, on the mountain's south side, you'll find one of the coldest freshwater springs in the Western Hemisphere. The water is a teeth-cracking 42 degrees. A drink of something more than water: of earth juice, of nectar, of the essence and soul of the Trinity Alps.

EAST BOULDER CREEK TRAILHEAD

Access: 5.5 miles from Callahan on 40N17 through McKeen Divide. Watch or sign at road 39N10 and turn left. Nearest campgrounds are **Scott Mountain Campground** 15 miles away on Highway 3 and **Trail Creek Campground** below Carter's Meadow on the Callahan/Cecilville road.

Trails: Trail 8W042 is a relatively short two miles with connections to the PCT to the south, Little Mill Creek Trail (8W010) to the east and Middle Boulder Lake Trail (8W062) to the west.

Destinations: East, Upper, and Lower Boulder Lakes.

Elevation/Difficulty: 5,200 feet at trailhead. Moderate.

Summary: Quick hike to a panoramic alpine basin containing a good-sized lake and tumbling streams surrounded by jagged peaks.

EAST BOULDER LAKE

Elevation 6,700 feet; 32 acres; 60 feet deep. Six miles by road from Callahan and then one and a half miles by trail up East Boulder Creek to the lake. **East Boulder Creek Trailhead.**

Here's the lake for the angler bent on catching a good-sized brook trout. There is so much natural food and reproduction that the fish can all be called "wild," since they don't have to plant it any longer. They still aren't native to the Alps.

By Alps standards, this is a big lake. You'll find it in a spacious open basin often shared with cows and saddle stock, giving the place an Old West quality. In the glow of evening, the landscape can have all the Arcadian elements of a 19th century Romantic painting, a few silhouetted conifers framing the foreground, horses grazing in the middle distance, wispy blue smoke from a campfire drifting aimlessly, the faint softly lit mountains in the background.

Luckily, there's a lot of real estate around the lake available for a campsite removed from the olfactory experience of bovine byproducts.

The sagebrush in this area is a pleasant surprise. You wouldn't think this plant of the Great Basin would find its way into the Alps. Perhaps it was transplanted from the desert in the intestines of cows wintered in Nevada and summered in this basin.

Sagebrush is from the mint family (*Artemisia*). Take a couple of sprigs and rub it between your fingers and sniff deeply. That's an aroma you will never forget. Natives once burned bundles of sagebrush leaves as a purifying incense. Western cattlemen burned it as a mosquito-repellent smoke. In Europe it is known as wormwood. The smell of wet sagebrush:

> *"Hail Artemisia,*
> *aromatic in the rain,*
> *I will think of you in my other poems."*
>
> – Gary Snyder

EAST FORK COFFEE CREEK TRAILHEAD

Access: Located on Coffee Creek Road (County Road 104) just over the bridge crossing the East Fork of Coffee Creek. **Goldfield Campground** is just off Coffee Creek Road a couple of miles from the trailhead.

Trails: Trail 8W06 climbs through rocky terrain past the Holland Mine, which was destroyed by a landslide in 1983, to a junction with a spur trail to Stoddard Lake and continues on to the Doe Lake Trail (8W05).

Destinations: Stoddard Lake, McDonald Lake, Upper Stoddard Lake, Doe Lake, Stoddard Cabin, Granite Lake.

Elevation/Difficulty: 3,550 feet at trailhead to more than 6,000 feet at headwater lakes. Moderate steady-climbing trail.

Summary: There is the possibility of a loop hike via Doe and Granite Lakes to the North Fork of Coffee Creek. The North Fork trailhead is only a mile on up the road from this trailhead.

FISH LAKE

Elevation 6,050 feet; 3 acres; 4 feet deep. Cross the East Fork of South Fork of the Salmon River about one mile above the Trail Creek Campground. Then two miles on USFS 39N05 to Fish Lake Creek Bridge. A one and a half mile, one hour hike to the lake from the bridge. Contains a large population of Eastern brook trout. **Fish Lake Trailhead.**

Fish Lake? Seems the logical choice to catch fish, doesn't it? What could be a better choice from more than a hundred Alps lakes for catching a fish than one called Fish Lake? Fish Lake should have fish. And it does. It's just a shallow pond with enough natural reproduction that the Department of Fish and Game feels no need to stock it anymore. The angler who knows how to entice brookies to the hook in three feet of water will be rewarded.

Use a long cast and fast retrieve if you are using a small spinner. Fly-fishermen need a fine, long leader and floating line when trying to work a fly. After each strike, there is often a wait until the water calms down before you'll be able to get another bite.

Arctic grayling were introduced into Fish Lake in the 1970s, but it's been a long time since anyone reported catching one. Maybe nobody is talking. Maybe they aren't there any more.

FISH LAKE TRAILHEAD

Access: Take road 39N08 off the Callahan/Cecilville road 17 miles from Callahan. Watch for **Trail Creek Campground**. Less than a mile from campground, find 39N05 to trailhead.

Trails: Trail 10W200 passes Fish Lake at 3miles, continues to the divide, where it forks into Trail 9W16 to Rush Creek, Trail 9W04 down the South Fork of Coffee Creek, and Trail 9W14 down Trail Gulch.

Destinations: Twin Lakes, Fish Lake, Deadman Peak, Coffee Creek, Trail Gulch, Rush Creek, Rush Creek Lake.

Elevation/Difficulty: 5,300 feet at trailhead. Moderate to lake. Difficult from lake to ridge.

Summary: Fish Lake may disappoint. Trail from lake to ridgetop is steep and hard to find.

FOSTER LAKE

Elevation 7,250 feet; 5.5 acres; 20 feet deep. Named after a pioneer Trinity Center family. The main access route is up to Union Creek and then up the outlet to the lake; a distance of about 10 miles from Coffee Creek. A good brook trout lake. **Union Creek Trailhead.**

Foster Lake on the old *Know-It-All Guide* was called Bear Lake. The U.S. Geological Survey topographical and U.S. Forest Service maps label it Foster. Makes you wonder who is in charge of naming these places. Who knows why a name sticks or not.

Whatever its name, you'll find it on the divide between Union Creek and Boulder Creek. Come up either creek or make a loop out of it.

Union Creek is the easier way to do it because the elevation gain is less, plus it is shorter. The trail up Union Creek is more gentle than the Boulder Creek trail and has a few ghosts left over from the Dorleska Mine up through Bullard's Basin.

The Dorleska Mine first fired up in 1898 by R.D. Laurence, who named the site after his wife, Dorleska. Due to its extremely remote location, much of the heavy equipment had to be hauled in by mule teams. Probably no more than a couple of dozen people ever lived here, but there were a number of buildings, including a sawmill and two stamp mills for processing the gold ore.

Dump and tailing areas, as well as piles of scrap wood and metal, still remain. Close to 2,000 feet of tunnels were dug, and a snowshed was built over the tracks which brought the ore to the stamp mills in order to allow work to go on through the winter snows, often 25 feet deep. Mabel Steele, who was born over on the headwaters of Coffee Creek, lived at the Dorleska as a little girl and remembers Christmas in 1900 when the cabins were all covered with snow with only smooth mounds to show where they were. The windows were blocked with snow, and kerosene lamps burned all during the day.

It is said the ore ran up to $2,000 per ton. Mabel remembers the beautiful sight of candlelight on the white quartz, streaked with tellurium and encrusted with shining gold, hundreds of feet down in the face of the mine shaft.

Many years later, as an adult, Mabel visited the Dorleska Mine, noticing the old machinery she had seen shiny and new as a child when it was brought in to extract the gold from the ground. She commented:

"Last hunting season (1955) I rode by the old mine accompanied by my son and his wife returning from a cattle drive. It was dusk, and a party of hunters were camped in the old cookhouse and had built a large bonfire just outside. Hearing our horses approaching, they called a cheery greeting, and as we came up they informed us of their good luck in getting a large buck as well as a small bear. We stayed only a few minutes, and as it was late, we rode on.

Crossing the granite flats, I looked to the right toward where once stood the cabins that sheltered us all during that long snowy winter at the turn of the century. The cabins are gone now, and all is bare and lonely. I thought of the cold November evening when I saw the scene for the first time. It was cold and windy, with a sheet of snow falling, but through the windows shone the welcome lights of the kerosene lamps. I also thought of the ones who were our companions then, now all passed away except two or perhaps three.

A little later we paused at the summit of the pass and looked back. The flats lay gray and ghostly under the early moon, but the campfire burned brightly and it seemed to me a good omen that perhaps someday in the future, warmth and life may come again to the old Dorleska Mine."

Personally, I think that the mining era of the Trinity Alps is fading into the indiscernible past.

The last mile up to Foster Lake is steep enough to make you breathe hard. Just after crossing Union Creek, where the trail starts the final climb to the lake, you'll find a gushing stream that must come direct from an ice cave somewhere. Cold enough to crack your teeth. This is the last water there is until you get to the lake. Never pass up drinking water in the Alps, but filtering or other treatment is a good idea.

You might stumble upon Foster/Bear Lake from the Boulder Creek side. This approach was a lot more fun back when there was no trail over from Lion Lake. Now the Forest Service has constructed an Interstate-quality trail over the divide. In fact, more than one person has been on the way to Lion Lake, failed to look up while plodding along, and found themselves well past Lion and almost over the divide on the way to Foster. There is probably a need for an off ramp to Lion Lake. Why there is a need for more than a simple trail in a wilderness is a question we should all ask ourselves.

FOUND LAKE

Elevation 6,800 feet; 2.5 acres; 9 feet deep. This lake is situated above Lost Lake, which is above Big Boulder Lake. It is three hours to Big Boulder Lake and then another hour up to Found Lake. Marginal fish habitat. **Boulder Lakes Trailhead.**

Found Lake is the finale of Boulder Creek. The name "lake" may be a misnomer for the frog pond you're going to find at the end of a 45-minute hike up from Big Boulder Lake. There is no trail, but none is needed, as all you have to do is follow the stream (stream bed after mid summer) from Big Boulder Lake to Lost Lake (Tapie), and then up to Found Lake.

The late afternoon sun in 1958 was backlighting the airborne pine pollen that drifted through the forest. I was young enough to be able to linger that summer above Found Lake for no reason. I sat for a few hours on the granite boulders above Cub Wallow, watching a hawk climb the shadows up out of the canyon. The dark texture of trees beyond the hawk, covering the faraway ridge, was really the hair on my leg, only the hair on my leg wasn't my leg, it was the faraway ridge, and it wasn't the forest or mountains, but my body. People climb the shadows looking for places to camp in my brain, leaving their garbage in my bloodstream, digging a latrine near my heart.

Fortunately no one stays for long. Found Lake is open only four or five months of the year.

There's a little confusion concerning the three "lakes" to be found (no pun intended) in this area. There are actually three bodies of water and three names, but the names Lost and Tapie are used rather interchangeably, not to mention that at least one popular map labels one lake Found, one Lost, and one Tapie. Other maps have Lost where Tapie is. Some maps only have a Lost and Found and no Tapie at all. You'll have to decide what lake you are at when you get there.

FOX CREEK LAKE

Elevation 6,600 feet; 9.5 acres, 38 feet deep. It's seven miles by road from Callahan to the start of the Fox Creek Ridge Trail and about four miles to the lake via Mavis Lake. Eastern brook, rainbow, and brown trout are in the lake. This is a productive lake with good natural reproduction. **Fox Creek Ridge Trailhead**.

I never thought I'd ever see a three-pound brook trout, but that was before I knew of Fox Creek Lake. Fishing in the late fall in the Alps is often most productive, as trout seem to go on a feeding binge in preparation for the long winter under the ice soon to come. For years, knowledgeable anglers timed their trip to this lake for the last few days before the first snow of winter. Husky, brawny, one to three pound brookies were often the reward.

Once word got around, the big trout population diminished. There are still some lunkers in here. Late at night a distant crash, as if someone has thrown a refrigerator into the lake, startles light sleepers awake. Unable to fall back to sleep, you lie there in your sleeping bag, listening to the night sounds of a mountain lake.

Frogs squeak in unison, starting and stopping on queue; water lightly laps the rocky shoreline, a pine creaks and groans, a muffled hoof thuds the duff followed by a sharp snort, and a trout silently rockets upward through the black water, becomes airborne, stalls, and falls back to the surface with a flat smacking splat. Colossal fish finning through the dreams of sleeping anglers are common at Fox Creek Lake.

Lily pads push out from the grassy shoreline around most of the lake, making fishing difficult, but that's where the big ones are. Too many people camp where the trail hits the lake. It looks hammered. Superior and cleaner campsites with lake access await on the far side among the rock ledges.

I recently followed the old trail, now unmaintained, that follows the outlet stream from road 40N17. It's the shortest way. It took me about an hour and twenty minutes from the car, but I spent most of my time looking for the trail. Some tree blazes remain. With a little route-finding, it's possible to negotiate the swampy brush areas where the trail plays hide-and-seek.

FOX CREEK RIDGE/MAVIS LAKE TRAILHEAD

Access: Seven miles from Callahan on 40N17 through McKeen Divide. Parking and a stock unloading ramp. Nearest campgrounds are **Scott Mountain Campground** 15 miles away on Highway 3 and **Trail Creek Campground** below Carter's Meadow on the Callahan/Cecilville road.

Trails: Trail 8W102 climbs steadily 2.5 miles along ridge where spur trail forks right to several lakes. Straight ahead at top of divide it crosses the PCT at right angles and meets trail 8W03, which drops down Granite Creek.

Destinations: Mavis Lake, Fox Creek Lake, Virginia Lake, Section Line Lake, Pacific Crest Trail, and Wolford Cabin.

Elevation/Difficulty: 4,800 feet at trailhead. Moderate.
Summary: Several good fishing lakes in accessible country favored by horse packers.

GARTER SNAKE LAKE
Elevation 6,900 feet; .75 acres; 8 feet deep. A forty five minute hike from Middle Boulder Lake. This lake is not stocked by the California Department of Fish and Game. **East or West Boulder Creek Trailhead.**

If rattlesnakes were as prolific as garter snakes there'd be a whole lot more cases of snakebite in the Alps. You'll find harmless garter snakes at most Alps lakes. It's fitting to name a lake after the little guys. After all, there is a Rattlesnake Lake over on the western side of this wilderness.

Garter snakes (yes, it is two words) serve a vital ecological purpose as they streak around eating frogs, frog eggs, insects, bird eggs, and small rodents. Their speed is amazing, especially when compared to the slow, lumbering rattlesnake. But they aren't quite fast enough to avoid being a meal for raptors circling overhead.

Garter Snake Lake would be called Water Dog Lake if it were in the western Green Trinities. We know that all alpine lakes, in the evolution of the landscape, will become meadows. This one is almost there. Check back in a couple of hundred years and Garter Snake and its nearby buddy, Sage Lake, will be a lush green meadow.

GRANITE LAKE
Elevation 6,400 feet; 6.3 acres; 12 feet deep. From the Eagle Creek Ranch it is about a 12-mile, six-hour ride to the lake. Also reached by going up the North Fork of Coffee Creek and then up Granite Creek. Both brook and rainbow trout in good condition to 12 inches, caught in 1956. Some natural reproduction. Good campsites and limited feed. **North Fork of Coffee Creek Trailhead.**

Not to be confused with the Granite Lake up Swift Creek. On some maps it's called Little Granite Lake, in an effort to avoid the confusion, I suppose. Once you've seen both lakes, you won't ever get them mixed up. Granite Lake up Swift Creek is three times bigger, three times deeper, and 100 times more heavily hit by people. This Granite Lake, on a tributary of the North Fork of Coffee Creek, is a shallow, muddy little affair with some pretty good fishing for brookies, but not much else.

If you thought the trail up Granite Creek to the lake was steep, the trail that climbs the ridge from here to Doe Lake is even steeper: a gut-busting mile of switchbacking. Even if you are not going to Doe Lake, the hike is worth the view. Let's face it, there's only so much you can do at a Granite Lake and a hike up to look the country over is just what you need. Once up the steep first mile, the trail mellows out and contours along the south side of an unnamed peak (7,360 feet). Distinct and stupendous on the horizon are the heavyweights of the Alps: Sawtooth Peak, Thompson Peak, and Caribou Mountain. Continue a little farther on to the Doe Lake saddle and get a long clear shot of Mount Shasta, with Grey Rocks and Castle Crags in the foreground.

HIDDEN LAKE

Elevation 6,700 feet; 3 acres; 15 feet deep. Hidden Lake is situated almost at the top of the divide between the Salmon River and Scott River drainage. A 30-minute hike by trail from the heliport at the summit of the Cecilville/Callahan road. Contains Eastern brook trout. **Carter Meadow Summit Trailhead.**

Only have a day to spend? Here's your perfect picnic lake in the Alps. Of all the Alps lakes, Hidden is the closest to a trailhead. It's hard to remain hidden when a paved highway is less than thirty minutes walking time away, close enough to your car that you can carry a picnic basket to the lake, spend the day, and return just before dark.

Oddly enough, in spite of its proximity to civilization, not many people take the time to spend some time at Hidden Lake. Too bad. As Alps lakes go, it can hold its own in terms of location and alpine ambiance. Lounging on the grassy edge at the south end of the lake, I've been impressed that I am usually alone. Perhaps people are looking for more of a challenge and write Hidden Lake off as being too easy.

Looking for a challenge at Hidden Lake? Look no farther than the 7,900-foot, unnamed peak immediately south of the lake. It's the one that caught your attention while driving up from Callahan. Dramatic, dark and rugged, it's a short scramble, yielding exceptional views of the marvelous surrounding alpine landscape. The most reasonable route is to climb the steep scree slope south-southeast of the lake just as if you were going to the South Fork Lakes. Once on the divide where you can see the South Fork Lakes, start working the spine of the ridge, staying mostly on the south side, to the summit.

HOLLAND LAKE

Elevation 6,400 feet; .5 acres; 32 feet deep. No trail. Can be reached by following the outlet from the East Fork of Coffee Creek in the vicinity of the Holland Mine, or by following the ridge above Stoddard Lake southward for about two and a half hours. This small lake was stocked with brook trout in 1956. **Stoddard Lake or East Fork Of Coffee Creek Trailhead.**

I was with a U.S. Forest Service helicopter crew dismantling the Billy's Peak Lookout in the 1970s. The pilot gunned the Bell 205 Jet Ranger up Coffee Creek, skimming the treetops before pulling full power and pushing the stick to the right, bringing us up the East Fork and over the real Billy's Peak to the lookout. (The lookout was not on Billy's Peak, but on a lower peak to the southeast.) What caught my eye was a speck of blue tucked in tight below the saddle of the southernmost collection of spires collectively called Billy's Peak. Making a mental note of its location, I put it on my future hit list of lakes to visit.

There are two ways to hike into Holland Lake, both difficult and demanding cross-country route-finding skills. About three miles up the East Fork of Coffee Creek, the remnants of a huge mountain slide mark where once the Holland Mine was. This is where you'll start climbing up the obvious gulch to the south that leads to Holland Lake. It's steep, very steep, and brushy, very brushy, but the most direct way. The other choice is to bushwhack and contour your way over from Upper Stoddard Lake. You don't have to gain as much elevation, but as you contour, err on the side of going too high. Contour too low and you'll miss the lake and whack a lot of brush before discovering your error.

Contour high. The lake is a lot higher than you think.

The easiest route would be from a helicopter, but where's that U.S. Forest Service 'copter when I need it?

Guess you could camp at Holland Lake if you wanted to, but the few people who find it are day hikers who have accepted the challenge of finding the darn thing.

HYLA LAKE

Elevation 6,400 feet; 1 acre; 2 feet deep. This lake lies adjacent to Sedge Lake. It is not suitable for trout and has not been planted by the California Department of Fish and Game. **Fish Lake Trailhead.**

Sometimes called one of the Twin Lakes along with nearby Sedge Lake, Hyla is well named. It's not much of a fishing lake, but it has an abundance of frogs of the genus *Hyla*. It's a stiff little climb on a faint trail of about a mile from the Fish Lake Creek Trail. It's the perfect place for those seeking a wilderness frog pond. And, you might catch a trout in nearby Sedge Lake.

JOSEPHINE LAKE

Elevation 5,800 feet; 17 acres; 47 feet deep. Josephine Lake is located near the headwaters of the South Fork of the Salmon River. Being privately owned, it is *not* stocked by the Department of Fish and Game. **Big Flat Trailhead.**

It's a shame, but this lake somehow ended up in private ownership. Deplorable as this is in the eyes of wilderness lovers, the lake is not available to the public. If someone can own a lake in the Alps, they might as well own the clouds, the rain, the thunder of a summer storm.

Josephine Lake is like a fjord fitted into a tight granite slot adjacent to Caribou Mountain. High walls of rock on either side keep the sunshine hours to a minimum and may bring out latent claustrophobia in some people.

Drive to the end of Coffee Creek Road. If you come to a locked gate, that's it. Park and start walking. If you are overnighting, leave your car at Big Flat Campground. If the gate is open, drive to Josephine Creek Lodge and ask for permission to leave your car there. It is private property, but don't be intimidated. They own only a very small chunk of the canyon (Section 31) and can't prevent you from free travel through the area. The southwestern end of the lake is public land and can be used by you and me.

There are several pieces of private land within the Wilderness Area called "in holdings." Long before there was even a U.S. Forest Service, people were able to establish ownership on property that ended up inside the established wilderness boundaries. Attempts by the government over the years to either purchase or trade with the owners have failed. Most likely these inholdings are permanent fixtures in the Alps. Other notable areas under private ownership are Morris Meadow and Emerald Lake on Stuart Fork and several sections (one square mile each) north and south of Coffee Creek.

Josephine Lake

LADY GULCH TRAILHEAD

Access: On Coffee Creek Road (County Road 104) 14.5 miles from Highway 3. Watch for sign on left. **Big Flat Campground** is at the end of Coffee Cr. Road.
Trails: Trail 9W05 climbs steeply 2.4 miles to the ridgetop, where it junctions with McNeil Creek Trail (10W250) and the Rush Creek Trail (10W02).
Destinations: Packers Peak, Rush Creek Lake.
Elevation/Difficulty: 4,100 feet at trailhead. Difficult, but short.
Summary: Startling beautiful views of Caribou Mountain and the Central Alps. Massive white firs, several cold springs and the pungent smell of azaleas in the spring and early summer. Loop hike over Packers Peak and back to trailhead on Coffee Creek Road possible.

LANDERS LAKE

Elevation 7,100 feet; 6 acres; 17 feet deep. The level of Landers Lake fluctuates considerably, as the bottom is not sealed. A 10-mile trip via the Swift Creek and Landers Creek trails, and about the same distance up Union Creek from Coffee Creek. Also reached from Big Flat. Has some fair-sized rainbow trout. **Swift Creek or Union Creek Trailhead.**

Red. Red is the color of the rocks that tumble down off the mountain and surround Landers Lake. When you see the mountain, you'll know what its name is.

Landers Lake is right up close to the top of things–kind of a mountaintop lake where a short walk in several directions yields long views. Over to the north you can prop up against a rock and let your eye hike off down Union Creek and to Battle Mountain. Or, with a little exertion, you'll be up on Red Rock Mountain (7,853 feet) to the west, watching dangling skirts of thunderstorm scrape the peaks of the Marble Mountains far and way to the north. Those dark valleys seem to swallow, in quick great gulps, the jags of lightning. Dead ahead to the west and nose to nose with you is Caribou Mountain (8,875 feet). Were there ever caribou in these mountains?

Still looking north, below you from left to right, is a valley that looks as if a giant finger pushed through the primeval clay of the Alps, leaving a canyon for the South Fork of the Salmon River. This is an example of stream piracy where the upper South Fork of the Salmon River has beheaded Coffee Creek at Big Flat. Geologists guess that this happened in the early or middle Wisconsin period, somewhere around two million years ago, and that it was a direct result of glaciation. As the glacier moved northward down the valley of Coffee Creek, marginal melt waters spilled westward over a low divide between the Coffee Creek drainage and the headwaters of the South Fork of the Salmon River. This new stream cut rapidly into the low ridge as it fed into the steeper gorge, and it was able to maintain its course after the glacier receded. As you can see, the upper South Fork of the Salmon River makes an abrupt westward turn and flows at a right angle to the trend of the valley only about a mile from where Coffee Creek now heads at the same elevation.

There is much to be learned from sitting on mountain tops.

Lilypad Lake and Ycatapom Peak

LILYPAD LAKE

Elevation 6,300 feet; 2 acres; 8 feet deep. This lake is at the head of Poison Canyon, a tributary of the North Fork of Swift Creek. The best fishing in this lake is in the early summer, since later the surface becomes completely covered with lily pads, making it nearly impossible to fish. Eastern brook trout are plentiful, and some are of fair size. **North Fork Swift Creek or Lake Eleanor Trailhead.**

Yes, there are a lot of lily pads on this lake late in the summer. Best time, unless you plan to study lily pads, is about mid-June until mid-July.

There are several ways to get to Lilypad Lake. From the Lake Eleanor trailhead hike past Eleanor Lake, past Shimmy Lake, and cross the divide between Ycatapom Peak (7,596 feet) and Thumb Rock (7,735 feet) dropping down past some ponds to the lake. It's little more than a stroll to the summit of "The Why Cat" from the divide and the view from the top offers a heart-stopping look down the north face. Ycatapom is an tribal name that means "mountain that leans to the north."

Some people choose to visit Lilypad from the trail into Big Boulder Lake. This is big deer-hunting country. One autumn we came upon a deer hunter in Poison Canyon who had wandered over from Big Boulder Lake and spent the night after breaking his leg. Our plans to climb the Ycat were canceled as we helped him back to our car and on down to medical attention.

The main trail comes right up the North Fork of Swift Creek from a trailhead reached from the Lake Eleanor Road. Poison Canyon got its name from the sheep men who lost a lot of sheep in the canyon when they ate black laurel. My youngest daughter was stung by yellow jackets here one afternoon. Luckily, she didn't eat any black laurel.

There are two trails that find their way to Lilypad Lake in a roundabout way from Parker Creek. The longer route stays high above the headwaters of Boulder Creek and Cub Wallow. There is an opportunity to climb a good-looking unnamed peak (8,037 feet) that dominates the divide. One map names this peak "Mount Daisy," but I doubt that it has been cleared with the U.S. Geological Survey. Thumb Rock is an easy climb from this trail. The other trail leaves Parker Creek at Sandy Canyon and goes through Deer Flat, joining the route from Lake Eleanor described above.

LION LAKE

Elevation 7,000 feet; 3 acres; 37 feet deep. A four-hour, seven-mile trip up the Boulder Creek trail to the lake. Brook trout are plentiful. **Goldfield or Boulder Lakes Trailhead.**

The trail up Boulder Creek is the long way, used mostly by people on horseback. An alternative for the backpacker is to drive to the trailhead for Big Boulder Lake and hike into Big Boulder Lake. A little less than a mile downstream on the lake's outlet stream is a trail that works around to the west and drops down into Boulder Creek. The pointy knob you see to the west is Sugar Pine Butte (7,861 feet), best climbed from the other side from Sugar Pine Lake. If you can't find the trail, contour anyway. You can't miss hitting Boulder Creek eventually. Actually, once in Boulder Creek, some people prefer to follow the creek up to the outlet stream and then follow the outlet stream up past a couple of ponds to Lion Lake.

You might be surprised at the fish you can catch by casting into that pond right below the lake.

There is a lot of white granite and blue sky here. A short jaunt up over the low gap beyond the lake will put you on Foster/Bear Lake.

Lion Lake receives a fair amount of traffic, especially from the dude ranches down on Coffee Creek. While at Lion you would be remiss not to explore the upper reaches of Boulder Creek for some off-trail adventure. You'll find small feisty trout to catch in the stream. Follow the stream far enough and you'll be in another of those secret places of the Alps that were at one time known only to the sheep herders and cattlemen. Solitude guaranteed. The place is called Cub Wallow. The experience is lonesome. The animals match the meadow at the very headwall of the canyon. Both are wild!

LITTLE BOULDER LAKE

Elevation 6,350; 4.5 acres; 19 feet deep. Located about two miles by trail to the east of Boulder Lake. Also accessible by trail from Carrville and the North Fork of Swift Creek. Good population of both brook and rainbow trout. **Boulder Lakes Trailhead.**

I was sixteen years old when I peeled off my clothes and plunged into the crystalline waters of Little Boulder Lake. The first six inches were warm, but deeper it was close to 39 degrees. Later there was time to lay shivering on warm granite slabs and dream of golden-haired women.

Once, too early in the spring, we tried to follow the old trail from Carrville to the lake, lost the trail in the snow, and ended up down at the bottom of Buckeye Creek.

Timber-product companies, aided by the Forest Service, did their best to render this area unfit for wilderness status by building a maze of roads and chopping down all green things over six inches in diameter. They punched a road to within a 30-minute walk of the lake.

Nearly every other *square mile* in this part of the Trinity County belongs to a private timber company. How so much public land ended up in the hands of private individuals is one of those stories about your government in action that you don't want to hear. Seems that the U.S. government felt a need for a north/south railroad between California and Oregon. As an incentive to the railroad company, the government offered to give them a gift, every other square mile of land on either side of the right-of-way where the railroad would run.

So a route for the railroad was surveyed up through this country. The Southern Pacific Railroad was given every other square mile of land. Where's the railroad today, you ask? Oh yeah, they decided to build the actual railroad over on the Sacramento River. Meanwhile, Southern Pacific formed the Southern Pacific Land Company and kept the thousands of square miles given to them by the government in return for a railroad they never built.

Southern Pacific officials will tell you that they actually did eventually pay for the land by providing free shipping of war munitions for the government during World War II. Over the years, ownership of this land has passed from one timber-products company to another; and each in turn has clear-cut huge areas of it.

Lest anyone feels the public got snookered on the deal, remember that our government got blowout bargain prices on Manhattan Island for $24 from the natives and picked up Alaska from the Russians for a mere two cents an acre. It seems only fitting that someone should clip the government now and then, but we all lose when the forest is abused by cutting all of the trees. With establishment of the wilderness boundaries in 1984, efforts to trade private land within the wilderness for Forest Service land outside the boundary have moved slowly along.

To reach the trailhead for Little Boulder Lake, take the Carr Road, half a mile south of the Highway 3 bridge over Coffee Creek, and follow it until it ends. There may or may not be signs to direct you. They come and go over the years. The trail takes off at road's end and forks after a mile or so (to Big Boulder Lake). Stay left and soon you'll drop gently down to Little Boulder Lake.

Recently I sat by Little Boulder during a swirling snowstorm in early December, listening to the throaty sound of the wind in the pines, and thought about that kid jumping into the lake those many years ago. I could barely make out the granite boulders across the slate-gray water. Vision was dimmed and blurred by snowflakes riding the wings of the wind. My dreams have ceased to be of golden-haired women.

LITTLE MARSHY LAKE

Elevation 6,200 feet; 1.5 acres; 6 feet deep. This tarn lies just below Big Marshy Lake on the trail. Open shoreline and a good Eastern brook trout producer with flies. **Tangle Blue Lake Trailhead**.

There's not much reason to spend a lot of time at Little Marshy except to see if it will give up a brookie or two. It doesn't take long to find out. It's an easy 4.5-mile hike from the trailhead through wet meadows and soaring incense cedars. There's a lot of cattle and kids from Camp Unalayee grazing in the area, making all drinking water suspect.

LITTLE MILL CREEK TRAILHEAD

Access: From Callahan on road 40N16 past Bolivar Lookout Road.
Trails: Trail 8W010 follows canyon past Mill Creek Lake to East Boulder Lake.
Destinations: Mill Creek Lake, Washbasin Lake, Klatt Mine, East Boulder Lake.
Elevation/Difficulty: 5250 feet at trailhead. Easy for two miles, Moderate to lake at 6,600 feet.
Summary: Gentle meadows, scenic rock formations on Craggy Peak. Beautiful lake in granite setting.

LITTLE SOUTH FORK LAKE

Elevation 5,950 feet; 9 acres; 21 feet deep. Located at the head of Little South Fork Creek, a tributary to the South Fork of the Salmon River. No trail. From the Salmon River side, take the trail to the Caribou Basin; from where the trail leaves Little South Fork Creek make your way up the creek to the lake. You'll encounter considerable brush. The terrain is very rough between the Caribou Basin and the lake. Stocked with rainbow trout. **Big Flat or Stuart Fork Trailhead**.

There are several ways to reach this productive lake. All of them are tough, and none can be recommended. Previous guidebooks to the Trinity Alps don't even mention this lake. However, if you are dead set on catching huge fish, or want to step into a time machine and see what the Alps looked like 50, 75, even 175 years ago, then Little South Fork should be on your list.

My friend Gary Martin used to bust directly up Sawtooth Ridge from Emerald Lake, then drop down to L.S.F.L. That's 3,000 feet up and 3,000 feet down in less than a mile. Devastating.

Some deranged souls find their way in from Caribou Basin. But what a price to pay. A long, killing contour around the headwaters of Middle Fork of Little South Fork, followed by a 1,500 foot up-and-down over a ridge to reach the lake.

I contoured in from Grizzly Lake once when snow levels were low. The elevation loss/gain was physically challenging. Being on a north-facing ridge, this route always seems to have snow to some degree.

My friend Dick Everest is probably right. There ain't no good way to get to L.S.F.L., but if you have to go, take the drive around to Cecilville, find the Summerville Trailhead, and hike up the Little South Fork Trail for about four miles. From here you head upstream with no trail. The right side of the stream is rough and steep, but better than the left. In a little over a mile you'll hit the waterfall. Pass it on the right. The left side may be more tempting, but will add several exhausting hours to your hike. From the falls to the lake is another healthy mile of slow, tough grinding in low gear.

My Gawd! This is a tough lake.

Another acquaintance, Tom Stienstra, chose to hit Little South Fork Lake from

Caribou Basin. Faced with an altitude drop of 2,500 feet, then a climb of 3,500 feet without benefit of trail, they plunged off into the "considerable brush." Feeling like trailblazers back in the 1830s, they soon ran into a swarm of bees that sent them scattering in all directions. At one point the stream bed looked like an inviting avenue to the lake, but they ran head-on into a 100-foot waterfall. They named it Crystal Falls and then had to backtrack and climb up and around to get to the lake. Reaching the lake just before sunset after a two-mile hike that consumed some 10 hours, they were too tired to fish. But the next morning they were rewarded for the previous day's labor. In one stretch of seven casts, Tom reports five strikes and three landed rainbow trout measuring 12, 13, and 16 inches. The biggest of the day was over 17 inches. Another stripped off 20 feet of line before spitting the hook.

Yes, there are big fish in Little South Fork Lake. The Alps saves them for those willing to struggle.

LONG GULCH LAKE

Elevation 6,400 feet; 10 acres; 47 feet deep. The trail up Long Gulch from the access road off the Cecilville-Callahan Road is about a one-hour ride or hike to the lake. Eastern brook and rainbow trout are present. Large trout have been landed trolling from a raft with flasher lures. **Long Gulch Trailhead.**

If you've been to nearby Trail Gulch Lake you may experience *déja vu* upon arrival at Long Gulch Lake. The rocky cirque is darker in color than its neighbor, but with similar size and terrain it's surprising that they were not called Twin Lakes, Sister Lakes or Brother Lakes. It's a shorter hike to Long Gulch Lake than to Trail Gulch Lake, which is puzzling. Since the lakes are lookalikes, it seems sensible that the longer hike would be to Long Gulch and the shorter to Trail Gulch.

Speaking of long, you'll run into some folks who got here from the North and South Fork of Coffee Creek trailheads, a good six miles over the ridge to the south.

The 2.5 miles to Long Gulch Lake are short miles by USFS standards. It takes about 40 minutes of steady walking from the trailhead near Carter Meadow, spacious and well watered with grassy feed, which hosts large horse groups all summer long. Horses churn and stir their special equine signature with the soft trail dirt, leaving ankle-deep mulch for the hiker to wade through.

A favorite with inflatable raft enthusiasts, an armada of neoprene ships often ply the waters of Long Gulch Lake. By August the lake is warm enough for swimming.

This is not a destination for seekers of solitude.

LONG GULCH TRAILHEAD

Access: Just over the summit at Carter's Meadow on the Callahan/Cecilville Road 12.5 miles from Callahan on Highway 3, take loop road 39N08 and watch for sign. **Trail Creek Campground** is on down the road a way.

Trails: Trail 9W150 leads to Long Gulch Lake in 2 miles. Connects to Trail Gulch Trail (9W14), and Trail 8W902 down the North Fork of Coffee Creek, and Trail 9W61 through Steveale Meadow and the South Fork of Coffee Creek.

Destinations: Long Gulch Lake, North and South Fork of Coffee Creek, Buck Lake, Trail Gulch Lake.

Elevation/Difficulty: 5,100 feet at trailhead. Moderate walking in rugged country.
Summary: Loop trip possible to Trail Gulch Lake, as trailheads are less than a mile apart.

LOST LAKE (TAPIE LAKE)
Elevation 6,700 feet; 1.75 acres; 15 feet deep. It is a fifteen-minute climb (no trail) up to this lake from Big Boulder Lake. Eastern brook trout are plentiful. **Boulder Lakes Trailhead.**

On the U.S.G.S. topographic map this is called Tapie Lake. Tapie or Lost Lake causes some confusion depending on what map you are looking at. There are a number of ponds in the Alps of this caliber, but they are not fortunate enough to receive a name. Here sits a lake with two.

To get to Lost/Tapie, work your way up through the rock outcroppings above Big Boulder Lake. In spite of its name, it's not hard to find.

After you've had your fill of Lost Lake, there'll be plenty of time left over to do a little scrambling on the unnamed peak to the south. You might call it Tapie Peak, as one map does. Once on top, give yourself a nice geography lesson. Way over across Poison Canyon is Ycatapom Peak (7,596 feet). Ycatapom is an tribal name that means whatever a native wants it to mean. "Mountain that leans to the north" is one given meaning.

Due north you can study the route followed by the old trail/jeep road into the Boulder country.

Off to the west you can peek into Cub Wallow.

Way to the north is Mount Shasta.

Mount Shasta is California's Fujiyama, its Kilimanjaro, its Mont Blanc. It's said to be the most massive peak in the contiguous United States, containing over 80 cubic *miles* of material. "White as the winter moon and lonely as God" is an apt description penned by 19th-century poet Joaquin Miller.

Closer in, still looking north, is Billy's Peak. No, the lookout is no longer manned (womaned; see Big Boulder Lake). In fact, the lookout was dismantled in the '80s by the U.S. Forest Service. All the pieces not hauled off by helicopter were burned.

After the time you've spent on this unnamed peak, you'll feel that your trip to Lost Lake was not lost after all.

LOWER BOULDER LAKE
Elevation 6,300 feet; 4.5 acres; 3 feet deep. This lake is not stocked by the California Fish and Game Department. **East Boulder Creek Trailhead.**

Just when you think there can't possibly be another Boulder Lake, there is. With not much of an inlet or outlet, and no trail, it remains pretty much ignored except by grazing cattle in the East Boulder Creek drainage. Pollywogs, salamanders and a zillion frogs call it home.

It's only a few hundred yards off the trail through the timber about a mile shy of East Boulder Lake. To get a visual fix on its location, climb the trail past East Boulder that goes to Mill Creek Lake and look back down the canyon.

MAVIS LAKE

Elevation 6,700 feet; 3.5 acres; 16 feet deep. A fork about two and a half miles up the Fox Creek Ridge trail goes directly to Mavis Lake. Contains brook trout in good condition. **Fox Creek Ridge Trailhead.**

Mavis doesn't get nearly the traffic that Fox Creek Lake does. Just off the main trail, it's like a town just off the main highway; travelers have their destination in mind, and few are inclined to opt for a side trip. That's just as well; most would be disappointed with Mavis Lake. It's a little shallow, not much of a view, and cluttered with bleached blowdowns along the shoreline.

I've stopped at Mavis during the peak of several summers and found it devoid of people. Maybe what they don't know is that on the left-hand side of the lake is one of the finest sandy beaches of decomposed granite in the Alps. The summer sun stays on the beach until late in the afternoon, allowing a person to read and doze the slow hours away. Now and then you can hear horse traffic over on the trail to Fox Creek, but mostly it's just you and the soft lapping of the water against the sandy shore.

Mavis Lake Trailhead (see Fox Creek Ridge/Mavis Lake Trailhead)

McDONALD LAKE

Elevation 6,000 feet; 4 acres; Formerly called Middle Stoddard Lake. About a 10-minute walk up from Stoddard Lake. Populated with brookies. **Stoddard Lake Trailhead.**

Wander through the thick forest south of Stoddard Lake and perhaps escape the crowds of people, horses and cows draped around Stoddard's shoulders. Flies, horseflies, deerflies and mosquitoes love the piles of animal droppings produced by the menagerie the large lake attracts all summer long. They'll love you, too.

A rock outcropping at the upper end of McDonald affords stimulating plunges into delightfully nippy water and a place to soak up the sunshine afterward to smooth out the goose bumps. There are a few campsites. Fortunately, the big horse parties don't get beyond Stoddard, making it cleaner. But until midsummer, there's little relief from the mosquitoes.

McDonald and Stoddard lakes

MIDDLE BOULDER LAKE

Elevation 6,500 feet; 6.5 acres; 12 feet deep. Six miles by road from Callahan, then a four-mile hike up the West Boulder Creek trail. **West Boulder Creek Trailhead.**

Boulder Lakes redux. The rocky headwall above the lake, the mixed fir and pine forest laced with fields of sage brush and manzanita it's *déja vu* all over again. This could be any one of a half a dozen lakes in the Scott Mountains. A broad meadow borders the lake, inviting grazing by both human and bovine visitors.

Day hikes from a camp at Middle Boulder can take you to the Pacific Crest Trail to the south. It's a stiff pull of a thousand feet elevation in less than half a mile to the ridgetop. On the way, stop and catch your breath at the two sub-alpine ponds named

Garter Snake and Sage Lakes on some maps. Once on the ridgetop, and the PCT, go west to see if you can find the Shasta View Mine and the 42-degree spring near there, or make a stab at knocking off 7,789-foot Eagle Peak. Views from the ridgetop and Eagle Peak are in the stunning category, notably Mount Shasta to the north, Billy's Peak and the central Alps to the south.

Another day of hiking can be occupied by taking the trail around the shoulder of the mountain, through some fine sagebrush fields, to East Boulder and Upper Boulder lakes. It can be your bolder-boulder day.

MILL CREEK LAKE

Elevation 6,600 feet; 3 acres; 16 feet deep. Take the Mill Creek access road from Callahan five miles to the trailhead. Trail goes up Little Mill Creek three miles to the lake. Lake contains good population of Eastern brook trout. **Little Mill Creek Trailhead**.

From the Little Mill Creek Trailhead it's two miles of easy walking along an old logging/mining road through green meadows and tall timber under the brooding spires of Mount Craggy (8,089 feet). The last three-fourths of a mile climbs steeply over the granite boulders to the lake.

The lake offers a deluxe diving rock, small intimate campsites, and a marshy inlet meadow slowly pushing its way into the middle of the lake. The granite headwall above the lake is spectacular. Firewood is a bit scarce, but if you do choose to gather enough for a small fire, there is sagebrush to flavor the smoke.

The volcano you can see on the horizon is Mt. McLoughlin (9,495 feet) near Medford, Oregon.

This is a popular day hike from East Boulder Lake. The trail is super steep as it climbs up and over the divide to Little Mill Creek. Not the kind of trail you want to lug a pack over. Not when you can take a much kinder and gentler trail up Little Mill Creek from the trailhead.

Set deep down in a granite pocket, the lake is worth a few casts. Before long, you'll want to see if you can find Washbasin Lake. Turn to Washbasin Lake description elsewhere in this book.

MOSQUITO LAKE

Elevation 6,600 feet; 5.5 acres; 12 feet deep. Located in Tangle Blue Creek drainage. Contains brook and brown trout. **Tangle Blue Lake Trailhead**.

You won't be spending any time at this lake on account of Camp Unalayee, a private inholding in the Alps established forty years ago. All summer long there are roaming bands of young people from different racial and economic backgrounds living on the lake working on "wilderness skills, environmental education, and cooperative, multicultural living situations." Just what the Forest Service had in mind when they coined the term *multiple-use*.

However, prior to June (if it has been a light snow year) or after the end of August, this is a splendid lake to while away a day or two and perhaps catch a few fish.

From Scott Mountain there is a road to the lake, but a locked gate at the wilderness boundary, three miles from Highway 3, will put you afoot. Even if the gate is open, DO NOT drive into the wilderness. Severe penalties may be applied.

MUD LAKE

Elevation 6,600 feet; 1 acre; 3 feet deep. This very shallow lake is able to maintain fish because of the constant flow of water through it. It is nearly covered with water lilies, but does provide some brook trout fishing. It is located on the bench at the end of the trail below Lion Lake. **Goldfield or Boulder Lakes Trailhead.**

If the Alps has a forgotten closet way back in the rear of the house somewhere, this is it. Mud Lake by any other name would still be a mud lake. It is not very high on anyone's priority list of must-see lakes.

I first came across it while on the way to bigger and better (so I thought) Lion Lake. We had lost the trail coming over from Big Boulder Lake and were fighting our way cross country to Lion Lake when we stumbled upon Mud Lake.

So what the heck, said I. A #2 gold Mepps spinner cast casually among the lily pads brought everyone to their feet instantly. It almost seemed that the lake was full of piranha, so vicious was the attack on the lure. A fish, though hooked, would be assaulted by other fish as they tried to get the same lure. It was crazy. Sometimes a fish would get free, but another one would grab the spinning gold lure. We stayed and caught fish until our arms and wrists gave out from fatigue.

We went on up to Lion Lake, but between four of us we only caught one fish!

On the U.S.G.S. topographic map this lake is called Conway. Frederick Edmond Conway was an early miner on Swift Creek born in 1856. Neither Conway nor Mud is a very descriptive name for this lily-pad pond.

NO FISH LAKE

Elevation 6,900 feet; 1 acre; 7.5 feet deep. A small pond above Upper Boulder Lake. **West Boulder Creek Trailhead.**

Actually, there are two ponds above Upper Boulder Lake. Take your pick as to which is No Fish Lake. Neither pond has fish, they're just pretty little slips of water on the trail to the Pacific Crest Trail or over the ridge to Marshy Lakes and the Tangle Blue country.

NORTH FORK OF COFFEE CREEK

North Fork of Coffee Creek Trailhead. This is the place for lovers of historic cabins, with the value-added attraction of good fishing, perhaps the best fly-fishing stream in the Alps.

Francis Cabin, Hodges Cabin, Schlomberg Cabin, Wolford Cabin and a couple of others without names are reminders of a time when people meant to spend a lot of time here and needed permanent shelter. A small community once thrived at the mouth of Saloon Creek, known as Saloon City. Election records show that 700 votes were cast there in an 1850s election. It was never big enough to have a post office or school, but mining relics bear mute testimony to the sweat and toil poured into the ground to eke out a living in the wilderness. Nearby, up Milk Ranch Creek, there once lived about 300 people, and we suspect they had a pool hall because the billiard-type balls have been found in Chipmunk Meadows.

The cabins still standing date from the 1920s and the Depression years that followed. The handsome two-story Hodges cabin is the largest and is occupied some summers by volunteer U.S. Forest Service personnel who welcome company.

A Forest Service mile past Hodges Cabin, hang a right on Granite Creek and follow it to Wolford Cabin. It's in good enough shape to spend some time if you want to play pioneer and sleep in a log cabin. With an aluminum roof, it would be a fine place to listen to an afternoon thunderstorm or snuggle down cozy and awaken to the drumming of rain in the night.

In the valley of the North Fork of Coffee mountains are assumed, not seen, and the only long view is vertical to the sky beyond tall trees. A few miles from the trailhead the trail passes Douglas-firs, *Pseudotsuga menziesi* (which translates as "false hemlock"), too immense to walk by without pausing to take a look at, to touch. An occasional ancient cedar, with massive root buttresses, fire-blackened trunk and broken top, displays life-and-death struggle shaped by centuries of slow growth interrupted by sudden violence.

When the miles and shadows grow long in the afternoon and you think surely the forest and stream are without end, it's time to find a creekside bench with humus for a mattress, a gravel bar for a kitchen, a log for a seat, and a fire for warmth and light, as cool darkness fills the valley even before the sun has left the treetops.

There are numerous ideal campsites up and down the creek, and no sleep is so peaceful as a wilderness sleep by a creek. The usual things that bump and screech in the night are submerged in the sound of water plunging over smooth stones too deep to clutter or muddle the calm flow of your wilderness dreaming. Yet it is never a deep sleep, but rather a shallow blend of REM mixed with the fragrances and sounds of forest and falling waters, the steady pulsation of the creek and dreams of a hundred other remembered rivers and streams, and as you dream, the scent of fir needles just inches from your nose, the cool breeze on your cheek, all this and much more enters the dreamer into the snug dreams of other times, all flowing into a whole and complete dream of present and past.

NORTH FORK COFFEE CREEK TRAILHEAD

Access: Just a mile up the road from the East Fork of Coffee Creek Trailhead on the Coffee Creek Road (County Road 104). **Big Flat Campground** is at the end of the Coffee Creek Road and **Goldfield Campground** is four miles from the trailhead.

Trails: Trail 9W02 follows the North Fork of Coffee Creek past the historic Hodges and Schlomberg Cabins and eventually winds up over on the South Fork of the Salmon River. Trail 8W09 branches off to Granite Lake. Trail 9W03 climbs Saloon Creek to the ridge where it meets the Pacific Crest Trail. Trail 9W01 on Saloon Creek is used to reach the South Fork Lakes over on the South Fork of Scott River.

Destinations: Hodges Cabin, Schlomberg Cabin site, Wolford Cabin, Granite Lake, Buck Lake, Pacific Crest Trail, streamside camping.

Elevation/Difficulty: 3,580 feet at trailhead to 7,000- foot ridgetops. Moderate hiking except in upper areas of drainages, where trails become more difficult.

Summary: Lightly traveled trails in deep forest. Several old cabins to visit. May run into grazing cattle at times.

NORTH FORK SWIFT CREEK TRAILHEAD

Access: 29.5 miles north of Weaverville on Highway 3, just north of Swift Creek Bridge, watch for sign on left. Follow Lake Eleanor Road for a couple of miles and then turn right on 37N55 just past Gratton Creek. Trailhead is alongside the road past Lick Creek. **Preacher Meadow Campground** is nearby on Hwy. 3.
Trails: Trail 8W10 climbs up the North Fork of Swift Creek through Poison Canyon to Lilypad Lake and on over the divide to Deer Flat. The Tracy Trail (8W26) leads to the Boulder Lakes and/or Thumb Rock and Parker Creek.
Elevation/Difficulty: 3,400 feet at trailhead. Moderate with some difficult sections.
Summary: Wet meadows and boggy ponds. Lilypad Lake is well-named. Tracy Trail is a rough and eroded connection to the Boulder Lakes.

PACKERS PEAK

(7,828 feet) Packers Peak or Lady Gulch Trailhead. This is a big, broad-shouldered mountain at the head of Coffee Creek. The most direct trail to the summit up Packers Gulch is a gut-buster, climbing almost 4,000 vertical feet in 2.5 miles. Look for the sign marking the start of the trail about a mile and a half north of Big Flat Campground near Mountain Meadow Ranch.

If you've not in the mood for a direct assault, consider a gentler and kinder loop. You still have to gain almost 4,000 vertical feet, but it's spread over a few more miles. About 15.5 miles from Highway 3 on the Coffee Creek Road, find the *Lady Gulch* sign. The trail starts as a gentle road, but soon gets serious and climbs up Lady Gulch, crosses the upper reaches of Adams Creek, and finally tops out in open meadows where a sign points north to Rush Creek, Taylor Creek and Carter Meadow; south to Packers Peak (where you are headed, three miles away) and Big Flat Campground; and west to Rush Creek and the town of Cecilville.

It's a fascinating hike south from this intersection along the spine of the divide in a series of successively higher timbered saddles. After about a mile, you can swing over to the east and peek into Adams Lake. It's easy to lose the trail along this ridge, but just try to stay astraddle the divide. You'll come to Packers Peak Cabin, an old unoccupied cabin at the edge of a meadow where it is easy to lose the trail. About all you can do is keep above the meadows and continue south. The trail will reappear once you get back to drier ground.

Once you break out of the timber on Coyote Peak (really just a named bump) you see the final switchbacks up the northwest slope of Packers Peak. Compared to the sharply dropping north and west sides of the mountain, this is a pretty gentle approach.

There are two summits. On the lower one you still find the leftovers– glass, metal scraps, and lumber–of a fire lookout abandoned years ago. The higher summit will deliver the views you've been waiting for. Simply magnificent. The white granite bulwark of the Trinity Alps stares back at you from across the canyon of the South Fork of the Salmon River. Caribou Mountain, huge, gray and snowy-cold, humps against the sky. Running left and right behind Caribou Mountain are the spiked turrets of Sawtooth Ridge, terminating on the west with Thompson Peak. Off down the South Fork of the Salmon, and to the west, is the continuing crest of the Salmon Mountains, with roads and clearcuts nipping away at the edge of the Wilderness Area.

Below your feet at the juncture of Coffee Creek and the South Fork of the Salmon is a visual display of "stream piracy." The Salmon River, a swift, fast-cutting stream, dug into the low ridge holding Coffee Creek and thus made what used to be the upper portion of Coffee Creek the headwaters of the Salmon.

Near the summit, take a look at the foxtail pine. It's the Alps equivalent of the bristlecone pine. It actually is a close relative of that species. You can identity it by the cluster of five needles resembling a bottle brush. It's found in a couple of other places in the Alps and elsewhere, but is extremely rare.

PACKERS PEAK TRAILHEAD

Access: Watch for 18 miles from Highway 3 on Coffee Creek Road. Trailhead is about 1.5 miles from **Big Flat Campground.**
Trails: Trail 9W06 goes up the rocky open hillside to the summit of 7,828 foot Packers Peak.
Destination: The top of Packers Peak.
Elevation/Difficulty: Strenuous, almost 4,000-foot vertical climb in 2.5 miles.
Summary: A challenging hike to a fabulous viewpoint. The old fire lookout tower was taken down years ago, but the view remains as grand as ever.

POISON LAKE

Elevation 7,000 feet; .75 acres; 7 feet deep. A small population of rainbow trout may remain from a plant made in 1960. This small lake is probably best reached off the trail from Trail Gulch Lake to Rush Creek Lake. **Taylor Creek Trailhead.**

Now here's a lake not covered in any guidebooks until now. It barely made it inside the Trinity Alps Wilderness boundary, let alone into anyone's book. It's not exactly a destination lake at less than an acre in size, but nonetheless a couple of wandering anglers find their way to Poison Lake each summer.

You have to have extraordinary determination to get there, because no one likes to drop down to a lake and then have to climb back out again. On the trail between Trail Gulch Lake and Rush Creek Lake, start looking for a faint trail on the divide between South Fork of Coffee Creek and Taylor Creek. Make like you are climbing the bare knob to the north, but slip around to the west side. Climb higher than you think you need to. Once you're pretty sure you are in the Poison Creek drainage, head down to the lake. Game trails help in places, but mostly you'll be on your own.

The satisfaction of finding this lake is its own reward. Fish were planted in the lake nearly forty years ago. You'll have to check it out yourself to see how they are doing.

Note on the map that a road comes up Taylor Creek from the Cecilville/Callahan Road to within a mile and a half of the lake. The problem is that there's no trail, and a couple of thousand vertical feet of timber and brush might just be more than a sane person can endure in pursuit of such a small lake on the back side of nowhere.

PREACHERS PEAK

(7,180 feet) Big Flat or Union Creek Trailhead. It sounds a lot more interesting than it is. How it came to be called Preacher's Peak involves the winter crossing between Swift Creek and the Salmon mines by a man of the cloth who didn't make it. After winter passed, his watch and gun were found, but not his bones.

The weathered remains of the Dorleska Mine, a booming mining community at the turn of the century, hug the mountainside. Many a citizen of Dorleska, young and old alike, climbed up to the top of old Preacher's Peak.

It's a great picnic peak, only a couple of hours by trail from Big Flat at the head of Coffee Creek. On the way you'll pass through the ruins of the Yellow Rose of Texas Mine with its leftover tailings and assorted rusty machinery. One winter night an avalanche roared down on the Yellow Rose, smothering the buildings and men inside under tons of snow. They dug themselves out and struggled barefoot over the divide to the Dorleska, seeking help. It's only about a mile, but barefoot, darkness and winter make for a tough hike.

RUSH CREEK LAKE

Elevation 6,600 feet; 2.5 acres; 15 feet deep. Easiest access is to take Trail Gulch Lake trail to the summit, then take the trail skirting the east side of Deadman Peak to Taylor Saddle, then take the trail straight ahead to the large meadow encountered upon entering the Rush Creek drainage. Lake is located in next pocket to south of and across meadow. Lake is not visible from the trail. This lake can also be reached via the Rush Creek trail from the East Fork of the South Fork of the Salmon River or via trails from Coffee Creek. A large population of brook trout is present. Also present are campsites and feed for stock. **Lady Gulch Trailhead, Rush Creek/South Fork Salmon River Trailhead, Trail Gulch Trailhead, Taylor Creek Trailhead.**

Regarding the suggested routes to Rush Creek Lake (not to be confused with the *Rush Creek Lakes* near Weaverville), I prefer the Lady Gulch Trail from Coffee Creek. A little steep at first, gaining over 500 vertical feet right off the bat, the trail soon enough eases off and works its way through the large white firs and wild azaleas of the North Fork of Adams Creek. Another steep pull and you're on the divide, actually a surprising plateau of meadows and ribbon streams. It may be an exhausting climb from Coffee Creek to this point, but the gorgeous ocular delights distract your mind from how tired your body might be.

The views and scenery will continue to sustain you as you climb north another thousand vertical feet to the saddle on the ridge where you will begin your final descent into Rush Creek Lake. The hike, as is so often the case in the Alps, is more than just a way of getting somewhere; it's a major part of the pleasure of the trip.

The lake is a real alpine beauty, with a white rock headwall, meadow-edged on the east, steep rocks on the south, and wooded campsites on the north among firs and cedar. Best of all, the place is obviously under used.

I have not fished Rush Creek Lake, but my guess is that you could find a few brookies here. There is abundant feed. The surface of the lake is frequently dimpled by trout sucking down some of that abundance.

SAGE BRUSH LAKE

Elevation 6,900 feet; 1 acre; 5 feet deep. This lake is a 45-minute hike from Middle Boulder Lake and lies adjacent to Garter Snake Lake. Stocked with Eastern brook trout. **East or West Boulder Creek Trailhead**.

By the time you get to Sage Brush Lake you've already noticed sagebrush along the way and pondered the curious question of why this plant, ubiquitous in the Great Basin, makes an appearance here in the Alps. I've always associated sagebrush with cows and sheep and figured that given the right conditions of soil acidity, moisture and climate, sagebrush would flourish.

Aromatic after a rain, provocative when burned, it's a welcome addition to the diversity of plant life found in these mountains. Old-timers will tell you that it makes an outstanding mosquito-repellant smoke; others say that as an herbal tea, it will cure whatever ails you.

Not named on most maps, Sage Brush and its buddy, Garter Snake Lake a few feet to the west, are two frog ponds south of Middle Boulder Lake almost on the Scott Mountain Divide. The Pacific Crest Trail lies in the wide gap above the lakes.

If you came via the West Boulder Creek Trail, consider hiking up to the county line, and walking the PCT for a mile west, taking the trail past Telephone Lake and making a loop out of your trip by returning to your vehicle that way. Even if you don't return that way, a hike to 7,789-foot Eagle Peak from the lakes is a rewarding day hike. By far the highest point for miles around, Eagle Peak is an outstanding place to give yourself a geography lesson on the surrounding terrain. Eagle Creek and the Eagle Creek benches, scarred by forest fires, draw the eye to lush green valleys and the granite escarpments shielding Tangle Blue and Big Bear lakes to the east. Northward, Mount Shasta, bare or snowclad, dominates in all seasons as only a 14,181-foot mountain can. Off to the west, that's Deadman Peak, with the green-hued labyrinth of upper North and South Fork of Coffee Creek filling the void with a complex array of blue-green ancient forest.

SECTION LINE LAKE

Elevation 7,100 feet; 2.5 acres; 12 feet deep. No trail. The outlet stream can be followed just over a small rise to the east of Fox Creek Lake. About a 30-minute walk from either Mavis or Fox Creek Lakes. Contains Eastern brook trout. **Fox Creek Ridge Trailhead**.

There are the granite peaks of the White Trinities, the metamorphic rocks of the Red Trinities, the heavily forested Green Trinities, and now, since the Wilderness Act of 1984, the Gentle Trinities here along the Scott Mountains. Without visual reference, off-trail navigation is dicey here in the Gentle Trinities. Strike out across country and downed timber, dense forest and boulders hide the true shape of the land. The high Alpine mind may experience claustrophobia after a time in this land of short views. The cure is to take a day and get up on the Scott Mountain Divide and get a long view.

Perched high up among the granite knuckles between Mavis and Fox Creek Lakes, you'll find this exquisite personal-sized lake, which we can imagine got its name because you cross the invisible line between section 25 and section 36 to get to the lake.

Most people heading directly to Section Line Lake strike out directly southwest of Mavis Lake and gradually gain altitude until the lake is in view. And some pick up the outlet stream on the trail between Mavis and Fox Creek Lakes and follow it to the lake. From Fox Creek Lake, it's a cross-country climb through heavy timber and boulders. A few find their way from the Pacific Crest Trail just over the ridge to the south.

SEDGE LAKE

Elevation 6,400 feet; 1 acre; 3 feet deep. Slightly over one mile up the Fish Lake trail a trail forks to the right. Sedge Lake is about three-fourths of a mile up this trail. It is the westerly of two ponds and contains Eastern brook trout. These two ponds have been called the Twin Lakes. **Fish Lake Trailhead.**

The reason you would make Sedge Lake your destination is not because you are seeking a wilderness experience, although you can get that here. No, people figure that nobody goes to Sedge Lake, therefore the fishing will be outrageous from lack of fishing pressure. Maybe. Remember the rule of thumb about fish and fish size. The larger the body of water, the larger the fish will be. Look closely at Sedge Lake. Do you think any lunkers lurk in its three-foot depth?

SHIMMY LAKE

Elevation 6,400 feet; 1.5 acres; 10 feet deep. Because this lake is so open and shallow, it gets rather warm during the summer. Reached by continuing on the trail past Eleanor Lake, or from Lily Pad Lake. Stocked with brook trout. Winter kill noted following severe winters. **Lake Eleanor Trailhead.**

Shimmy Lake is usually dead water with respect to fish, but it opens early in the spring and makes a great place to camp, swim and lounge about while exploring the Thumb Rock/Ycatapom country. As the summer wears on, the water warms and breeds some nasty little bugs that will bite.

In the 1950s, when we still carried air mattresses, we would inflate them and navigate the lake as bare-bottomed Vikings. Fishing while prone on an air mattress can be tricky. We worked on the technique at Shimmy Lake, but never really perfected it. Sit up and the mattress jackknifes in the middle. Then, should you be lucky enough to hook a fish, it is difficult to release it while flat on your back. Izaak Walton probably never fished nude on an air mattress.

The hike to Shimmy Lake is a nice walk from Lake Eleanor, with wide handsome views of Mount Shasta off to the northeast. Imagine! That hunk of mountain contains 80 cubic *miles* of material! The land you walk through was once in the hands of private logging companies that tried to improve the view by cutting down many of the larger trees that had become "overripe" and were just "wasting away." The stumps remain for your enjoyment.

There used to be an interesting trail down from Deer Flat that would take you back to the Gratton Flat trailhead, but the chaotic labyrinth of logging roads makes it a challenge to find.

SLIDE CREEK TRAILHEAD

Access: Off Callahan/Cecilville Road on road 40N17.

Trails: Trail 8W08 follows Slide Creek to top of Blue Jay Ridge and down to Loftus Mine, connecting with Noland Gulch Trail (no #).

Destinations: Loftus Mine, South Fork Scott River.

Elevation/Difficulty: 4,800 feet at trailhead. Difficult.

Summary: Evidence of cattle grazing and logging. Solitary hiking.

SNOWSLIDE LAKE

Elevation 6,700 feet; 10 acres; 42 feet deep. Another of the popular lakes in the Caribou Basin. A good brook trout producer, rainbow present also. About a four-hour ride from Big Flat. **Big Flat Trailhead.**

Here is the only lake in the Caribou Basin not named Caribou something. Apparently after Big, Little, Upper, Lower, and Middle, the mapmakers couldn't think of any more prefixes to nail onto the word Caribou.

Snowslide Lake is a pretty good choice of name, I'm sure. The lake is right smack dab at the bottom of a steep slope that begins at the summit of 8,575-foot Caribou Mountain. You can bet that plenty of snow slides down that slope.

It is at this lake that you'll most likely lose the trail to Big Caribou Lake. It's easy to do among all the little campsites and spur trails that litter the shoreline along the west side of Snowslide. A lot of people wander too far west, go over and take a look at Lower Caribou, and then, realizing the trail has been lost, follow the stream rather than the trail up to Big Caribou.

Not that it matters a whole lot, but stay close to the shoreline of Snowslide as you pass by and you'll pick up the real trail at the south end of the lake.

I would advise camping at Snowslide only if you enjoy life in the middle of a freeway. There are people traveling back and forth through here day and night.

SOUTH FORK COFFEE CREEK TRAILHEAD

Access: Fifteen miles up Coffee Creek Road (County Road 104). **Big Flat Campground** is another five miles up the road from the trailhead.

Trails: Trail 9W04 follows the creek gently until climbing steeply to the South Fork Divide. Intersects trail 9W61 to Steveale Meadow and Trail Gulch Lake and Long Gulch Lake.

Destinations: Deadman Peak, streamside camping and fishing.

Elevation/Difficulty: 3,590 feet at trailhead. Easy, except for the pull up to the South Fork Divide which is moderate to difficult.

Summary: Rolling, easy walking country, but usually a lot cows or evidence thereof.

SOUTH FORK LAKES

Elevation 6,720 feet; 6.4 acres; 34 feet deep. An easy five-minute walk from Lower South Fork Lake. Rainbow and Eastern brook trout present.

UPPER SOUTH FORK LAKE

Elevation 6,700 feet; 4.4 acres; 23 feet deep. Easiest approach is to climb through rocky crags to south of Hidden Lake and drop down to South Fork Lakes. Can also be reached by a three-mile trail up the South Fork of the Scott River from the Cecilville-Callahan road. Contains both rainbow and Eastern brook trout. Campsites present. **Carter Meadows Summit Trailhead or South Fork of Scott River Trailhead.**

LOWER SOUTH FORK LAKE

Elevation 5,850 feet; 3 acres; 18 feet deep. The first of three lakes on the headwaters of the South Fork of Scott River. Shortly after leaving the Pacific Crest Trail on the South Fork Lake Trail, bear south to the lake.

LITTLE SOUTH FORK LAKE

Do not confuse this Little South Fork Lake with the one described in the North Central Alps section of this book. This one is just a puddle below and off to the side of the upper and lower lakes. The Little South Fork Lake over on the South Fork of the Salmon is perhaps the toughest, most remote lake in the Trinity Alps, and it is not to be trifled with.

Upper and Lower South Fork Lakes–here–are two green sockets set at the base of an unnamed 7,794-foot peak, the source of the South Fork of Scott River. Surrounded by thick timber and grassy meadows, the upper lake has cliffs breaking straight down into the water. Afternoon shadows come early and long at these north-facing lakes.

There are several ways into these lakes; hop off the Pacific Crest Trail onto the short but steep outlet trail; toil the long scenic trail up the North Fork of Coffee Creek and Saloon Creek; or be adventurous and take the short direct cross-country route from Hidden Lake.

Hidden Lake, a brisk twenty-minute walk from the Carter Meadow Summit Trailhead brings you to where the work begins. A near-vertical talus slope rises south and east of the lake. Aim for the gap. From the gap it's a tricky and steep contour around the top of the gulch; you may have to use your hands for support in places, to reach the next gap. Don't try this one alone or without previous climbing experience. Watch for traces of trail others have left. Once in the second gap, you'll be rewarded with the sight of two lakes gleaming green and cool in the distance. From here, you can use visual flight rules to make a descent into the basin. Without a pack, it won't take an hour; with one, a little longer.

Plenty of firewood and plenty of places to camp here. Wildflowers, tall timber, bold meadows–this is a place to spend a few days. Perhaps the best use of the upper lake is for fishing. It's deeper, and the diminutive brookies will almost strike at a bare hook. Use the lower lake for swimming; it's shallower and gets a lot more sunshine than the upper one.

SOUTH FORK OF THE SALMON RIVER

Big Flat or Salmon River Trailhead. This is the stream that stole the headwaters of Coffee Creek (see Packer's Peak). Hard to figure why the road was never completed along the South Fork of the Salmon between Big Flat and Cecilville. For many years it saw a lot of pack train traffic due to the mining activity in the area. Once the mining played out, there was no reason to haul supplies on a large scale, and by the time the thought of connecting the two came around again it was too late, a Wilderness Area had been established, banning further road building.

Speaking of Coffee Creek, the stream didn't have a name until the 1850s when one of James Abrams' mules loaded with sacks of coffee fell into the stream while packing into his trading post at Big Flat. The mule was rescued, the coffee dried and saved.

The Coffee Creek Road pokes a 16-mile-long nose into the wilderness until it hits the locked gate at Big Flat, where you will find campsites overlooking the South Fork of the Salmon. The road from the Cecilville side heads upstream and gives you the impression that it's going all the way to Big Flat, but it ends at the Rush Creek/Salmon River Trailhead six miles short. If you want to get to Big Flat from this way, you have to walk.

There are two South Fork of the Salmon experiences.

Upstream from Big Flat the valley is an open U-shape reminiscent of Yosemite valley; lots of granite domes, aspen trees, flat camping sites, and easy trails along both sides of the creek that tangles its way through the forest. There's a road (for walking, not driving) to a private lodge once called Carter's, now named Josephine Creek Lodge.

Downstream, the creek becomes a river plowing through a deep, heavily forested canyon. The trail stays on the north side, well above the water, with occasional peeks at the high Alps to the south. The "glacier" on the north side of Mount Caesar must have given Glacierview Ranch its name. Glacierview and Lakeview Ranches are private inholdings.

Lakeview Ranch, about four miles downstream from Big Flat, was built in 1854 by Francis (Frank) Abrams, James' brother. Frank never married, but James' wife and one of his children, who both died in 1879, are buried at the ranch. The house you see today at the ranch, owned by an Abrams' descendant, was built in 1898.

It's pleasant and easy hiking in either direction along the stream, whether you choose the valley or the canyon. Stream fishing can be good in either direction too. Downstream, it's large rocks and pools, while upstream, in the open valley, the South Fork of the Salmon River becomes a creek. Great peaks tower over crinkled cliffs, and soft grass carpets the pines at the edge of the twisting silver ribbon of the river. Late on a summer afternoon it fills the silence with liquid chatter. Puffs of cotton from cottonwood trees drift in the sunlight shafts. A cool breeze, scented damp, springs from the canyon shadows. The water, shrugging the sun off its back in shards of gold, gives color and an aura of timelessness to the smooth pebbles on the creek bottom.

Dozing at streamside one afternoon, I watched a spider on a cobweb high in the sky caught momentarily in the sun. As I watched, the spider cut loose a strand in the wind and rode it like a hang glider off through the pines, trusting chance to find a new home. It might be a reckless way to travel, but anyone who hikes the back country can relate.

SOUTH FORK SCOTT RIVER TRAILHEAD

Access: Find road 40N17 9.5 miles from Callahan on the Callahan/Cecilville road. Trailhead is on east side of South Fork of Scott River at road crossing.

Trail Creek Campground is four miles further on the Callahan/Cecilville Road.
Trails: Trail 9W131 climbs steeply to the South Fork Lakes. Intersects PCT.
Destinations: Pacific Crest Trail, South Fork Lakes, Saloon Creek, North Fork of Coffee Creek.
Elevation/Difficulty: 5,200 feet at trailhead. Begins moderate and then turns difficult.
Summary: A tough way to hike to South Fork Lakes. A better approach is from Carter Meadow Summit on the PCT. Or over the ridge from Hidden Lake.

STODDARD LAKE

Elevation 5,900 feet; 25 acres; 84 feet deep. Either go up the East Fork of Coffee Creek trail (about three to four hours walking), or go in from the trailhead on Ripple Creek (about a ninety-minute hike). A popular and productive lake for brook and rainbow trout. Campsites and feed for stock. **Stoddard Lake Trailhead**.

Lucky this lake is as big as it is, considering the amount of traffic it sees every summer. What with the cattle grazing and the horse packers, it's a miracle there is any green grass or clean places to camp by midsummer. All this livestock, combined with the buggy ground around the south and western edges produces swarms of mosquitoes.

Stoddard Lake, where the aroma of all things bovine and equine wafts on the evening breeze.

But the wise woods person can find some rocky ground at the east end of the lake back in the trees with a waterfront view out of sight of the rodeo scene and protected from the bugs.

It's a big lake. To fish it effectively, many use a rubber raft or a float tube. The flotilla can be quite impressive at times.

The lake is named for John R. Stoddard, who owned the ranch near the mouth of Ripple Creek in 1878. It's now called Eagle Ranch. Before he owned it, it was Iowa Ranch, settled in the 1850s. Stoddard grazed cattle for many summers around here and you can still find remnants of drift fences along the trails.

Cowboys staked their territory here long before backpackers showed up.

STODDARD LAKE TRAILHEAD

Access: Take Eagle Creek Loop 2.5 miles north of Coffee Creek and watch for signs. You can park alongside Forest Road 38N27. **Trinity River Campground** and **Eagle Creek Campground** are nearby on Highway 3.
Trails: Trail 7W06 begins climbing moderately to the top of the ridge and then gradually drops to its junction with Doe Lake Trail (8W05). It then climbs up rocky slopes and meadows through increasing brush and drops to Stoddard Lake.
Destinations: Stoddard Lake, Upper Stoddard Lake, McDonald Lake, Holland Lake, Doe Lake, Bloody Run Creek, Eagle Creek Benches, Eagle Peak.
Elevation/Difficulty: 5,300 feet at trailhead. Moderate to Stoddard and McDonald lakes. Difficult to strenuous to Upper Stoddard and Holland lakes.
Summary: Short; popular day hiking area.

SUGAR PINE LAKE

Elevation 6,600 feet; 9 acres; 43 feet deep. About a three-hour, eight-mile trip up the Sugar Pine Creek trail from Coffee Creek. Brook trout and rainbow trout to 10 inches were reported in 1958. **Sugar Pine Trailhead.**

Sugar Pine Lake is another of the secret places in the Alps. And for good reason. The lake nestles at the head of a long, steep, one-way canyon. From the time you leave the trailhead on Coffee Creek until six miles later when the lake is glimpsed through the trees, the trail climbs relentlessly, one of those trails that mean business.

There's another way to get to Sugar Pine Lake, but it's seldom used. From Union Creek, a trail climbs steeply up over the ridge into the headwaters of Battle Creek, and then climbs another ridge to get into the Sugar Pine Creek valley and intersects the trail about mile or so below the lake.

Sugar Pine Lake is loaded with fish, has campsites that catch the early sun from the east, and normally nobody is camped there.

One of the pleasures of going to this lake it that you can concentrate on just going to the lake. No decisions to make about alternate routes or destinations. Once you leave the trailhead, you are committed to Sugar Pine Lake.

Notice the change of forest cover as you steadily gain altitude up the trail. Notice the scattered oaks become scarce and give way to the evergreens. Notice the ridgelines on either side of the canyon. To the west there are open green spaces, while the east is more timbered, with craggy rocks jagging the skyline. Notice the meadows you pass through, each a different size, with different textures. Notice that the key words in the first sentence of this paragraph are *steadily* and *up*.

In late summer, water along the trail is difficult to obtain. Unless you carry some, the best you can do is leave the trail and find the stream, which never comes close to the trail until you are almost at the lake.

The cirque holding the lake makes for interesting exploring, as do the imposing cliffs to the west and Sugar Pine Butte (7,861 feet) to the east. Sugar Pine Butte is a walk-up offering grand and sublime views, especially toward the north and east.

It's possible to go through the gap south of Sugar Pine Butte and visit Conway and Lion lakes. It's even possible to make this a loop trip without a car shuttle, because the trailheads for Sugar Pine and Lion are only a mile and a half apart back down on Coffee Creek.

SUGAR PINE LAKE TRAILHEAD

Access: About six miles west on the Coffee Creek Road (County Road 104) from Highway 3 out of the town of Coffee Creek, a mile past the Coffee Creek Ranch. Watch for sign. Bridge across Coffee Creek washed out in 1997, making access difficult during high water. Nearby **Goldfield Campground** is off Coffee Creek Road on the way to the trailhead.

Trails: Trail 8W07 follows Sugar Pine Creek 5.5 miles to Sugar Pine Lake. Trail 9W59 takes off at Cabin Flat and climbs over the ridge to the headwaters of Battle Creek and on over to Union Creek 4.3 miles away.

Destinations: Sugar Pine Lake, Sugar Pine Butte, Battle Creek, Battle Mountain, Union Creek.
Elevation/Difficulty: 3,570 feet at trailhead. Moderately steep.
Summary: A steep hike to a solitary lake.

TAPIE LAKE (see LOST LAKE)

TELEPHONE LAKE

Elevation 6,900 feet; 3.5 acres; 30 feet deep. Located at the head of West Boulder Creek out of Callahan. **West Boulder Creek Trailhead.**

Your guess is as good as anyone's. Why a lake named "Telephone" in an area where "Boulder " is obviously the name of choice? Perhaps there was once a phone line from Callahan to the Shasta View Mine? Perhaps someone thought this dry socket (no inlet or outlet) lake resembled the shape of a telephone?

If you do want to make a "call" at Telephone Lake, it's a brisk hike of about an hour from the trailhead up East Boulder Creek. The lake gets a few calls from people on the Pacific Coast Trail just over the ridge to the south.

However you place a call at Telephone Lake, you can't go wrong stopping here for a day to enjoy a swim or try your luck with the brookies that occasionally swirl the surface.

THUMB ROCK

(7,735 feet) Swift Ceek, North Fork Swift Creek, or Lake Eleanor Trailheads. I can't say it reminds me of a thumb, but it does make a good lookout for the eastern Alps and Mount Shasta on a clear day. This is not a particularly difficult climb from the trails to Lilypad Lake. Knock off the unnamed 8,037-foot peak next door while you are there.

TRAIL GULCH LAKE

Elevation 6,450 feet; 14 acres; 21 feet deep. From Carter Meadow it's a three-mile, ninety-minute hike up the Trail Gulch Creek trail. About seven miles from Coffee Creek. Contains naturally reproducing Eastern brook trout. Campsite and feed for stock present. **Trail Gulch Trailhead.**

A twin to nearby Long Gulch Lake, only a little longer hike, Trail Gulch Lake is the place for a gentle Alps trip. It's where you'd take a Boy Scout troop, or first-timers in need of a positive wilderness experience.

Authentic backpackers will feel out of place in this area once known as the Scott Mountains. Long before it was designated official wilderness, people came to places like Trail Gulch Lake to kill things: animals, fish, a case of beer. They still do.

That's Deadman Peak (see description and discussion under Eastern Alps section) soaring over a thousand feet above your campsite along the north side of the lake. Some mornings you'll watch the sky ripen into daylight as the sun gently kisses the mountaintops and leisurely sends caressing fingers of warmth and light down to where you lie in your sleeping bag. It may take until noon to finish breakfast; by then it's time to swim to the island on the other side of the lake and laze away a summer afternoon draped like a sea lion on the solar-heated rocks.

Other mornings you'll be up before the sun sipping a cup of Earl Grey, waiting for just the right moment to snap the sun-splashed reflection of Deadman Peak in the smooth face of the lake. Later, as the day warms, you'll throw a few things to eat into a day pack and tackle the talus slides of the mountain and feast at noon on the summit. While you're dining on salami, cheese, crackers and cookies, mountains and rivers without end will stretch beyond your vision in all directions.

On the descent, the bare bones of the mountain lie open for easy examination. All afternoon you'll be a student of mountains, a millennia of living rock your classroom.

Back in camp, supper done, you'll sit and set the sun.

TRAIL GULCH TRAILHEAD

Access: Just over the summit on the Callahan/Cecilville road 12 miles from Callahan on Highway 3 at Carter's Meadow. Take loop road and watch for trailhead sign. **Trail Creek Campground** is on down the road a way.

Trails: Trail 9W170 is a moderate 4.5 miles to Trail Gulch Lake and then a steep climb over the ridge to Long Gulch Lake. Intersects on divide with Taylor Creek Trail (10W230), Fish Lake Trail (10W200), and South Fork of Coffee Creek Trail (9W04).

Destinations: Trail Gulch Lake, Long Gulch Lake, Deadman Peak, South Fork of Coffee Creek.

Elevation/Difficulty: 5,100 feet at trailhead. Moderate to Trail Gulch Lake, difficult over ridges.

Summary: Popular area, especially for horses. Loop hikes possible.

TWIN LAKES (See Sedge and Hyla lakes)

UNION LAKE

Elevation 6,050 feet; 3.5 acres; 14 feet deep. Located about 10 miles up the Union Creek trail from Coffee Creek. A somewhat shallow lake that supports a good population of brook trout. **Union Lake Trailhead.**

The Union name you find pinned on geographical features in this area comes from an early venture known as the Union Consolidated Mining Company.

The hike up Union Creek follows the faint traces of the wagon road that once served the Dorleska Mine. Late in the evening, when the sun cuts long slanted shafts of light through the gloaming, it seems you can hear the clatter of wagons and shouting of the teamsters and smell the sweat of horses as another supply train passes by on its way to the mine.

Dorleska was the wife of R.D. Lawrence, discoverer of the mine in 1898. It went broke after a few years. The sixteen feet of snow each winter did not contribute to the success of the effort to extract gold from the 2,000 feet of tunnels that were dug in the mountainside. It was profitable until 1912, sometimes yielding a profit of $200 a day from ore that netted $1,100 to $2,000 per ton after expenses.

There is a photograph taken of a group of young people on the shore of Union

Lake in 1906. They may have been from the Dorleska Mine for all I know. I saw the photograph on display in Weaverville's Jake Jackson Museum. It is a timeless black-and-white portrait. In the foreground are people in turn-of-the-century clothes: poofy dresses, baggy pants, floppy hats. The group consists of three men with wicker fishing creels, five women and one dog all sitting at the edge of Union Lake, frozen in time. Behind them you can see the lake, the lily pads, logs at the water's edge, the hillside, all exactly as it is today. As I look at the photograph it occurs to me, that if it were possible, I could walk into their 1906 world, sit down next to them, and feel very welcome and comfortable.

Perhaps this is the real message of the Alps: wilderness transcends time. The most precious gift that wilderness can offer is an elegantly simple sense of timelessness.

The people at Union Lake in 1906 were having a wilderness experience within the framework of their lives, just as people in 2006 will. Nothing lasts forever, but the Alps can last much longer than our human lives. We know the sun will eventually explode into a Red Giant star and consume the earth along with the entire solar system. The rocks, trees, streams, meadows, lakes, peaks, snowbanks, thunder, wildflowers, sunsets, brook trout, campfires, everything will become "star stuff." However, before that happens the Alps will be a common thread of experience weaving through the minds of many people of many years.

Envision, if you can, a group of young people, three men, five women and a dog on the shore of Union Lake in the year 2406!

The hike to Union Lake is easy, but it can be metaphysical.

UNION CREEK TRAILHEAD

Access: About 12 miles west on the Coffee Creek Road (County Road 104) from Highway 3 out of the town of Coffee Creek. Watch for signs. **Big Flat Campground** is at the end of Coffee Creek Road and **Goldfield Campground** is on the same road before you get to the trailhead.

Trails: Trail 9W07 follows an old logging/mining road above Union Creek, crosses the creek and continues 7.8 miles to Union Lake. Trail 9W65 branches to the Dorleska Mine site and Trail 8W12 goes to Foster Lake. Trail 9W09 heads to Landers Lake, and Trail 9W19 over to Parker Creek and Swift Creek.

Destinations: Union Lake, Landers Lake, Dorleska Mine, Preachers Peak, Foster Lake.

Elevation/Difficulty: 3,710 feet at trailhead. Moderate hiking in all directions, except for the climb up to Foster Lake, which is difficult.

Summary: Dorleska Mine site is of historical interest. Nice trails through tall timber and open meadows.

UPPER BOULDER LAKE

Elevation 6,850 feet; 7 acres; 11 feet deep. A 15-minute walk up trail from East Boulder Lake. **East Boulder Creek Trailhead**.

Yet another "Boulder" lake for your atavistic perusal.

Upper Boulder, a short hike from East Boulder Lake, is one of several lakes in this area where the brookies do so well on their own that there is no longer any need to stock. Linger for a few hours making a mental note to come back with a big pack next time to explore for a few days.

Upper Boulder and East Boulder lakes

And explore you can, from a camp at Upper Boulder Lake. Just a short push over the divide and you're on the Pacific Coast Trail, that Interstate Walking Freeway from Canada to Mexico.

Go a mile or two east and treat yourself to views down Eagle Creek, Marshy Lakes and Tangle Blue. The trail stays high on the ridge before dropping down to Mosquito Lake Creek. From above Big Marshy Lake look for the tumbled remnants of the Grand National Mine far across the canyon.

Go a mile or two west and skirt or climb Eagle Peak. Find that spring near the Shasta View Mine and plunge your face in and drink deep down to your boot heels. Be warned, the water temperature of the spring is mind-numbing.

If you do climb Eagle Peak it's a 360-degree panorama from a heaven-scraping summit. You'll be gasping anyway, so save one last deep intake of breath for the awesome view that will reward your effort.

UPPER STODDARD LAKE

Elevation 6,400 feet; .5 acres; 14 feet deep. Approximately a 50-minute hike up from Stoddard Lake. Populated with brookies. **Stoddard Lake Trailhead or East Fork of**

Coffee Creek Trailhead.

In contrast to the heavily timbered Stoddard and McDonald Lake, Upper Stoddard is a little spot of water high up on the ridge, a day-hike destination or private campsite away from the often crowded basin below. There are granite spires to climb, even the real Billy's Peak if you figure out which one it is, and the adventure of trying to find Holland Lake. Afterward, a plunge in the lake puts lead back in your pencil.

WARD LAKE

Elevation 7,100 feet; 5.5 acres; 23 feet deep. Ward Lake is 9 miles up the Swift Creek trail. Also accessible by trail from Big Flat. A good brook trout lake. **Swift Creek or Big Flat Trailhead.**

During what geologists call the Wisconsin ice age, there were at least 30 valley glaciers in the Trinity Alps. The longest glacier, thought to have been about 13.7 miles long, occupied the valley that is now Swift Creek.

The glacier left a dandy route into Ward Lake, named for Whit Ward, William Foster's number one cowhand. Sure, you can come in from Big Flat on Coffee Creek via a shorter, steeper trail. If you are in a hurry, maybe you should. But when you consider how long it took for that last glacier to move down Swift Creek, any pace you choose will be meteoric by comparison.

Travel in Swift Creek canyon is to be savored. There are no gut-busting grades on the ambling trail that winds and wanders through meadow after meadow, among stands of large trees, and skipping across occasional streams. High up on many of the trees along the trail you'll see automobile license plates from the 1940s nailed twenty to thirty feet from the ground. These were to mark the trail in winter when U.S.F.S. snow survey teams trekked into this drainage to measure the depth and water content of the snow. No, they don't mark the depth of the snow, but were placed high enough above the snow so as to allow navigation when the trail was buried under the snow.

It was August nearly 40 years ago when we first wandered through the long shadows of a never-ending warm summer evening along Swift Creek and found a grassy knoll near the creek in Mumford Meadow. Sounds seemed to be muffled by the stillness of the air. And as night crept into our campsite, it was too warm for a sleeping bag. Lying on top of our bags, we peered deep into the space between the stars, talking of mysteries of the universe and swapping lies to bolster our young lives.

The next morning we found that the two or so miles to Ward Lake were laughingly easy for boys as young and tough as we were. To prove it, on the way back to our campsite in the meadow, we ran all the way.

Ward Lake or any part of the Swift Creek area makes for good running and day hiking. Jog up from the trailhead, spend the day, and jog back to your car before dark.

WEST BOULDER CREEK TRAILHEAD

Access: 6 miles from Callahan on USFS 40N17. Closest campgrounds are **Scott Mountain Campground** on Highway 3 and **Trail Creek Campground** on the Cecilville/Callahan road.

Trails: Trail 8W062 follows the creek for a couple of miles before forking left to Middle Boulder Lake and right to Telephone Lake on Trail 08W050. Trail above Middle Boulder Lake forks left to East Boulder Lake and right to the PCT.
Destinations: Middle Boulder Lake, Telephone Lake, Eagle Peak, West Boulder Lake, Shasta View Mine, Pacific Coast Trail, Eagle Creek Benches
Elevation/Difficulty: 4,800 feet at trailhead. Moderate with a couple of steep pitches.
Summary: A lot of cattle grazing and horse-riding evidence. Good brook trout fishing in lakes.

Ycatapom Peak from Lilypad Lake

YCATAPOM PEAK

(7,596 feet) North Fork of Swift Creek Trailhead. The Ycat (pronounced why-cat), as most people call it, spends its time watching the traffic below its rocky brow in Poison Canyon. Many, many days go by with nothing to watch. Local lore has it that the name means "mountain that leans to the north" in the ancient native language of the area.

The west side is nasty brush and the north face is cliffy. The obvious way to get to the summit is from the saddle on the Lilypad/Shimmy Lake trail. From that point it's just a matter of picking your way along the ridge to the summit.

Chapter Seven

EXTREME NORTHEAST ALPS

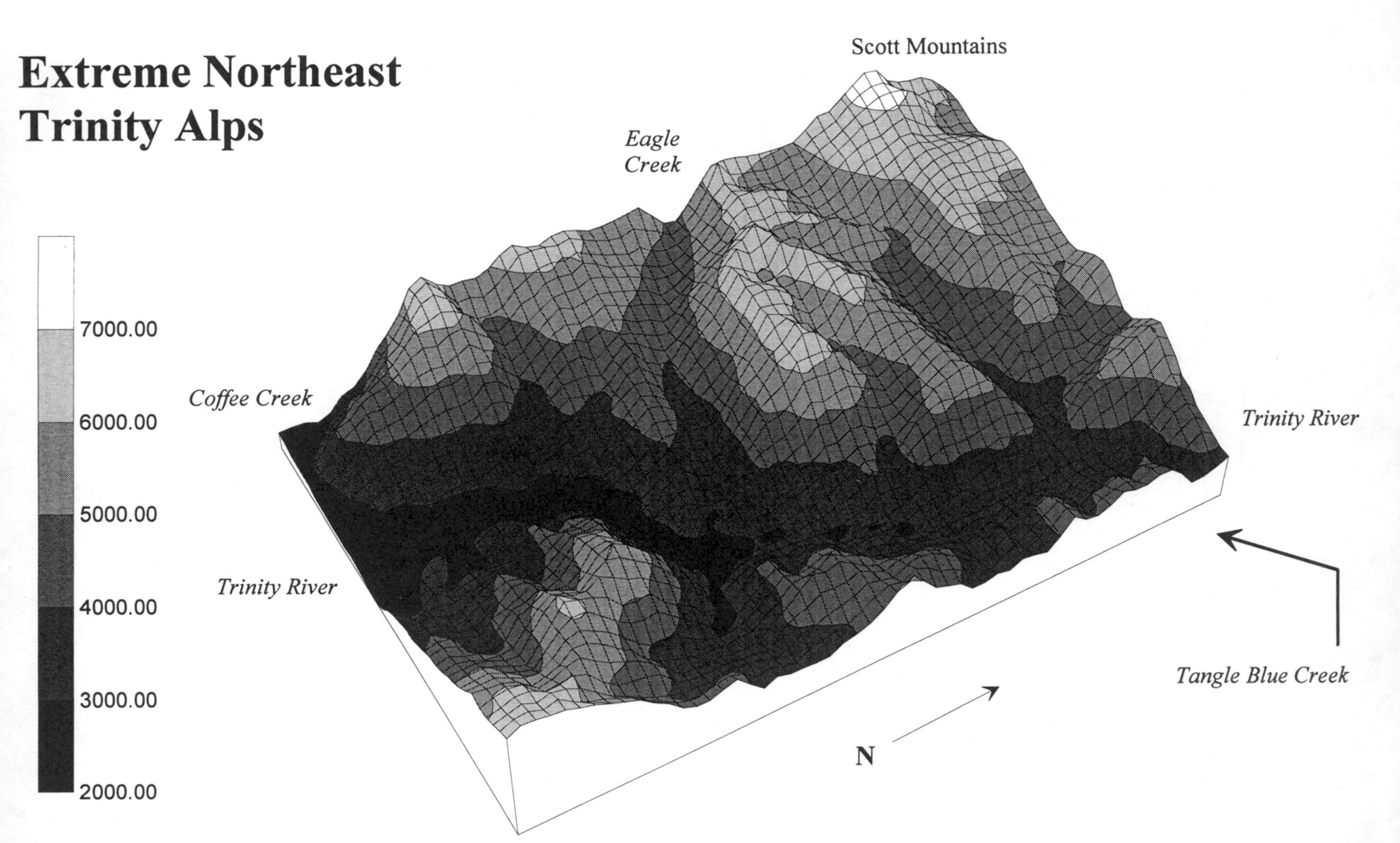
Extreme Northeast
Trinity Alps
7000.00
6000.00
5000.00
4000.00
3000.00
2000.00
Scott Mountains
Eagle Creek
Coffee Creek
Trinity River
Trinity River
Tangle Blue Creek
N

Extreme Northeast Trinity Alps

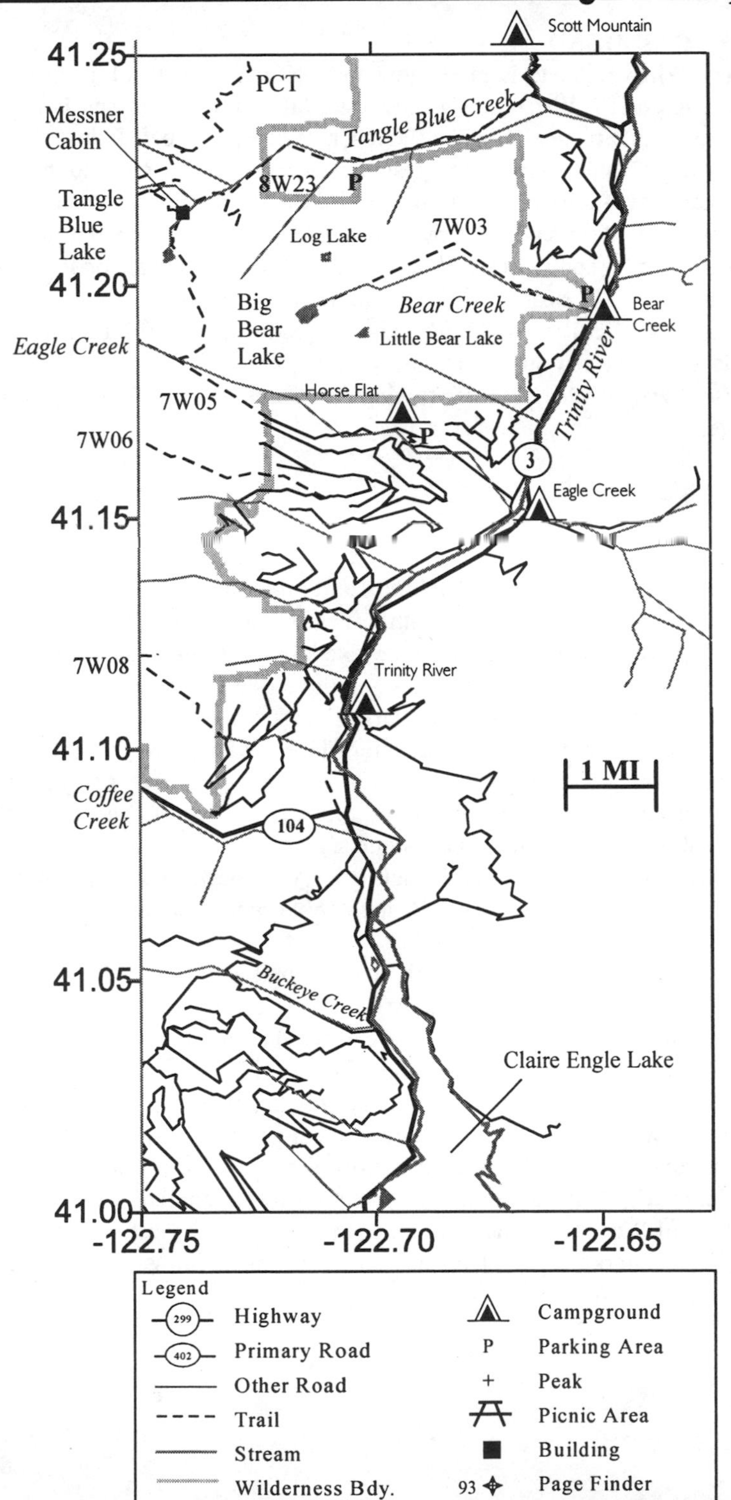

BEAR LAKE TRAILHEAD

Access: This trailhead is off Highway 3, 47 miles north of Weaverville on County Road 137. Watch for signs. **Horse Flat Campground** and **Eagle Creek Campground** are nearby on the Eagle Creek Loop just off Highway 3.

Trails: Trail 7W03 climbs steeply, switch backing for 4.5 miles to the outlet of Big Bear Lake. A one mile cross-country hike to the cirque containing both Little Bear and Wee Bear is accessed by climbing up and around the east ridge of Big Bear Lake, then contouring east and south into the outlet canyon to the lakes.

Destinations: Big Bear, Little Bear and Wee Bear Lakes.

Elevation/Difficulty: 3,300 feet at trailhead to over 6,000 feet at lakes. Moderate with a few steep sections.

Summary: Fairly easy access to elegant mountain lakes in a rugged granite cirque.

BIG BEAR LAKE

Elevation 5,800 feet; 28 acres; 73 feet deep. One of the larger lakes, and picturesquely situated in a deep granite basin. Six miles, or about three and a half hours by trail, up Bear Creek from the Trinity River Road. Both brook and rainbow trout plentiful and in good condition in 1957. Campsite at lake. Very little feed for stock. **Bear Lake Trailhead**.

If you've ever wondered what a cirque lake looks like, this is the classic example. High-angle granite slabs surround the deep lake on three sides. Most people camp near the outlet, and you'll be lucky if you are alone during the summer.

At the upper end of the lake is a better place to camp, and you have excellent rocks for diving, sunning and swimming. A short swim across the bay and you can bask your shivering naked body on warm monolithic granite plates etched by glaciers thousands of years ago, like an insect on a stone skillet.

Lie on your belly and while the sun dries your backside, look closely at the smooth rock and see the scratches carved by the pebble-toothed glacier from the last ice age.

Got a day to kill? It's a challenging hike to Log Lake, less challenging to Little Bear and Wee Bear. To reach Log Lake, make a mental note in your mind where the low point is on the ridge to the northeast. Go back down the trail less than a mile and start angling upward to the low point. Use your route-finding skills to avoid as much brush as possible. You won't be able to avoid much. It's a true bushwhack all the way.

To get to Wee Bear and Little Bear, you can go on up past Big Bear Lake and circle around through the gap, but it makes more sense to take off climbing the ridge above the outlet of Big Bear and gradually work your way around to where you can see the outlet stream of Wee Bear. Once you've got that spotted, head for it. You may see rock ducks trying to mark the way. Destroy them and strike a blow for the wilderness.

Big Bear Lake

BIG MILL CREEK TRAILHEAD

Access: Forest Service road less than a mile south of junction of Highway 3/ Gazelle Road intersection.

Trails: Trail 8W02 enters Wilderness Area at extreme eastern boundary and climbs to the Pacific Crest Trail near Black Rock. Trail is faint in places.

Destinations: Pacific Crest Trail, Black Rock.

Elevation/Difficulty: 3,760 feet at trailhead. Moderate.

Summary: Nice ridgetop views in seldom visited country.

BILLY'S PEAK

(7,343 feet) Billy's Peak Trailhead. This often confuses people. The prominent peak you can see from the Coffee Creek area, the one that had a USFS fire lookout on it for years, is called Billy's Peak. But the *real* Billy's Peak is couple of hundred feet higher and a mile or so to the northwest of the one that used to have the lookout. If you want to be sure you have climbed "Billy's Peak," do them both.

The former lookout Billy's Peak is a short, steep hike of about three miles from the trailhead. The trailhead can be found by turning at the sign just north of Trinity River Campground on Highway 3. It's one of the tougher three-mile hikes in the Alps with a vertical gain of more than three thousand feet. Near the summit, loose rock, no water and no shade add spice to the challenge.

The view from the summit will explain why there was once a lookout here. Magnificent in all directions. Little evidence remains of the fire lookout. It was dismantled and helicoptered to the dump in the 1970s by the U.S. Forest Service.

Now, to nail the real Billy's Peak takes a bit more work than the hike to the former lookout peak. First get to Stoddard Lake and then up to Upper Stoddard Lake. As soon as you get over the hump above the lake you'll see two distinct peaks, and the closer one looks the highest, but isn't. It'll take you a couple of hours of contouring, climbing and whacking a little brush to work your way into the saddle between the two peaks. The one to the west is 17 feet higher than the other one and is the real Billy's Peak. Actually this whole massif of jagged peaks is often referred to as "Billy's Peak."

BILLY'S PEAK TRAILHEAD

Access: A couple of miles north of Coffee Creek find 34N34 on Highway 3. Watch for sign. **Trinity River Campground** is close by.

Trails: Billy's Peak Trail (7W08) begins climbing steeply from an old logging deck and tends to be very steep and rocky. About 3 miles up the trail lies a boulder with the phrase "The spirit is indeed willing but the flesh is weak" painted on it. A series of switchbacks and a scramble up a talus field leads to the peak.

Destination: Only one. Top of 7,274-foot-high Billy's Peak.

Elevations/Difficulty: Strenuous, steep 4,000-vertical-foot climb in 3.1 miles.

Summary: Incomparable views in all directions. The lookout tower was dismantled and removed in the 1970s.

BLACK ROCK

(7,486 feet) Scott Mountain Trailhead. This is the massive, volcanic-looking mountain at the headwaters of Mill Creek. Of the two main summits, the southern is the high point. From Highway 3 at the Scott Mountain Summit, drive three miles on the road leading to Mosquito Lake/Camp Unalayee to the locked gate. Walk on the road beyond the locked gate another mile to the Tangle Blue divide. Leave the road and follow the divide around the head of Mill Creek to the south side of the mountain and work your way to the top. Stunning views to the north.

EAGLE CREEK TRAILHEAD

Access: Located off Forest Road 38N70 at Horse Flat Campground 2.5 miles north of Coffee Creek on Highway 3. **Horse Flat Campground** is located at the trailhead and **Eagle Creek Campground** is nearby on the Eagle Creek Loop.
Trails: Trail 7W05 enters a series of meadows called Eagle Creek Benches approximately five miles from the trailhead. Cattle grazing in the meadows has resulted in multiple trailing. The trail eventually meets the Pacific Crest Trail after 8.2 miles. The trail is rocky and heavily eroded.
Destinations: Eagle Creek Benches, Eagle Peak, Shasta View Mine.
Elevation/Difficulty: 2,700 feet at trailhead. Climbs moderately and steadily.
Summary: Some areas still show the effects of the fires of 1987. The Eagle Creek Benches area is used by horse-packers.

LITTLE BEAR LAKE

Elevation 6,200 feet; 6 acres; 74 feet deep. A deep blue-water lake. No definite trail. Fifty-minute walk from Big Bear Lake by contouring in a southeast direction to the lake. Not advisable for stock. A good trout lake with both brookies and rainbows. **Bear Creek Trailhead.**

Of the three lakes in this basin, Little Bear Lake is the winner for several reasons: stunning scenery similar to Big Bear, better campsites, easier to fish, and fewer people.

Off alone, I sleep among boulders moved by glaciers. Green streaks of fir and pine climb the rockfall, and when I see the reflected sunrise splashing the surrounding headwall, I wonder why the last ice age left this all just for me.

"The 1.5 billion cubic kilometers of water on the earth are split by photosynthesis and reconstituted by respiration once every two million years or so."

– Gary Snyder

LOG LAKE

Elevation 6,050 feet; 4.6 acres; 18 feet deep. Formerly called Moss Lake. No trail. Drive up the Tangle Blue Creek access road. The route leaves the road on a switchback just after the road crosses the creek. Follow Horse Creek about one mile to meadow. Steep tributary stream entering from the south is the lake's outlet. Considerable brush to negotiate before reaching open rocky terrain below the lake. At least a two-hour hike from the road. Log Lake is over a granite ridge about one-half mile below Big Bear Lake on the trail. Brookies to 11 inches reported in 1965. **Tangle Blue Lake Trailhead**.

Whichever of the two routes described above you choose, be prepared for a couple of hours of hand-to-hand combat with vicious brush.

The most direct approach, but also the most brushy, is from the Tangle Blue Trailhead and up Horse Creek to the obvious outlet stream. Most people stay to the right of the stream as they sweat and swear through the foot-tripping, face-slapping brush fields.

The Big Bear Lake trail approach is a lot longer in distance, but there's less brush to fight if you have good route-finding skills. Just below Big Bear Lake, about a quarter mile or so, start for the low point on the ridge to the north. With some luck you can pick your way from open space to open space, but you'll never get there without thrashing in the incessant underbrush thickly coating the near perpendicular slope.

Is it worth the effort? Oh yeah. It can feel like you have your own private alpine lake tucked high in the granite and pines if you're lucky and have the place to yourself. It's an outstanding one-party lake, because there are only a couple of campsites.

SCOTT MOUNTAIN TRAILHEAD

Access: At Scott Mountain Summit on Highway 3, 54 miles north of Weaverville. **Scott Mountain Campground** is at the trailhead. Or drive three miles to locked gate on road to Mosquito Lake/Camp Unalayee and walk on road to the divide and intersection with the Pacific Coast Trail.

Trails: The Pacific Coast Trail crosses Highway 3 at the summit and heads west for 18.4 miles to the Carter Meadow Summit Trailhead.

Destinations: East Boulder Lake, Middle Boulder lake, Telephone Lake, West Boulder Lake, Mavis Lake, Fox Creek Lake, Section Line Lake, Virginia Lake, upper and lower South Fork Lakes, Mosquito Lake, Big Marshy Lake, Little Marshy Lake.

Elevation/ Difficulty: 5,401 feet at trailhead. Easy, well-maintained trail.

Summary: Ridgetop walking with splendid views of Mount Shasta and mountains in all directions. Opportunity to visit many lakes. Shuttle with trailhead at Carter Meadow possible.

TANGLE BLUE LAKE

Elevation 5,700 feet; 12 acres; 17 feet deep. An access road goes up Tangle Blue Creek from Highway 3. A popular and productive lake. Both brook and rainbow trout present to 14 inches. Campsites. **Tangle Blue Lake Trailhead**.

The name is poetry. It ripples off the tongue with a rhythm and meter that conjures up provocative images of twisted color. Local legend says an early miner traveling between Callahan and the Trinity Mines got seriously drunk one night while camped along the creek, and the next morning the trail and stream he saw through a foggy hangover appeared to be a tangle of blue.

The lake you find after an easy 3.5-mile hike lives up to its picturesque name. Nestled in a wildflower strewn basin, surrounded by a serrated granite ridge, an idyllic stream wanders through a green grassy meadow before slipping into the lake. Brook trout often congregate at the inlet.

It's a place where a kid can catch his first fish and feel the tingling thrill of a fighting eight-inch trout on two-pound line. A place where the lesson of catch and release can be taught.

While in the area, check your map and take a look back into history by visiting the Grand National Mine. Lots of rusting machinery, including a stamp mill, and collapsing derelict buildings stare vacantly out over the spectacular valley and distant red ridges of the Scott Mountains.

There are two unnamed peaks towering over the lake well worth scrambling up. The higher craggy one to the south yields splendid views of Eagle Peak and Eagle Creek drainage, while the lower, sharp-pointed one provides vistas across the Tangle Blue canyon and the lakes and ridges to the north.

TANGLE BLUE TRAILHEAD

Access: 50 miles north of Weaverville on Highway 3 the road narrows as it begins climbing up over Scott Mountain via Tangle Blue Creek. If northbound, watch for sign and turnoff on switch back corner just after highway crosses Scott Mountain Creek. Follow road 39N20 to the trailhead. **Scott Mountain Campground** on the Highway 3 summit is nearby, as is **Eagle Creek Campground** on the Eagle Creek Loop.

Trails: Trail 8W23 is actually a road for a couple of miles until it connects with the Tangle Blue Trail (8W01), which forks to Tangle Blue Lake to the left or continues on to Big Marshy Lake and the Pacific Crest Trail. Trail 8W23 is a 1.3 mile spur trail (actually an old roadbed) to the Grand National Mine.

Destinations: Grand National Mine, Tangle Blue Lake, Little Marshy Lake, Big Marshy Lake.

Elevation/Difficulty: 3,900 feet at trailhead. Easy walking trails in this area.

Summary: Beautiful incense cedar trees. Grand National Mine is well worth a visit.

WEE BEAR LAKE

Elevation 6,150 feet; .5 acres; 14 feet deep. Located about 100 yards below Little Bear Lake. Populated with Eastern brook trout to 12 inches. **Bear Lake Trailhead**.

You can't miss this lake on your way to and from Little Bear Lake. Hopefully you noticed the rock ducks you didn't need on the route from Big Bear and kicked them over.

Just a pond, really, on the outlet stream, Wee Bear gets little camping pressure because its more spectacular brother is so close by. A natural jacuzzi bath is possible in the small gushing stream above the lake. Just the thing you need to lower your core body temperature on a blistering summer day.

Chapter Eight

THE SOUTHEASTERN ALPS

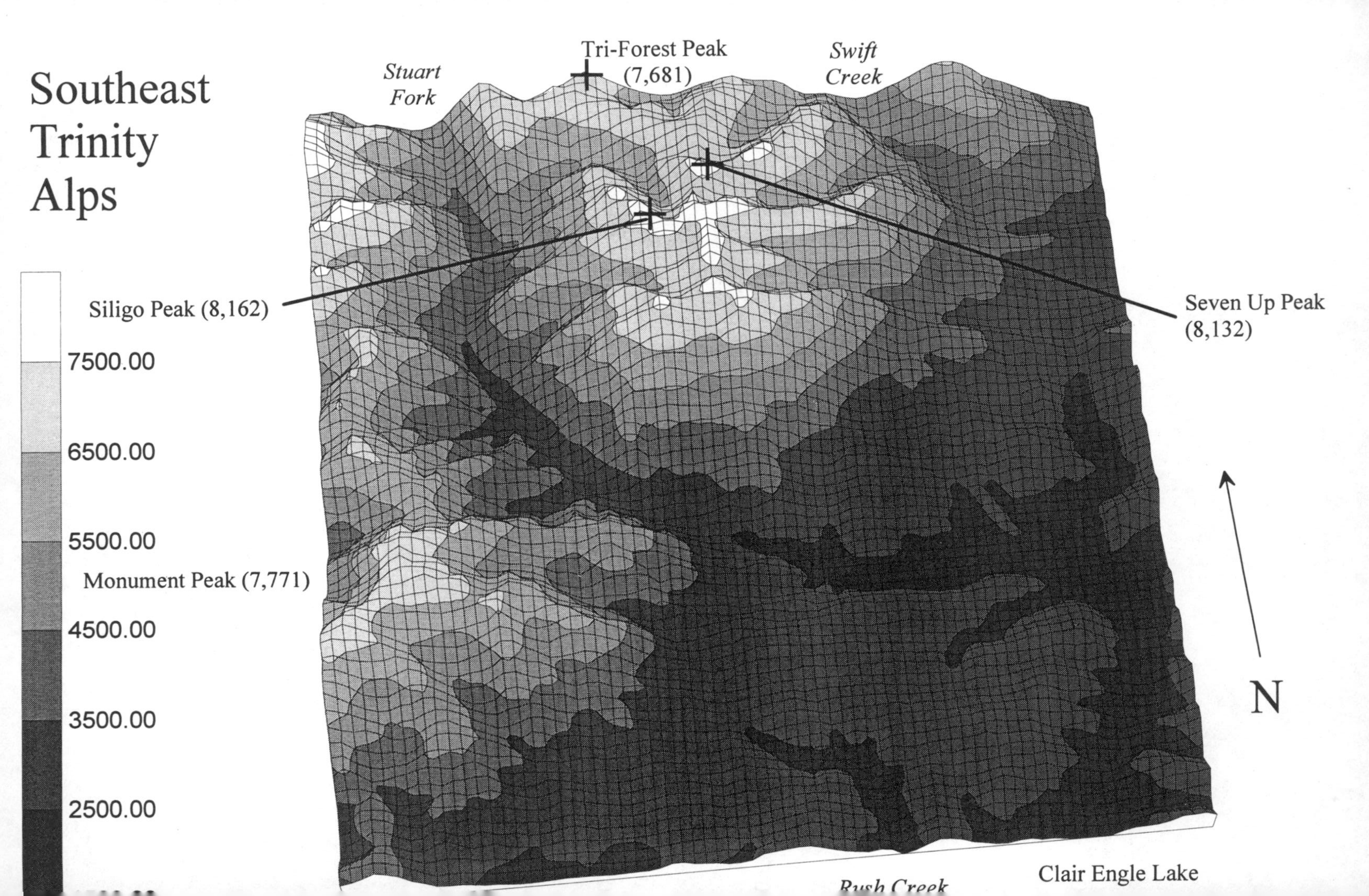
Southeast
Trinity
Alps
Tri-Forest Peak
(7,681)
Stuart
Fork
Swift
Creek
Siligo Peak (8,162)
Seven Up Peak
(8,132)
7500.00
6500.00
5500.00
Monument Peak (7,771)
4500.00
3500.00
2500.00
N
Clair Engle Lake
Rush Creek

Southeast Trinity Alps

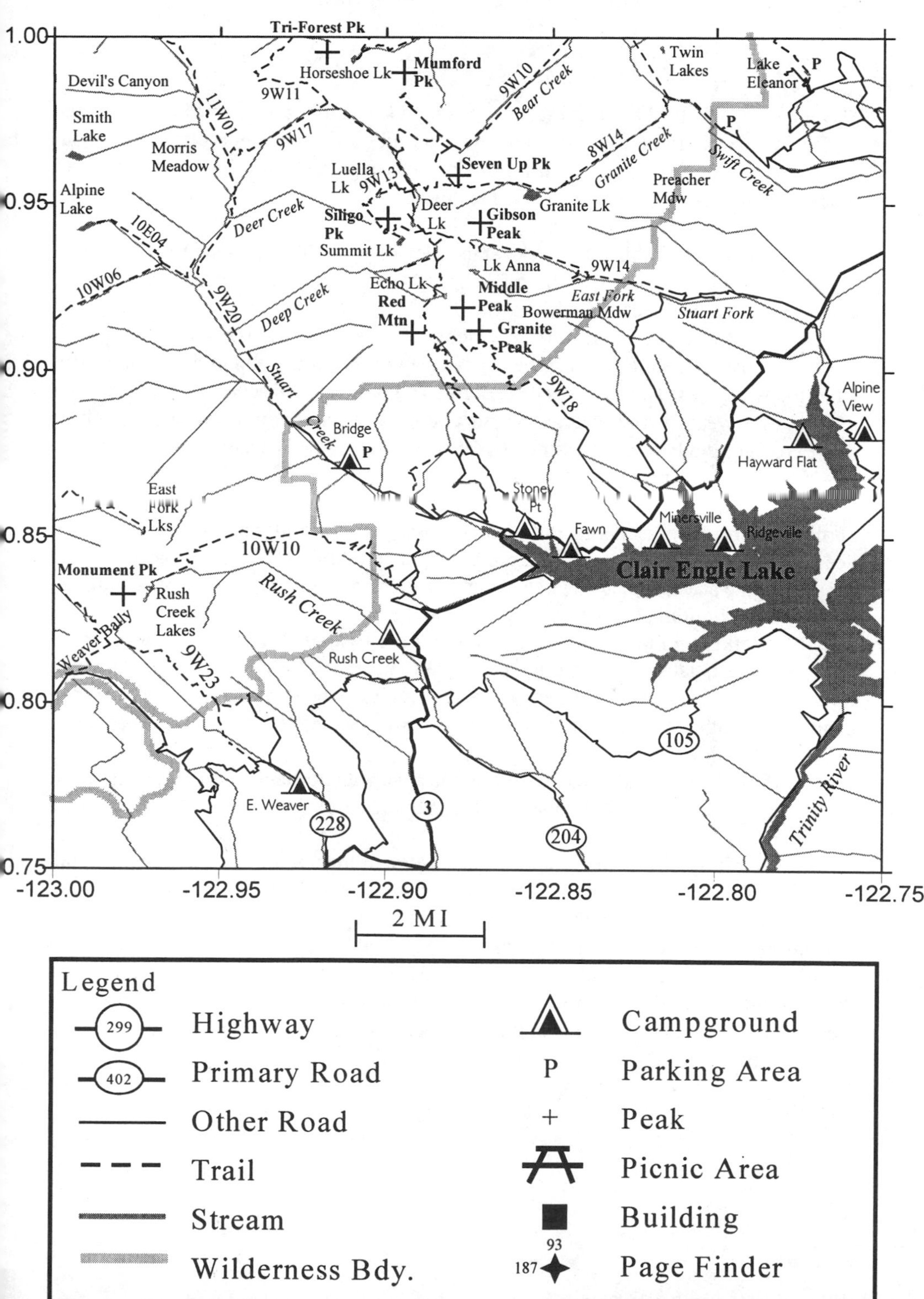

ALPINE LAKE

Elevation 6,150 feet; 14 acres; 26 feet deep. About seven miles up Stuart Fork trail, take the Boulder Creek trail for two miles to where a trail goes up the outlet stream for about two more miles to the lake. The last mile is very rough and rocky. Both rainbow and brook trout do very well. **Stuart Fork Trailhead**.

One wouldn't think that a lake at this elevation would be particularly difficult to get to. Wrong! Once you cross Stuart Fork, if it's even crossable, a pretty stiff climb of almost 3,000 vertical feet to the lake awaits.

Getting across Stuart Fork takes some effort if the water is high.

Crossing Stuart Fork can be tricky early in the spring and early summer. If it looks too wide, deep, and swift to cross, don't. The best bet is to scout downstream for a big log. Most years there is a large log jam about a quarter of a mile downstream where a safe crossing can be made anytime of year. However, streams change, and by the time this is read the logs may be long gone.

Once safely camped at Alpine Lake, an enormous ridge of delight stretches to the north. The prospect of exploring this high, treeless, granite world is enough to ferment the yeast of adventure in the most lethargic mountaineer. Alpine Lake is an excellent base camp for some peak bagging on three mountains with no names, or, if just passing through on the way to Smith Lake, the first night's stop.

Working northeast of the lake, around the base of Peak 8203, leads to Smith Lake. This peak, 8203, was years ago unofficially named Trinity Journal Mountain by a former editor of the local newspaper. There are still a few people who call it that, but the name didn't really stick. The summit is an interesting scramble if you're in the area and in the mood.

Directly north of Alpine Lake is a fine peak with no name. Climb it and name it. On the topographic map it is labeled 8071. Southeast of the lake is 8,083-foot Little Granite Peak.

North of Smith Lake is a marvelous ridge of high granite that makes one think of walking on a gigantic tilted parking lot. At the south end of the parking lot is Sawtooth Peak, 8,886 feet. Sawtooth Peak is a must climb on every hiker's life list. There are several approaches to the split and splintered pinnacle. Some route-finding skills are required near the summit. Once on top, there are several "tops." The highest, by a couple of feet, is probably the one farthest south with a summit register. There are brass caps from the U.S. Geological Survey on the north peak, so that may be the official Sawtooth Peak summit.

Near the summit of Sawtooth Peak

North of Sawtooth Peak is a fantastic aerie offering aerial views of Mirror, Emerald, and Sapphire Lakes. It's all contouring at the 7,500 foot level on clean granite above the headwaters of Devil's Canyon with its gargoyle ridges, and then around Peak 8415 to a slab shelf above the lakes. There is usually ample water from snow melt year-round. Real danger lurks for anyone trying to drop down to Sapphire Lake, due to limited visibility over the cliffs below. The prudent route is to work back toward Emerald Lake or even back to and down Devil's Canyon. Be warned. Devil's Canyon cultivates some nasty brush fields near the bottom.

Alpine Lake is the door to a vertical wilderness.

BIG EAST FORK LAKE

Elevation 5,850 feet; 2 acres; 11 feet deep. Since this small lake is out of the way, it is seldom visited. Has both brook and rainbow trout. From Dedrick on Canyon Creek a trail follows up Big East Fork of Canyon Creek to the lake. **Big East Fork Trailhead.**

The actual trail to starts at Buck's Ranch. There's a road to Buck's Ranch, but you can't use it any more since the new wilderness boundary, drawn in 1984, has blocked off the road permanently. So actually, the route to Big East Fork Lake starts somewhere along F.S. Road 35N47Y. Sometimes there is a sign marking the way to the Maple Mine. The trail to the Maple Mine eventually hits the old road, now a trail, to Buck's Ranch taking you to Big East Fork Lake.

The road to Buck's Ranch is very steep. Once past the meadow marking the old mining claim, the trail is every bit as steep as the road. The last mile or so across a brush field reaches skin-scalding temperatures on a summer afternoon.

Another alternative is to get dropped off or do a car shuttle from the East Weaver Lake trailhead on the Weaver Bally Lookout road and cross over to the Rush Creek Lakes. From Lower Rush Creek Lake it is a short way down the trail to a point near the gap west of Peak 6844. From this gap it takes less than 30 minutes to contour around to Big East Fork Lake. Use a topographic map to navigate. Then you can exit *down* the steep trail and road to Dedrick.

Fishing for those little brook trout is always good at this lake. However, the real charm of the place is that it is de facto wilderness. Because of the remote location and lack of access, it would have remained wilderness even without federal protection, at least for a while. I've made several trips to this lake over the years and have yet to see anyone there even in the middle of summer.

Walk up the ridge to the east and look down into Van Matre Creek. Now *there's* some de facto wilderness.

BILLY-BE-DAMNED LAKE

Elevation 7,530 feet; 1 acre; 8 feet deep. No fish. **Long Canyon Trailhead.**

People find their way to Billy-Be-Damned from one of three directions: 1) over the little rise from Lake Anna; 2) cross country through the rocky notch in the ridge from Echo Lake; or 3) by mistake from Bowerman Meadows because they veered to far to the west, lost the trail to Lake Anna, and ended up at Billy-Be-Damned.

From the Long Canyon trailhead a fairly easy hour of hiking delivers the upper Bowerman Meadows, ensconced in an amphitheater formed by the charcoal-gray cliffs of Granite Peak and the red-orange ramparts of Lake Anna. Groves of cottonwood trees offer inviting campsites.

While climbing around on the almost treeless slopes of the basin, the thought occurs that this area might be a good site for some skiing. In the 1950s, Guy Covington, owner-operator of Covington Mill back when it was a working sawmill, envisioned a ski resort in Bowerman Meadow. Data on annual snowfall depths and length of snow on the ground were studied. A road was punched in as far as the Bowerman Meadow fork on the Long Canyon Trail. Permits with the USFS were filed. But nothing ever materialized. It takes a lot of money and patience to build a ski resort in a National Forest, especially if that section of the forest is under consideration for wilderness status. About this same time the original Mount Shasta Ski Resort opened. Potential investors and developers were pretty sure there was room for only one ski resort in this part of the state. The idea was dropped, the road grew over and the whole deal was forgotten.

Billy-Be-Damned Lake is shallow, barren and rocky, with an iceberg in it until sometimes late in July. But on a hot day in August, there's not a better place to take a swim. Bring shade, however.

Jagged view from near Deer Lake

DEER LAKE

Elevation 7,150 feet; 4.5 acres; 19 feet. Accessible by trail up Stuart Fork and thence up Deer Creek, up the Stoney Creek Ridge trail from Stuart Fork, or by way of Long Canyon. Brook trout to 10 inches common. Other lakes nearby. **Long Canyon, Stoney Ridge, or Stuart Fork Trailhead.**

If you come into Deer Lake from Deer Creek Pass before mid-July you'll be able to use the Gratton Flat Gang's "slide for life." Most years it is possible to glissade 300 to 400 feet down the steep snow slope to the lake. Five minutes down. Thirty minutes to hike back out. Take an ice axe to slow your descent.

We were there once when only a thin sliver of the lake was unfrozen. The entire lake was ice-covered except for a 15-foot strip along an edge. Putting salmon eggs on hooks and casting out onto the ice, we'd pull in line until the egg fell off the ice into the lake. WHAM! Every time a fish. Two kids caught and released about fifty fish in an hour.

Firewood is nonexistent at the lake. There is only one tree available for shade, so if you are the first one there, the only campsite is yours.

The enormous mountain massif of exquisite gray granite to the east has no name. At 8,207 feet high, it is often mistaken for Seven-up Peak. Seven-up Peak is lower (8,132 feet), red-colored, and farther north.

To the west, towering over the lake, is Siligo Peak, 8,162 feet.

The practical way to reach Deer Lake is to come up Long Canyon from the East Fork of Stuart Fork trailhead, cross Siligo Meadow to Deer Creek Pass, and drop down to the lake.

But if you love long walks, come up Deer Creek from Morris Meadow on Stuart Fork. It'll take you all day.

Many of the place names in the Alps come from the pioneer cattlemen who used this country for years for summer grazing. Until the 1940's, stock raising was a big business in Trinity County. Siligo Meadow and Siligo Peak were named for Louis Siligo, a Lewiston cattleman. Seven-up Peak was given its name by Irvin and Stanford Scott of Scott's Ranch in Trinity Center as they were playing a card game, Seven-up, while tending their cattle nearby.

DIAMOND LAKE

Elevation 7,250 feet; 2.5 acres; 13 feet deep. Best approach is up Stuart Fork and Deer Creek trails, then take the trail to the west just past Round Lake, continuing past Luella Lake to Diamond Lake. Excellent fly fishing for naturally reproducing brook trout. **Long Canyon, Stoney Ridge, or Stuart Fork Trailhead.**

Diamond Lake is a place to dream. To the west the arena of the Alps provides the stuff from which dreams are composed. A place to dine on clouds. You can dine on clouds and know you are growing older by the way the moon makes lines on your face with no lines. But clouds don't taste bad when the dining room is Diamond Lake.

The warm runny days of summer seem never to end. The sun hangs forever in the west and the temptation to look has to be resisted.

In the late '50s we killed a lot of fish in Diamond Lake. We were young and foolish, but even then knew better. Today, we release most fish so we and they can enjoy the lakes forever. When we tired of fishing, we stripped off our clothes and swam in water more fit for trout than humans. We were going to live forever as we stretched out naked on the grass to dry in the sun.

But Diamond Lake is not forever. Love it while you are there, eat a few clouds. If it's a warm day, take a dip. Stay as long as you can. Nothing lasts. I may be wrong about the whole thing.

The best approach is not from Stuart Fork and Deer Creek. A much shorter and direct way is via Long Canyon on the East Fork of Stuart Fork, through Bee Tree Gap, Siligo Meadow and the trail near Summit Lake, contouring around Siligo Peak and thence down to Diamond Lake.

ECHO LAKE

Elevation 7,250 feet; 2.5 acres; 17 feet deep. The best route is up the Stoney Creek trail through Stonewall Pass and past Van Matre Meadow. Just below Little Stonewall Pass, a dim trail goes in a southerly direction past a small pond to the lake. Stocked with brook trout. **Stoney Ridge Trailhead.**

The geologists probably have a name for it, but I call it a balcony lake. You can sit on the bank of Echo Lake, as if in a balcony, and dangle your thoughts, if not your feet, out over Deep Creek and that giant emptiness of Stuart Fork. The best show from this balcony starts at sundown each evening.

But a moon down can be just as rewarding. I recall a night when the moon was full–one of those huge moons at high altitude that makes it impossible to sleep because of the brightness. Maybe it's not just the brightness, but a full moon can breed some primeval stirrings in the heart of a wilderness wanderer.

It was a gargantuan hubcap of a moon. There was no doubt you could read a newspaper by the light of the moon that night. There are few trees for shade from such a moon. It isn't often that a person has to seek shade from the moon. When it finally set that night at Echo, we all felt relief, turned back into our kapok sleeping bags and tried to sleep until noon the next day.

The classic approach to Echo Lake is through Stonewall Pass from Red Mountain Meadow. The trailhead is pretty well marked, but you can only reach it between May and October, because the Forest Service locks the gate on the road at Highway 3 for six months of the year.

The East Fork of Stuart Fork Trailhead is open year-round. It's the long way around, but you can get to Echo via Siligo Meadow and Little Stonewall Pass.

The Stoney Creek Trail and Red Mountain Meadow approach offers the chance to climb the three fine peaks in the area: Red Mountain (7,928), Middle Peak (8,095), and Granite Peak (8,091). Middle Peak, the highest by four feet, gives a bird's-eye view of Echo Lake. Granite Peak used to have a fire lookout, but only the foundations remain. There is a summit register that provides amusing reading while you rest from your labor of reaching the summit.

GIBSON LAKE

Elevation 6,400 feet; .25 acres; 7 feet deep. Gibson Lake is a small body of water that can be reached by taking the Swift Creek and Granite Creek trails to the lower end of Gibson Meadow and then making one's way south from the lower end of the meadow. This is another lake whose ability to support fish is questionable. **Swift Creek Trailhead.**

Gibson Lake is one of those hide-and-go-seek lakes. It's hidden out there, and your task is to go seek it if you want to play the game.

Start by finding your way to Gibson Meadow. This is actually a good quarter of a mile downstream from the area marked "Gibson Meadow" on the U.S.G.S. topographic map. Across the stream from the trail to the south you see an open patch of hillside. Wander around the open area until you find a small outlet stream, and follow it uphill to a small boggy pond. You might assume this is Gibson Lake.

Maybe. If you contour around to the east, there is yet another lake of small proportions that could be Gibson Lake. Take your pick.

The value of Gibson Lake is that it offers an alternative to an otherwise overused area. Granite Creek and Granite Lake are trampled to death all summer long. But just a few minutes from this inter-Alps freeway is a personal one-person lake almost totally ignored.

But there may be some truth in the argument that .25 acres of seven-foot-deep water does not a lake make.

Whatever your reason for going to Gibson Lake, you'll have to look for it. No trail. A nice test of your route-finding skills.

GIBSON PEAK

(8,400 feet) **Long Canyon Trailhead, Swift Creek Trailhead.** This is the peak dominating Long Canyon and Granite Lake. You can gain the summit from either side. The approach from Long Canyon is the steep, direct route. From near Bee Tree Gap it's a matter of picking your way along the long, rocky (or snow-filled in early season) face and scrambling to the summit. From Granite Lake, there are several ways up. Use your route-finding skills to find the one that works for you.

I was sitting on top of Gibson Peak one day having come up from the Long Canyon side, when a man and his dog arrived from Granite Lake. A dog on top of an Alps peak is not a common sight.

Gibson Peak

GRANITE LAKE

Elevation 5,950 feet; 18 acres; 64 feet deep. It is about a half-hour hike up the Swift Creek trail to Granite Creek, and then another three miles up the Granite Creek trail to Granite Lake. Granite Lake is one of possibly two lakes in the Siskiyou-Trinity area to contain Lahontan cutthroat trout. The predominant fish in this water, though, are brown trout, and some are reported to be "big enough to tow a raft around." Some fair-sized rainbows are also present. **Swift Creek Trailhead.**

If Canyon Creek is the supermarket of the Alps, Granite Lake is the used-car lot. All summer long backpackers clutter up the shoreline like a bunch of old used cars waiting to make a deal.

People who have heard of the Alps expect spectacular scenery. Especially those who get their info from *Sunset* magazine. Granite Lake fills the bill, and, as a result, people fill the scenery. Yet by picking carefully the time and season, you can avoid the crowds. Try anytime before Memorial Day if the winter has been mild, or after Labor Day during Indian summer when crisp black nights alternate with warm hazy days.

This is azalea heaven from the end of June into July. The pungent smell, sweet and thick in the air, provides the incentive to wander farther and farther up the trail.

The trail is but five miles in length from car to lakeside. During the three to four hours required to walk it, you'll see waterfalls, luxuriant meadows, deep woods, sky scraping peaks. It's all here. Just like it said in *Sunset*.

Only have a day? You can run and jog into this lake in a little over an hour, spend the day, and allow 45 minutes in the evening to return.

Don't miss the view from the rock promontory just across the outlet on the east side of the lake. This is the place to sun, swim, and eye-climb Gibson Peak (8,400 feet). Gibson Peak rears up so suddenly on the far side of the lake that you risk getting whiplash from looking too quickly.

Gibson Peak is a moderate scramble from a campsite at Granite Lake. You can plot your entire route, over rock slabs and boulder fields, from the lake before you start. Once on top the view is rewarding in all directions, but especially to the east where you can see the upper Sacramento Valley, Mount Lassen, and northward to Mount Shasta.

Seven Up Peak (8,132 feet) is another peak to bag while you're in the area. Continue on the trail up Granite Creek to the pass leading over into Deer Creek. From the pass it's a stroll to the top. Interestingly, the rock on Seven Up is red in color, contrasting with the gray granite on the other side of the canyon and Gibson Peak.

A third and challenging peak can be found at the head of Granite Creek south of Seven Up and west of Gibson Peak. Marked 8207 on the U.S.G.S. topographic map, it has no name and is approached on its north face over glacier-like snow that never melts. One map marks this peak as the high point on a ridge labeled *Dolomites*, but I have no idea what that means. My guess is that when this ridge is viewed from Siligo Meadow on the south side it reminded someone of the famous Dolomites in Europe. This leaves us wondering where we would be if the 1930s resort owner, who came up with the name Trinity Alps, had been partial to the Dolomites rather than the Alps. Would we be hiking in the Trinity Dolomites Wilderness Area?

If Granite Lake is only a station on your way and not your destination, at the pass into Deer Creek you have a couple of choices.

One, you can drop down into Deer Creek, do the lakes in that area: Round, Luella, Diamond, Summit, and Deer. These lakes can all be found like a necklace draped around Siligo Peak (8,162 feet). Siligo Peak is an easy hike from all sides except its east face. Once your trip is over you have four choices to exit: 1) back the way you came to Granite Lake and the Swift Creek trailhead, 2) down Deer Creek and out Stuart Fork to the Bridge Camp trailhead (it's the longest way), 3) through Bee Tree Gap and down Long Canyon to the trailhead, 4) Little Stonewall and Stonewall Pass down Red Mountain Meadow to the Stoney Ridge trailhead. A slight variation would be to get back up on Seven Up Peak and down into Bear Basin and then to the Swift Creek trailhead.

Two, from the pass, there is a trail that contours around Seven Up Peak into Black Basin, where you'll find the remains of Long Cabin, an abandoned gold mine. Black Basin is named for an early Trinity Center sheep man. You'd have to guess that Long Cabin is named for a guy who built it and staked a mining claim here.

Black Basin is one of those secret places in the Alps where you can spend some time without other backpackers. It's well off the beaten path, has many campsites, abundant firewood, and offers the opportunity to read an entire novel without being interrupted.

From Black Basin you might continue on down into Deer Creek, go over the low pass into Bear Basin, or find the faint trail that angles up to the ridgetop and drops into Mumford Basin in Swift Creek. Should you choose the Mumford Basin route, you can easily knock off Mumford Peak (7,346 feet) on the way. If you choose Bear Basin (yes, it's really good bear country) you might visit one of the few places I've never seen, Elderberry Duff. I await your report. I can readily identify elderberries, but "duff" has got me stumped. We might speculate that Elderberry Duff was the name of an early Trinity Center sheep man, I suppose, who wouldn't get off his...duff?

GRANITE PEAK

(8,091 feet) Granite Peak Trailhead, Stoney Ridge Trailhead. The USFS fire lookout, a landmark for many years, is now long gone, a victim of the 1970s Forest Service purge of old buildings in the Shasta-Trinity National Forest. The government claimed that "undesirable" people were using places like the lookout to live in. This, said the feds, was a use violation of the forest and a potential legal liability. The lookout was leveled and burned. The foundation and a few burned scraps are all that remain.

Two trails lead to the top; steep and direct from the Granite Peak Trailhead and the more roundabout way via Stoney Ridge and Red Mountain Meadows. The two nearby peaks, Middle Peak and Red Mountain, can also be climbed the same day you climb Granite Peak.

Years ago there was a summit register on Granite that provided some amusing reading. Look around and see if it is still there, and make your contribution to the literature of Granite Peak.

Perhaps the most unusual use of Granite Peak was by the young couple in the '70s who used a helicopter to transport their wedding party to the summit and were married 8,000 feet in the sky. I wonder if they are still married.

GRANITE PEAK TRAILHEAD (STONEWALL PASS TRAILHEAD)

Access: 16.5 miles north of Weaverville on State Highway 3 turn left on road 35N28Y. This is just south of the Mule Creek Guard Station and directly opposite the road to **Minersville Campground** and **Bushy Tail Campground.** Trailhead is about three miles at end of road.

Trails: Trail 9W18 is steep all the way to the top of Granite Peak 4.6 miles away. Joins the spur trail (9W18A) to Red Mountain Meadow about one mile before the summit.

Destinations: Granite Peak, Red Mountain Meadow.

Elevation/Difficulty: Very difficult and strenuous with an elevation gain of more than 4,000 feet.

Summary: This is the most direct route to climb Granite Peak. Portions of the foundation of the old fire lookout remain on the summit. A superb view of Trinity Lake and the Alps awaits.

Panoramic view from near Thumb Rock

HORSESHOE LAKE

Elevation 6,850 feet; 6 acres; 22 feet. Situated at the head of Swift Creek, it is 12 miles from the end of the road. Brook trout are abundant. **Swift Creek or Big Flat Trailhead.**

Horseshoe Lake is a nifty little lake tucked away under the watchful eye of Tri-

Forest Peak at the headwaters of Swift Creek. The sun goes down early, but jumps up early, like a red rubber ball.

The route up Swift Creek is a piece of cake. Only the last mile or so involves any sudden elevation gain.

On the way from the Swift Creek trailhead the landmarks pass easily: Granite Creek, where probably 80 percent of the traffic turns off, Steer Creek (to be waded in early season), Parker Creek with its bomb-proof bridge, Foster Cabin near Parker Meadow, and finally the long sloping beauty of Mumford Meadow. A campsite in Mumford Meadow allows a good base to wander this gentle country. Stroll up into Mumford Basin, where the feeling of the Alps of 100 years ago prevails. A day hike from here over into Black Basin, Long Cabin, and then down Bear Basin provides a wilderness experience so exquisite you'll swear it's illegal.

But pushing on to Horseshoe Lake, the granite is white and clean. There's plenty of firewood, should you feel the urge to build a bonfire.

From a lakeside camp, be sure and get up on Tri-Forest Peak (7,681 feet).

Of course, you can come into Horseshoe Lake via Kidd Creek over by Big Flat. It's like entering a huge house from the back door. You miss a lot of the good stuff. It is shorter and steeper, but could be used to complete a point-to-point trip if you've arranged a car shuttle.

Tri-Forest Peak takes its name from the fact that at one time there were three national forests: Klamath, Trinity, and Shasta. The boundaries of these forests met at the summit. Two of the forests were combined into the Shasta-Trinity National Forest. Perhaps it's time to update the maps and call it Bi-Forest Peak.

LAKE ANNA

Elevation 7550 feet; 4 acres; 56 feet deep. There are two ways of reaching the lake: up the East Fork of Stuart Fork via Bowerman Meadow, and thence a steep climb up the outlet to the lake; or by way of Long Canyon, the most gradual climb, making your way over the last gap in the canyon leading to the left and down to the lake. Situated in a depression on the slopes of a steep mountain. Excellent angling for brook trout to 11 inches reported. **Long Canyon Trailhead**.

Prior to the advent of small gas stoves, people built two kinds of fires in the Alps; cook fires and bonfires.

It was in early October 1958 when we built a memorable fire at Lake Anna. A HUGE bonfire. All the wood we could muster was piled on at once, and the flames seemed to touch the full moon rising like a gigantic hubcap in the east. The four of us sat back about 300 yards from the blaze and marveled until way past midnight at how mild the night was for October at 7,000 feet.

That was nearly 40 years ago. Thank goodness for gas stoves. There is barely enough wood left at Anna to build a cook fire.

The lake hangs like a vest pocket on the coat of a very tall man. To get there you come in over the shoulder and drop into the pocket. From East Fork Stuart Fork trailhead it is a pretty steep pull up Long Canyon to Bee Tree Gap. Before you get to the gap, head for the skyline to the left up a rocky chute. Stay high and you'll hit in above the lake and will only have to drop down once you spot it. Probably only four hours from the car, but plan on four hours of hiking. Steep.

Yes, you can hang left at the Bowerman Meadow/Long Canyon junction and reach the lake via the outlet. It's a little shorter in distance but steeper than Long Canyon, and is often saved as a way to return. But the hike up through Bowerman Meadow is a seldom-used route. The trail is often overgrown from lack of use and eventually leads to a superb campsite at the base of the cliff band below Lake Anna. Plenty of wood and water is available. Camp here and experience secluded wilderness any time of year. A quick twenty-minute scramble up the cliffs gets you to the lake.

While at Lake Anna you are required to visit Billy-Be-Damned Lake. There are no fish in Billy-Be-Damned, but it offers superb swimming late in the summer.

Lake Eleanor

LAKE ELEANOR

Elevation 4,950 feet; 3 acres; 10 feet deep. The Lake Eleanor road goes nearly to the lake. Brook trout are present. **Lake Eleanor Trailhead.**

Eleanor, queen of the Alps. But the queen has been despoiled. Logging has taken place to within an ax throw of the lake. Because of its low elevation, Eleanor was always the first lake to open in the spring, and thus it was the first shakedown trip of the season. As went Eleanor, so went the rest of the summer.

When the final boundaries for the Wilderness Area were settled in 1984, Lake Eleanor was not included. Two related factors resulted in the exclusion. First, the section line dividing private land belonging to the Southern Pacific Land Company (see explanation under Little Boulder Lake) and the U.S. Forest Service goes right smack dab through the middle of the lake. That meant all the land on the west side was eligible to be logged prior to the final decision of what to include in the Trinity Alps Wilderness Area. And log it they did. Roads were built and the trees cut down.

So, when Lake Eleanor was inventoried to determine its worthiness for wilderness status, it failed the test on account of the recent logging activity in the area. A logging road will take you to within a 10-minute stroll to the lake. There's no opportunity for a wilderness experience anymore.

It was three miles by trail from Gratton Flat back in the old days. With the logging, a road has been built above the lake, like an ugly scar. They took the trees and left a road that goes nowhere. A double slap in the face to all of us who loved to listen to the frogs croak in the evening by Lake Eleanor.

In the 1950s we never took a tent. Just lay out under the stars there by the grassy inlet stream. Crawling into a tent in the Alps is akin to taking a shower with your socks on.

Later that day, flat on our backs floating on air mattresses in our underwear, we caught 26 trout.

Fred Conway was a pioneer cattleman from Trinity Center. He took credit for discovering Lake Eleanor and named it for his wife.

LAKE ELEANOR TRAILHEAD

Access: 29.5 miles north of Weaverville on highway 3, just north of the Swift Creek bridge (sign on left). Follow the road 36N24D and trailhead signs 7 miles to the trailhead. Preacher Meadow Campground in on highway 3, two miles south of Trinity Center.

Trails: Trail 8W13, a.k.a. Deer Flat Trail, passes Lake Eleanor after .25 miles and winds through a confusing series of logging roads to Shimmy Lake. From Shimmy Lake it climbs up the ridge to join the Lilypad Lake Trail (8W21). Left leads to Deer Flat Camp, right leads to Lilypad Lake. Beyond Deer Flat Camp it joins the Parker Creek Trail (9W19).

Destinations: Lake Eleanor, Shimmy Lake, Lilypad Lake, Ycatapom Peak and Thumb Rock. Parker Creek Trail leads to Swift Creek and eventually back to near trailhead for a loop hike.

Elevation/Difficulty: 4,850 feet at trailhead. Gentle country with easy to moderate grades.

Summary: Short, easy hike to Lake Eleanor. Good chance for solitude at warm, shallow Shimmy Lake. Climb Ycatapom Peak or Thumb Rock.

LONG CANYON TRAILHEAD

Access: North 23 miles from Weaverville on Highway 3. At Covington's Mill turn left and follow signs 4 miles to trailhead on 35N10A. **Alpine View Campground** is on Trinity Lake just beyond Covington Mill on Highway 3 and **Hayward Flat Campground**, also on Trinity Lake, is 4 miles south of Covington Mill on Highway 3.

Trails: Trail 9W14 is a steady labor intensive pull up Long Canyon to Bee Tree Gap 5.7 miles away. The Bowerman Meadow Trail (8W22) forks left a couple of miles from the trailhead.

Destinations: Bowerman Meadow, Lake Anna, Billy-Be-Damned Lake, Siligo Meadow, Gibson Peak, Siligo Peak.

Elevation/Difficulty: 3,800 feet at trailhead. All trails in this area are moderate to difficult with steady elevation gains.

Summary: Long Canyon is the gateway to a high alpine experience. Bowerman Meadow leads to solitude in a hidden canyon with a scramble up vermilion cliffs to Lake Anna. Long Canyon harbors high country meadows with an incredible array of wildflowers. Siligo Meadow offers camping in the heart of soaring peaks and shimmering lakes. Breathtaking views in all directions.

Long Canyon Trail

LUELLA LAKE

Elevation 6,950 feet; 2.5 acres; 13 feet deep. You reach this lake as you would Deer Lake, but should turn west near the pond (Round Lake) below Deer Lake. Both Eastern brook and rainbow trout are to be found here. **Stuart Fork or Long Canyon Trailhead.**

I was sure anxious to see this lake when just a kid. There was a restaurant in Weaverville called Luella's and it always flashed through my mind when I saw the lake on the map. Was there a connection? When I finally got to Luella Lake I could see no resemblance, but then things change, people change, restaurants change, lakes change.

Up above Deer Creek Meadow Luella squats, waiting. People rarely stay. Either they are passing through on the way to Diamond Lake or heading down to the meadow on their way back from Diamond. I have never met anyone who has actually camped at this lake. Maybe it's the Luella Restaurant connection I was looking for. No one camps in restaurants either. A change of name might change Luella Lake's life, as a change of name has done for a lot of people.

Like the other lakes in this area, the direct approach is from East Fork of Stuart Fork trailhead, up Long Canyon, across Siligo Meadow, and then either loop either left or right around Siligo Peak to the lake.

Other approaches are from Morris Meadow and up Deer Creek–a long, long way from the trailhead on Stuart Fork at Bridge Camp, or from Granite Lake and the Swift Creek trailhead.

MIDDLE PEAK

(8,095 feet) Stoney Ridge Trailhead, Granite Peak Trailhead. Middle Peak is the highest of the three sentinels standing guard over Red Mountain Meadows, but it got stuck with a rather mundane name. The easiest and most direct approach is from the meadow. It's not much more than a stroll from there.

The summits affords an aerial view of Echo Lake and a peek into Billy-Be-Damned Lake. I've often followed the ridge north to Billy-Be-Damned (good swimming in August) and Lake Anna and then returned via the notch in the ridge to Echo Lake. At Echo Lake you can pick up the trail and come back through Stonewall Pass and return to Red Mountain Meadows.

Deer Creek Meadow

MONUMENT PEAK

(7,771 feet) Weaver Bally Trailhead, Bear Gulch Trailhead, East Weaver Trailhead, Rush Creek Trailhead. This is the highest point on what is generally called Weaver Bally Mountain. It's a little over an hour's hike from the Weaver Bally Road bushwhacking cross-country from East Weaver Lake. This is also the preferred route to Rush Creek Lakes. Few people hiking into the lakes can resist bagging Monument Peak.

There is a bit longer route that avoids the brush. Drive as far as you can up Big East Fork of Canyon Creek and find the Bear Gulch/ East Weaver Trail. You may be stopped by a slide across the road that has been waiting years to be cleared. Follow the trail, if you find it, to the gap. From here it is a stroll along the gap northward and upward through big timber to the rocky summit knob.

Rocks on Monument Peak

The view from Monument Peak is superb. The Canyon Creek watershed stretches out below and reaches up to touch the base of Thompson Peak on the horizon.

You'll find brass caps placed by the U.S. Geological Survey on the summit. Early mapping efforts in these mountains required ground triangulation or sighting with surveying instruments from various peaks to establish anchor points from which to control distances and elevations on the map being drawn. Monument Peak was an important triangulation point. Surveyors would spend the night on the peak and build a bonfire visible from other peaks in the Alps where other surveyors were also spending the night building similar fires. During the night they would take accurate readings on their instruments of each other's pinpoints of lights in the darkness.

Spending the night on a high mountain peak is still a special treat. The stars are right there in your face, and as the morning twilight begins to pale the sky, meteors often flit and dart silently in milliseconds of fiery life.

MUMFORD PEAK

(7,346 feet) Swift Creek Trailhead, Big Flat Trailhead. Mumford Peak sits at the head of Swift Creek, waiting for visitors who seldom come. Those who do take the Swift Creek Trail to the point where it leaves the canyon and begins its climb to Ward and Horseshoe lakes. The route requires you to pick your way to the saddle south of the summit and then on up to the top.

There is a faint trail from Black Basin on Deer Creek that peters out on the lower peak south of Mumford Peak. By the time the trail disappears, you are high enough on the mountain that you can visually navigate your way to the top.

RED MOUNTAIN

(7,928 feet) Stoney Ridge Trailhead. Yes, it is red, an enormous dome of red rock almost eight thousand feet high. It gave its name to nearby Red Mountain Meadows, an ideal campsite from which you can knock off all three summits surrounding the meadow, Granite Peak, Middle Peak and Red Mountain.

Start up the trail from Red Mountain Meadow toward Stonewall Pass, but before you get to the pass, start a climbing contour to your left. This will avoid the minor summit between the pass and the top of Red Mountain. No use climbing any higher than you have to. No one likes to gain altitude and then have to give it up again.

There's a trail over from Siligo Meadow and Van Matre Meadow you can use to get to Stonewall Pass. The north side of the summit is pretty cliffy. You may want to get all the way up to Stonewall Pass before starting your contour to the right and eventually to the top.

ROUND LAKE

Elevation 6,400 feet; .25 acres; 9 feet deep. Despite its appearance, it has produced 12-inch brookies. The Deer Creek trail goes right past the pond. **Long Canyon or Stuart Fork Trailhead.**

Round Lake is like that throw rug in your hallway. You see it a lot, but only because it's on the way to somewhere else. People making the loop of lakes around Siligo Peak can't help but check in on Round Lake.

So Round Lake sits at the crossroads of Deer Creek. Anyone wanting to monitor the traffic in this area could not pick a better place to camp.

Evening comes early, and morning late, in this deep canyon. The sky cuts a blue gash between high forested walls and glaring gray granite. The west is blocked out by 8,162-foot Siligo Peak, and the east by 8,132-foot Seven Up Peak. Summer days are short and hot, mornings and evenings long and lingering. In winter, actual daytime is probably non-existent. It's doubtful that there is much traffic to monitor here in the winter.

Bill Horstman and I once camped near Round Lake. We found old bed frames left by some early mountain men. Seemed like a good idea to put our sleeping bags on the springs and sleep on the civilized comfort of a bed out in the wilderness. Wrong! We were suspended in the cold night air which could pass not only over us, but under us too. We set Jell-O out to cool under our makeshift spring beds. In the morning, both us and the Jell-O were frozen and stiff from a night in the deep freezer.

Deer Creek Trail

RUSH CREEK LAKE (LOWER)
Elevation 6,250 feet; .75 acres; 12 feet deep. A beautiful lake set deep between high granite walls bordered by meadows. Brook trout available. **Weaver Bally Lookout or Rush Creek Lakes Trailhead.**

You can't find more superb slabs of granite than those entombing the solitude at Lower Rush Creek Lake. Be sure to come in from the Weaver Bally Road via Monument Peak. The trail up from Kinney Camp should be declared illegal. It must have been designed by some dropout from trail-building school. Take it sometime and you'll see what I mean.

I sat in the fine meadow grass near Lower Rush Creek Lake one endless summer day and wrote:

When warm summer days
that pass through your fingers
begin to cover
brittle pine needles
with unbelievable urgency,
sit down,

take your mind in your lap
use your memory like
a paring knife
to open your mind and place it
next to mine.
Carefully
remove the remnants of any
love that may cling in
anxious chunks to your childish thoughts
of me.
Place them in a bottle
seal it with sweat that
pools between your breasts sending
it to me by floating it on the sea.
It may be that it will
rise
with the mists, become clouds,
which rush themselves
to the mountains and spend themselves
panting for days
making love to the peaks.
The climax becomes the pure streams
that spill over
into the canyons
where I lie
on brittle pine needles
covered with the warm
summer days of that time
when we
both drank from the same stream
but
not really.

RUSH CREEK LAKE (MIDDLE)

Elevation 6,540 feet; 1 acre; 12 feet deep. **Weaver Bally Lookout or Rush Creek Lakes Trailhead.**

Middle Rush Creek Lake has a fine granite cliff on one side. Get in the right place and you can bounce fine echoes. One evening we lay on our sleeping bags at one end of the lake and bounced .22 bullets off the lake to hear them splat against the rock wall. We didn't know anything back then, yet thought we knew it all. That was many years ago, back when we carried guns into the Alps to aid us in our conquering efforts. It was us against the wilderness in the Fifties. We were prepared to fight, if necessary, in order to return and report to President Jefferson what we had discovered in this part of the Louisiana Purchase.

I no longer carry a gun in the Alps and the only echoes I bounce off the cliff are my voice. Sometimes the silence is better still.

RUSH CREEK LAKE (UPPER)

Elevation 6,950 feet; 2 acres; 44 feet deep. A rockbound lake often frozen over until August. Contains both rainbow and brook trout. **Weaver Bally Lookout or Rush Creek Lakes Trailhead.**

Icebergs in August. That's Upper Rush Creek Lake. From the spring on Weaver Bally Lookout Road you can be on the lake in a little over an hour. The ice will be there even into late summer.

From East Weaver Lake head for the low gap to the north. Once in the gap, the way lies up over the right shoulder of Monument Peak (7,771 feet). You'll pass within a few hundred feet of the summit, so be sure to go on up and look around. Get the lay of the land. That's Upper Rush Creek Lake down there at your feet.

It may not be thawed out until July, but if it is thawed, you'll be able to catch fish.

Rush Creek Lakes are de facto wilderness. The area is rugged enough and obscure enough to protect itself. It was not included in the original primitive area, but fortunately made it into the final Wilderness Area when the boundary lines were drawn in 1984.

The ridge that runs roughly southeast from above the lake leads to two more secret places and isolated pockets of solitude. These nameless hideaways are seldom visited; places where you can spend a week and never see another human. Look for them below the north sides of Peaks 7364 and 7060 on the topographic map.

The lakes are tiny jewels tucked neatly in behind Monument Peak, pretty much isolated from the Alps in general. Only a few hours from the largest population area in Trinity County, they are seldom visited. It takes a bit of effort to reach them. The trail from Kinney Camp climbs high up the ridge rather than following the creek, resulting in a waterless trek until you are almost to the lower lake. The other route into the lakes is sans trail, requiring cross-country route-finding skills.

The cross-country route from the Weaver Bally Lookout Road is the best choice to reach the Rush Creek Lakes. It affords the opportunity to climb Monument Peak (7,771 feet) en route.

The view from Monument Peak will not disappoint. All of Canyon Creek lies exposed like an anesthetized patient on an operating table. You can visually dissect the landscape as your eyes wander past the waterfalls, meadows and dominating granite spires that stretch all the way to Thompson Peak on the horizon.

RUSH CREEK TRAILHEAD

Access: About 10 miles north of Weaverville on Highway 3 you'll pass through a huge road cut and drop into a hairpin turn to the right. In the middle of the hairpin turn 34N74B juts off to the left. It leads to Kinney Camp. The trailhead is a mile or so past Kinney Camp. Watch for sign. **Kinney Camp** has one campsite. **Rush Creek Campground** is nearby, just off Highway 3.

Trails: Trail 10W10 switchbacks up onto the ridge and then drops down to Lower Rush Creek Lake at 6.7 miles.
Destinations: The Rush Creek Lakes. Monument Peak. Cross-country to Big East Fork Lake on Canyon Creek.
Elevation/Difficulty: 3,600 feet at trailhead. Difficult to strenuous. No water.
Summary: Leads to a chain of four small isolated lakes surrounded by impressive granite walls. Snow remains until late in the season. Chances of seeing other people are extremely remote.

SALMON LAKE

Elevation 7,150 feet; 1.5 acres; 13 feet deep. Located at the head of the South Fork of the Salmon River. Reached by a beautiful and spectacular canyon ride that takes about four hours from Big Flat. The trail is clear and distinct to the divide between Willow Creek and the South Fork of the Salmon, then to the east there is a dim trail part way, but it is mostly a matter of picking your way to the lake. Stocked with brook trout. **Big Flat Trailhead.**

When you want to be alone, go to Salmon Lake. Weeks pass by, even in midsummer, with no human voices breaking the silence. There is no trail. Only the highly motivated person will ever see this secret jewel embedded in the dark cliffs at the headwaters of the South Fork of the Salmon River.

You'll park at the Big Flat Campground, even though a road goes three miles closer. For some unjustified and mystifying reason, private interests have been allowed to maintain a road with a locked gate inside the wilderness.

Just past Gullick Creek, look for a trail to your left. Less than a mile later, watch for another fork at Kidd Creek. Stay right this time.

After about four miles, you'll be wandering in the upper reaches of this fork of the Salmon River, now merely a creek. It's easy to lose the trail in this area, but it doesn't matter, since the country is open and you can see where you have to go. Yup! Head for the low point on the skyline dead ahead. That would be the Trinity-Siskiyou county line, which runs along the crest of the ridge.

Salmon Lake is over there at the base of Tri-Forest Peak (7,681 feet), so named because years ago there were Shasta, Trinity, and Klamath National forests, with boundary lines coming together on the summit. Be sure to climb Tri-Forest Peak while you're here.

You have to love this seldom-seen view of Sawtooth Ridge stretching out to the west. Stunning granite spires, snaggled-toothed multiangular monoliths scrape the sky like the backbone of an ancient dragon. You can give each spire your own name.

The meadow on the divide, the county line, is so wild, so beautiful, that you'll never be able to describe it to anyone. So don't even try.

SEVEN-UP LAKE

Elevation 7,350 feet; .5 acres; 6 feet deep. Situated high up on the southeast slope of Seven-Up Peak, just below a large outcrop of white talus. Best approached by a stiff climb north from Granite Lake. Good natural reproduction of brook trout. **Swift Creek Trailhead.**

This is, along with Gibson Lake, the other hide-and-go-seek lake. The lake was hidden several thousand years ago by geological forces in the late Jurassic period, and your task is to find it. No trail.

The best way to start your search is to leave from Granite Lake (which is very easy to find) and work your way at an upward angle along the red rock slopes of Seven-Up Peak. If you angle high enough, you'll find yourself above the lake and then can drop down to it. Lakes like this are much easier to spot from above, impossible from below, so a wise hiker always tries to err on the high side when contouring off trail.

When you leave Seven-Up Lake, merely drop straight down to the trail along Granite Creek. If you decide to spend the night at the lake, rest assured you'll have the place to yourself.

How can the rocks here on Seven-Up Peak be so red, while across the valley and all the way up to Gibson Peak, they are gray and white granite? Geologists call it a contact between two differing belts of rock types. The California Division of Mines and Geology has several books and papers dealing with Trinity Alps geology. Interested persons can read up on it.

I find satisfaction enough in lying down on the sun-warmed rocks and becoming a speck on a grain of sand on the shoreline of the cosmic ocean, a microscopic flash in geologic eons. Looking out over Granite Creek Canyon, my eyes can soar like a hawk. Let others catalogue and classify the world.

SEVEN-UP PEAK

(8,132 feet) **Swift Creek Trailhead**. This peak towers above and throws its shadow down Bear Basin, the one on Bear Creek, a tributary of Swift Creek. A trail connecting Bear Creek with Granite Creek loops around the western flank of the mountain. At several places where the trail is high up on the mountain you can make a break for the summit. This is one of the beautiful red rock areas in the Alps.

SILIGO PEAK

(8,162 feet) Long Canyon, Stoney Creek Ridge Trailhead. There's an 8,059-foot peak between Summit Lake and Siligo Meadow often mistaken for Siligo Peak. One hundred feet higher and to the north is the real thing. Siligo is skirted by five little lakes and a trail that circumnavigates it. Many people have walked completely around the mountain, but very few take the time to check out the top. Too bad, their loss.

Two places on the trail around the peak offer access to the summit. Try either the saddle between Summit and Diamond lakes or the saddle between Diamond and Luella lakes. You may even consider a traverse between the two saddles over the top.

Siligo Peak

STONEWALL PASS TRAILHEAD (see Granite Peak Trailhead)

STONEY RIDGE TRAILHEAD

Access: North on Highway 3, 13.7 miles from Weaverville and a few hundred yards south of the Stoney Swim Area, is road 35N73Y leading to the trailhead. It's about 6 miles from the highway to the trailhead. Follow signs. **Stoney Point Campground** is near where the road leaves the highway for the trailhead.

Trails: Trail 9W21 zigzags up through Red Mountain Meadow, past spur trail 9W18A to Granite Peak, through Stonewall Pass, where it contours above Van Matre Meadow, over Little Stonewall Pass to Siligo Meadow and Deer Creek Pass.

Destinations: Red Mountain Meadow, Granite Peak, Middle Peak, Echo Lake, Siligo Meadow and points beyond.
Elevation/Difficulty: 4,100 feet at trailhead. Moderate with lots of switch-backs.
Summary: Superb high mountain ambiance among 8,000 foot peaks. Echo Lake offers an abundance of seclusion. Stunning sunsets common.

STUART FORK
Stuart Fork Trailhead. By Alps standards, this is a river, one of the major drainages of the Wilderness Area. Beginning its journey to the sea in the heart of the Trinity Alps at Mirror Lake, Stuart Fork crashes and splashes for more than 20 miles before disemboguing into Trinity Lake. Along the way, at Morris Meadow, Deer Creek, Salt Creek, and Deep Creek, there opportunities to test your skill against trout from a wild mountain stream.

There is seldom an angler who doesn't discover something new about trout fishing in a wilderness stream. People a hundred years from now will find the answers to questions stumping today's anglers. The variables of water temperature, the moon and sun, the wind, the barometric pressure, bug hatches, are all too complex for one person to comprehend. Izaak Walton about three hundred years ago put it this way: "Angling may be said to be so like the Mathematicks, that it can never be fully learnt; at least not so fully, but that there will still be more experiments left for the trial of other men that succeed us."

A friend and I found a solution one evening. We could see trout rising to the hatch behind a large boulder midstream in Stuart Fork just below Deer Creek. Casting from the shore proved futile, since the swiftness of the water would take our fly downstream before the fish had a chance to see it. My buddy, Bobcat, went upstream and found some boulders to cross on and came down the other side opposite me. He cast his line over. I tied my line to his and dangled a woolly worm on about a yard of leader where the lines were tied. He then reeled his line back, and between our tied lines we were able to make the fly dance behind the boulder where the fish were feeding.

Success was instant. A 14-inch rainbow inhaled the fly and we both yanked the hook deep into its jaw. It was then a matter of deciding who should reel the fish in, since our lines were joined. We took turns reeling in four or five fish before moving to another pool and doing the same thing.

Sometimes while walking the long miles in twilight down Stuart Fork on my way back to the trailhead, I've thought about how enjoyable a trail like this can be if you actually enjoy the act of walking. I've felt it on other trails too, but especially along this stream. There are times when traveling through a landscape is to become empowered by raising its meaning. Walking along a trail, a line in space, the hiker travels a story, the trail gathering the momentum of the power of fiction as the arrow of time moves across a motionless mosaic of space out of time, here primeval and familiar. For a precious few hours the trail and the hiker and the mountains meld into a story imprinted on the mind, to be read again and again.

STUART FORK TRAILHEAD

Access: This major trailhead is at **Bridge Camp Campground** two miles from the Trinity Alps Resort, which is a mile off Highway 3, 13 miles north of Weaverville. Please drive slowly through rustic Trinity Alps Resort.

Trails: Trail 9W20 is like a 13.1 mile long interstate highway into the deepest recesses of the Trinity Alps. It follows an old wagon road once used for mining activity at Emerald and Sapphire Lakes. Trail 10W04 climbs sharply to Alpine Lake, trail 9W17 follows Deer Creek to its source, trail 10W01 is a vertical way to reach the Caribou Basin.

Destinations: Streamside fishing and camping, Morris Meadow, Emerald, Sapphire, Mirror Lakes. Numerous opportunities for cross-country hiking to remote locations.

Elevation/Difficulty: 2,660 feet at trailhead. The main trail is easy to moderate. The trails out of the drainage all range from difficult to strenuous.

Summary: Popular area offering meadows, streams, lakes, mountains, old mining equipment and ruins, with lots of room to roam and ramble in the heartland of the Trinity Alps. Some 1996 fire scars are evident in the Deer Creek/Morris Meadow area.

SUMMIT LAKE

Elevation 7,350 feet; 13 acres; 34 feet deep. Can be reached via the Long Canyon trail past Deer lake, or by a dim trail from Diamond Lake. A scenic lake surrounded by broken boulders and sparse vegetation. Brook trout to 11 inches. Rainbows also present. **Long Canyon, Stoney Ridge or Stuart Fork Trailhead.**

Summit Lake is aptly named. When viewed from some angles, it appears to be a lake filling the top a of a volcano. There is no apparent inlet or outlet, leaving to your imagination how it maintains itself as a lake.

To get to Summit Lake, you might choose to travel one of the outstanding routes in all the Trinity Alps: up Long Canyon, through Bee Tree Gap and across Siligo Meadow. From the trailhead on the East Fork Of Stuart Fork, it is only five miles to the heart of the Alps. Once you reach Bee Tree Gap and tire of the view eastward toward Mount Lassen, turn 180 degrees and behold the Trinity Alps! Mountains piled upon mountains entertain your eyes for as far as you can see, more mountains than you can hope to experience in a lifetime.

Siligo Meadow, named for Lewiston pioneer Louis Siligo, is a 7,500-foot lush verdant pasture you have to share with grazing cows in the summertime. If playing cowboy isn't for you, the place is big enough for you to move elsewhere.

Summit Lake, with its rocky shoreline and warm water late in the summer, invites lounging. Between lounging sessions, consider a stroll up the rock mass to the east (Peak 8059). Many people mistake this summit for Siligo Peak. Wrong! Siligo Peak (8,162 feet) is an interesting stroll to the north of the lake, also worth your time and energy to visit.

From either summit, while eating an orange, take a look around this microcosm of the Alps: red rocks and pinnacles, grizzled outcroppings of pearly granite, splashes of green meadow, streams twisted like ribbons in the gaping canyons, and a cobalt sky millions of times bigger than all of it.

SWIFT CREEK

Swift Creek Trailhead. Swift Creek was one of the main arteries for 19th century travel. You'll know why after spending a few days in this wide gentle canyon of colossal conifers and riotous meadows. Regular pack trains plied the trail from Trinity Center to the Dorleska Mine, Big Flat and the Salmon River mines beyond. After the miners came the cattlemen.

The Trinity Farm and Cattle Company, owned by William Foster, Sr. and his five sons, grazed cattle in Swift Creek for more than fifty years. There have been several structures called Foster's Cabin in Parker Meadows dating back to 1915. The one you see today was built in 1944 for both Foster and the U.S. Forest Service which used it for a snow survey shelter until the 1960s. Those automobile license plates you noticed nailed high up in the trees along the trail were for navigation to the cabin when deep snow covered the ground. Each winter a couple of Forest Service employees would snowshoe into Foster's Cabin and spend a week measuring the snow depth and water content, data needed to determine spring runoff and water availability. That's all done with technology now. The California Department of Water Resources maintains remote sensors called "snow pillows" at several sites in the Alps. Data on snow depth and water content are updated hourly and put on the Internet. Anyone with a home computer has access to the information.

No doubt it was a lot more fun to spend a week in Foster's Cabin up Swift Creek in the middle of winter than it is sitting in a stuffy office recording numbers on a computer hooked to a remote snow sensor buried out there in the wilderness.

Swift Creek is a pretty good address in the Alps. Fishing is usually good for bait snatchers in the main creek, with slightly larger fish to be had in Ward and Horseshoe lakes. There's ample firewood and many a campsite far removed from the trail.

Horse and llama traffic is a bit thick at times, which messes up the trail with clumps of that stuff that attracts flies. They also leave portions of the meadow chewed up and dusty.

SWIFT CREEK TRAILHEAD

Access: 29.5 miles north of Weaverville on Highway 3. Turn left just north of Swift Creek Bridge at Trinity Center and follow road 36N25 and signs 7 miles to trailhead. **Preacher Meadow Campground** is 2 miles south of Trinity Center on Highway 3.

Trails: Trail 8W15 climbs gradually along Swift Creek past a deep gorge to the junction with the Granite Lake Trail (8W14) to a three-way junction with Bear Basin Trail (9W10) and Parker Creek Trail (9W19) and continues on through Parker Meadow, past Foster's Cabin, into Mumford Meadow and a junction with Landers Lake Trail (9W09), and finally, after 9 miles, to Horseshoe and Ward lakes.

Destinations: Granite Lake, Gibson Lake, Seven-Up Lake, Ward Lake, Horseshoe Lake, Landers Lake, Twin Lakes, Bear Basin, Foster's Cabin.

Snowslide Peak, Mumford Peak, Black Mountain, Red Rock Mountain, Parker Meadow, Mumford Meadow.

Elevation/Difficulty: 3,900 feet at trailhead. Easy to moderate hiking in gentle country. Steep pitches up to lakes and peaks.

Summary: Amicable area of the Alps. Granite Lake suffers from overuse, but upper Swift Creek is an escape to simple pleasures.

TAPIE LAKE (see LOST LAKE)

TRI-FOREST PEAK

(7,681 feet) Swift Creek or Big Flat Trailhead. Three ridges converge on this peak. Prior to the 1950s, the three ridges carried the boundaries of three national forests on their backs: Klamath, Trinity, and Shasta. The Klamath National Forest is still valid, but the other two were combined into what is now known as the Shasta-Trinity National Forest, or Shasta-T. Which could mean that we should call this mountain Bi-Forest Peak.

From the Willow Creek Divide, it's a ridge walking task easterly, staying on the south side most of the way. The peak you first think is Tri-Forest is not. The summit is further to the east.

This is also a nice climb from either Salmon Lake or Horseshoe Lake. Pick your own route.

TWIN LAKES (LOWER AND UPPER)

Lower Twin Lake. Elevation 5,000 feet; .25 acres; 2 feet deep.

Upper Twin Lake. Elevation 5,100 feet; .5 acres; 3 feet deep.

About .5 miles above the mouth of Granite Creek on the Swift Creek trail is the outlet stream. Follow this for about a half a mile to the lakes, which have a small population of brook trout. **Swift Creek Trailhead.**

These lakes are really two brush-lined ponds with mud bottoms. Nobody else ever camps near them, but I did once. Sometimes in the mountains a person gets caught between places; too late in the day to make the destination, but early enough to at least go someplace else. Twin Lakes are, at least, someplace.

From the Swift Creek trailhead, it is an easy mile to the Granite Lake trail turnoff. Before the trail forks, you pass by an extraordinary gorge that Swift Creek has sculpted in sheer stone, with walls so vertical that even by leaning over the rim you can't see the creek below. During low water during the hot days of late summer, it is delightful to enter this gorge from the lower end and explore upstream on the cool damp boulders. Anglers can usually find a few fish, and swimmers can always find a secluded place to take a dip.

From the Granite Creek trail fork, stay right. In less than a mile the trail crosses a series of small seeping streams coming in from the slope on your right. This is the outlet from the Twin Lakes. If you don't mind wet feet, the best way to find the lakes is to simply walk up the stream until you hit the lower lake. The trees and brush are pretty thick, but with a little luck and imagination it is possible to avoid both wet feet and a brush-scratched face.

You can sometimes catch a couple of brook trout by using a stealthy approach and a *fast* retrieve. Remember, it's only two feet deep!

Chapter Nine

THE SOUTH CENTRAL ALPS

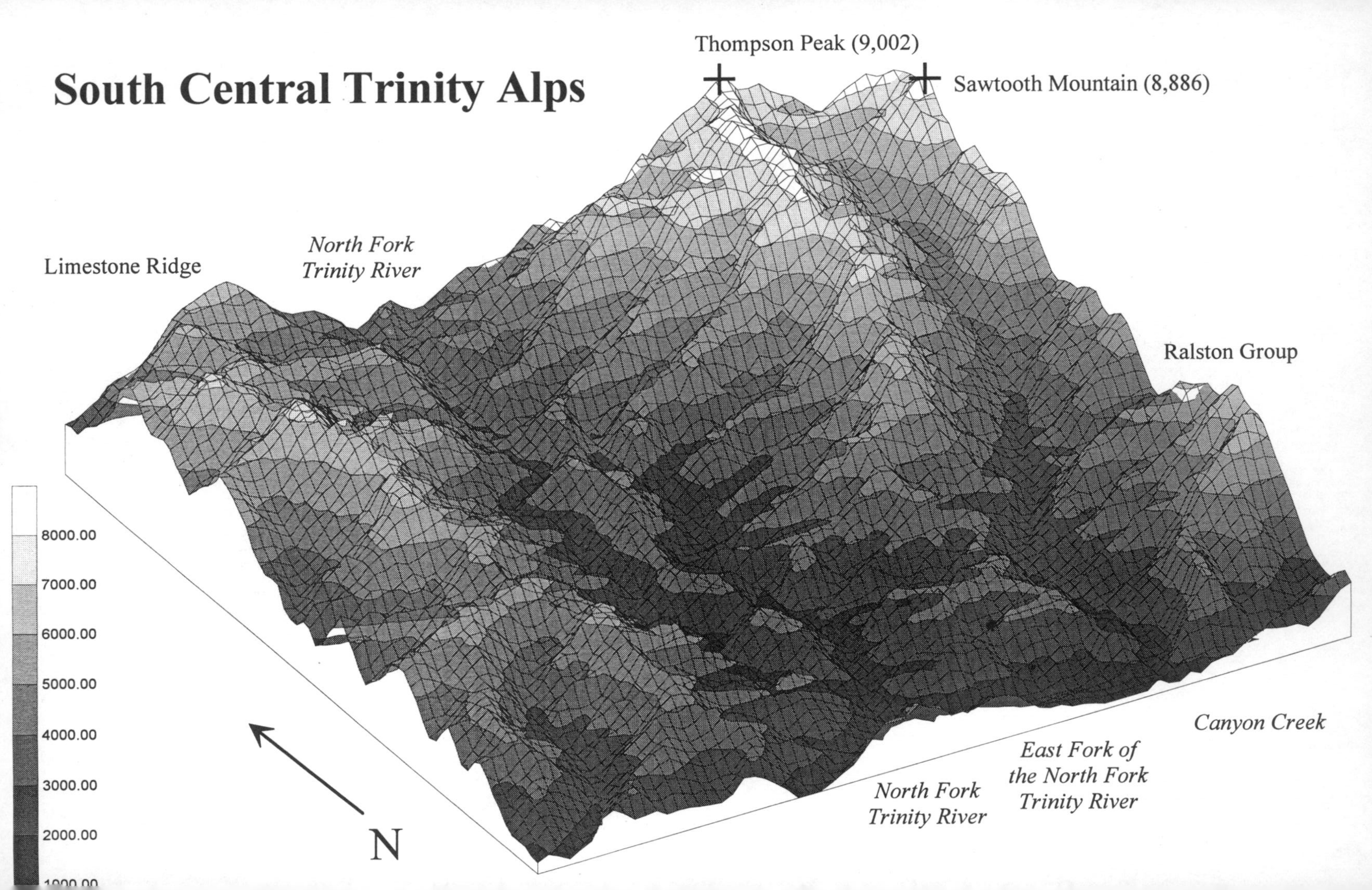
South Central Trinity Alps
Thompson Peak (9,002)
Sawtooth Mountain (8,886)
Limestone Ridge
North Fork
Trinity River
Ralston Group
Canyon Creek
East Fork of
the North Fork
Trinity River
North Fork
Trinity River
N
8000.00
7000.00
6000.00
5000.00
4000.00
3000.00
2000.00

South Central Trinity Alps

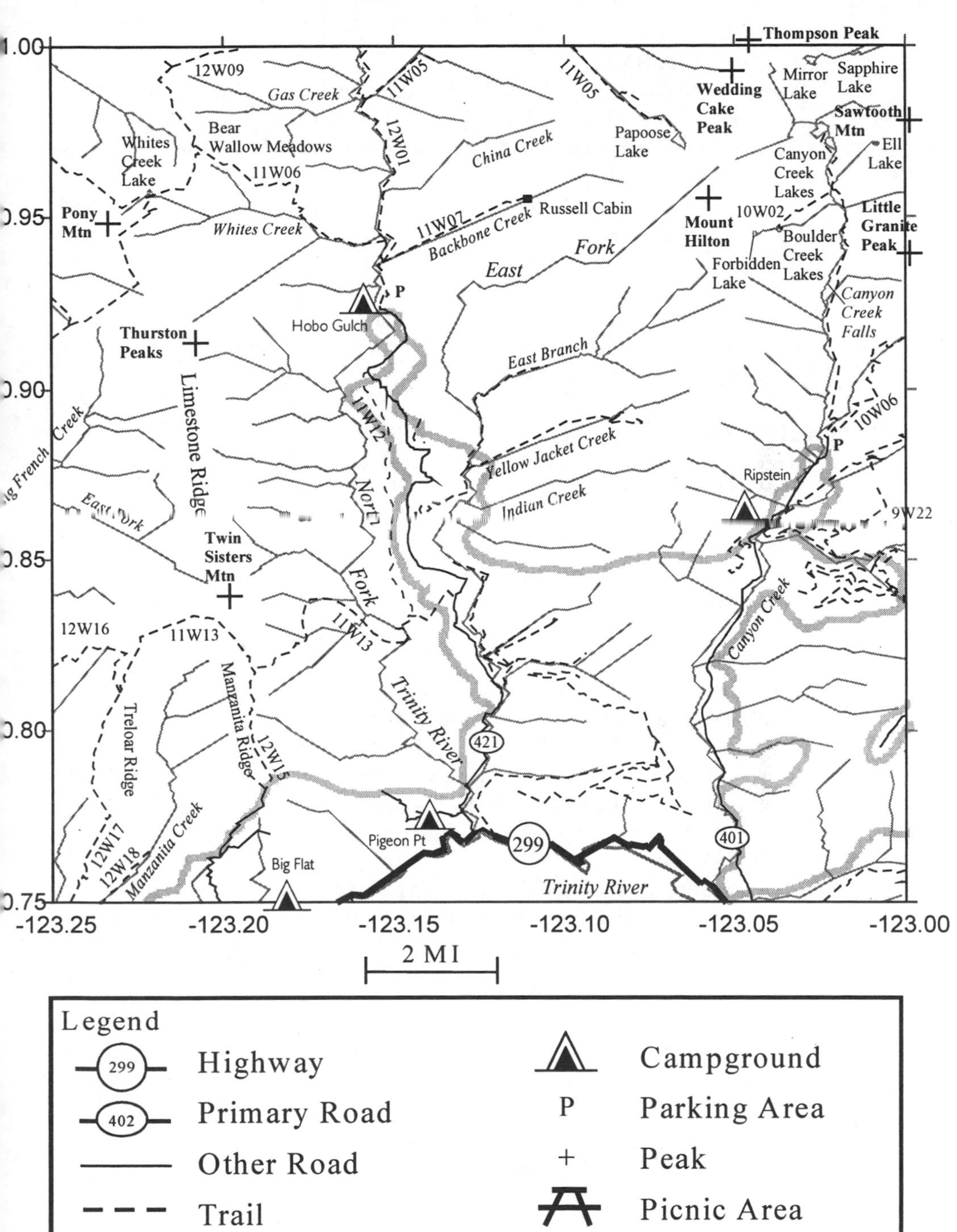

BEAR GULCH TRAILHEAD

Access: North on Canyon Creek Road at Junction City on Highway 299 for 12 miles. Right on Big East Fork Road about three miles. Just beyond crossing of Big East Fork Creek a slide blocks the road. Walk on road a mile and a half and watch for trail to left.

Trails: Trail 9W23 climbs steeply up north side of Bear Gulch to East Weaver Creek Divide in two miles.

Destinations: Monument Peak, East Weaver Lake.

Elevation/Difficulty: 4,100 feet at trailhead to 6,800 feet at divide. Moderate in length, difficult in elevation gained in a short distance.

Summary: Trail often not maintained. Provides fairly direct route to climb Monument Peak and Rush Creek Lakes.

BIG EAST FORK TRAILHEAD

Access: This trailhead can be difficult to find, depending on whether the sign is there or not. Turn right at the intersection 11 miles north of Junction City onto 35N47Y. Three miles up the dirt road start looking for a wide place in the road. There may or may not be a sign. It might say "Maple Mine." It might say "East Fork Lakes." It might say "Buck's Ranch." Usually there is no sign. Parking is on the road shoulder.

Trails: Trail 9W22 climbs up past the Maple Mine to the old jeep road on top of the ridge and follows it to Buck's Ranch. It then climbs steeply through brush and open country to Big East Fork Lake. Total length 4.6 miles.

Destinations: Big East Fork Lake, Buck's Ranch.

Elevations/Difficulty: 3,650 feet at trailhead. Difficult with little water.

Summary: A single-destination trailhead. **Ripstein Campground** is nearby, 13 miles north of Junction City.

CANYON CREEK

Canyon Creek Trailhead. The basic character and personality of Canyon Creek from the lower falls to its mouth was changed dramatically by the flood waters of 1964. Prior to the flood damage of that year, old-growth forest and fern-lined grottoes enclosed the stream. Now, more than thirty years later, the stream bed is choked with huge white granite boulders with scant vegetation on the shoreline.

Lower Canyon Creek Falls

The water still runs crystal clear, dashing white and wild over the boulders, resting momentarily in deep turquoise pools before plunging off down the canyon. Small rainbows can be caught in most pools. The trail doesn't approach the creek for the first four miles, except for a spur trail at The Sinks, about three miles from the trailhead.

The best time to work this lower part of the creek is mid to late summer, when you can rock-hop up or down from any point you choose to leave the trail and follow the stream. Once above the lower falls, the creek changes dramatically. Much calmer now, except at the middle and upper falls, the creek winds through meadows and pitches over large granite boulders. On warm summer afternoons, rainbow trout can be readily fooled, or you can peel off your clothes and plunge into the emerald pools and become trout-like yourself.

Small golden trout can still be found in a short stretch of Upper Canyon Creek above the last waterfall beyond Upper Canyon Creek Lake. Any golden trout you find here are the descendants of goldens planted in the 1950s. They have been able to maintain a population for almost 50 years.

CANYON CREEK BOULDER LAKE

Elevation 5,750 feet; 5 acres; 17 feet deep.
Go up the Canyon Creek trail from Dedrick for six miles to Boulder Creek; then another two miles up the Boulder Creek trail to a meadow at the base of a cliff below the lake. From the north side of the meadow the trail goes through dense brush to the bench where the lake is. Stocked with rainbows. **Canyon Creek Trailhead.**

A couple of hundred thousand years ago acres of ice came oozing down Canyon Creek, shearing off many of the side canyon entrances. C.C. Boulder is in a "hanging canyon." Thus the last mile below the lake is a steep climb up onto the shelf wherein lies the lake.

The turnoff to the lake is well signed on the Interstate-quality trail up Canyon Creek. Immediately past the fork in the trail, the crossing of Canyon Creek can be a problem during high water. Look upstream stream for a log. While searching for a crossing point, bear in mind that just in the last 10 years alone, three people have drowned doing just what you are trying to do.

After crossing the creek there are quiet meadows, but up ahead you'll see the cliff bands below the lake. The trail works up to the right to avoid the cliffs.

C.C. Boulder is a great mid-summer lake for swimming and sunning. Foot traffic is relatively light. The rocks are warm flat granite slabs, perfect for lounging away a lazy afternoon. The surface water gains warmth as the season wears on.

My halcyon summer days are still spent running from the trailhead to the lake (two hours), lounging the afternoon away at the lake, running back in the evening (1 hour 20 minutes).

Canyon Creek Boulder Lake sees a lot more people than it used to, but the vast majority of people who spend time in the Canyon Creek drainage never venture up to this lake. Recently the Forest Service has built a new trail that avoids the meadows and starts to angle up the last mile in an attempt to lessen the impact on the meadow and the impact of the sudden elevation gain on the hiker.

There is very little firewood at the lake and too many people still insist on camping too close to the lake. There's plenty of room away from the lake for a good campsite, and you may want to skip the fire, particularly in frequently used areas.

The huge peak to the north of Canyon Creek Boulder Lake is 8,964-foot Mount Hilton, a little higher than Sawtooth Peak, which you see across the canyon to the east. Speculation has it the mountain was named for James Hilton, author of *Lost Horizon*, who compared the town of Weaverville to Shangri-La, "that strange and wonderful somewhere which is not a place, but a state of mind." Hilton, only 38 feet lower than Thompson Peak and only two feet lower than Mount Caesar, is the third highest peak in the Alps, and makes a worthwhile and rewarding climb while you're at C.C. Boulder. There's a metal ammunition box with a summit register left there by a Boy Scout troop from Oregon. The view does not disappoint, and there's that wonderful lake waiting for your hot, tired body when you return from the top. The water is so clear that you might wade up to your knees before realizing you've broken the surface.

CANYON CREEK LAKE (LOWER)

Elevation 5,600 feet; 14 acres; 56 feet deep. From Dedrick is an eight-mile, four-hour trip up Canyon Creek to the lake. All three species, brook, brown and rainbow trout are present, including some large ones. **Canyon Creek Trailhead.**

This area is the supermarket of the Alps. It's all here. Canyon Creek uses its waterfalls, lakes, and magnificent granite to attract more shoppers than any other place in these mountains.

Obviously many people prefer a supermarket such as this. A trip to Canyon Creek Lakes between Memorial Day and Labor Day is strictly a social experience, not a wilderness one.

Like any good supermarket, Canyon Creek crowds are a varied lot. You'll see people packing in gas lanterns, lawn chairs, ice chests (with ice), and chemical toilets. They come with llamas, horses, and dogs. One backpacker once lost his pet monkey while camping here. In the evening kids often are chasing about with burning sticks, frisbee and hackysack games, and raucous music from tape decks.

A friend and I were once routed from our lakeside camp by a YMCA group from the coast playing a spirited game of flashlight tag.

Canyon Creek is where people come from the coast to get warm and dry out. You'll see buses parked at the trailhead. BUSES! Recently there was a herd of 52 Cub Scouts and their leaders ensconced at the upper meadow. The hills were alive with the sound of screaming.

If the Trinity Alps resemble the Sierra Nevada on a smaller scale, then Canyon Creek certainly is the smaller version of the Yosemite Valley.

To get to the lower lake, simply park at the Canyon Creek trailhead, usually overflowing, 13 miles north of Junction City, and follow the thundering brigades of people up the trail. After the dust settles you'll see the lake there, between the people.

Lower Canyon Creek Lake

Recently the Forest Service has made an attempt to route people the last quarter-mile to the lake via the meadows and trees at Stonehouse rather than the traditional trail that stays on the east side of the creek to the outlet of the lake. A couple of backpackers have bought the farm from falling into the outlet stream. Your choice: cross Canyon Creek to the west side or stick with the east side to the lake. The east side approach brings the suddenly dramatic view of Thompson Peak and Wedding Cake brooding over the lake. It is the quintessential picture in the Trinity Alps. The crossing of the outlet at the lake is straightforward except during high water. If it looks swift and deep, don't be stupid. Instead, walk back down below the rocky area and find a log to cross in the timbered area. If you fall off the log you'll only get wet; fall into the boiling caldron of white water in the rock chute and it may be a month before your body is retrieved. Use your head.

Canyon Creek is still being loved to death. The carrying capacity of the valley corridor is exceeded many times during the summer months. Large groups seems to be attracted. There's not a stick of firewood to be found at the lower lake, which is okay as it affords you the opportunity to see what Colin Fletcher is talking about when he recommends not building a fire in the wilderness. Sit next to a campfire at night and you are enclosed in a room that extends only to the edge of the firelight, completely blocking the world around you. Walk away from the fire, or better still, don't build a fire, Fletcher says, and the entire universe opens up.

Canyon Creek is for many the first and only trip they make into the Alps. However, if a person is going to make only one visit to the Alps, this would be the recommended one.

My introduction to the Alps was Canyon Creek. It was slated to be a weekend snowshoe hike and campout at Canyon Creek Lake with my Boy Scout troop during Christmas vacation in 1956. A dozen of us started out with snowshoes, on loan from the Forest Service, strapped to our backpacks, since there was no snow at the trailhead. By the time we got to McKay Camp, it had started snowing and we hit snow on the ground. Struggling with the rawhide-and-wood contraptions buckled to our feet and sloppy packs banging our backs, we struggled and staggered onward and upward. By late afternoon the trail from McKay Camp to the upper meadow was strewn with the bodies and baggage of the beleaguered scout troop. The scene resembled that famous photograph of miners crossing the Chilkoot Pass during the '98 gold rush to the Klondike.

Nightfall, which came about four o'clock at that time of year, found us gathering at a collapsing cabin near Upper Canyon Creek Meadow. All that remains of the cabin today is a pile of rocks that used to be the chimney. You have to know where to look to even notice them. But that winter night there was still a roof of sorts and some crumbling walls. We crawled inside and staked out space for our sleeping bags in the dark gloom on the dirt floor. A fire was built in the disintegrating stone fireplace. We took turns trying to warm beans and tamales in cans next to the sputtering fire.

The night was memorable because of the lack of oxygen and sleep. Smoke from the partly plugged fireplace soon filled the cabin. It was only by digging a hole in the dirt floor and putting our faces in the ground that anyone could hope to get air to breathe and relieve the suffocating sting of dense smoke filling the cabin. Sleep was interrupted by poorly conditioned Scouts suffering severe leg cramps from strenuous efforts on the trail. Those who were fortunate enough not to have leg cramps were kept awake by the frequent and sporadic screams of those who were not so fortunate. Start to drift off into troubled sleep and dreams of smoke suffocation jerked you awake. Deep in sleep, shrieks of pain from the campers sat you bolt upright.

It was a long dark sleepless night in the winter wilderness. When morning came it was still snowing, and any thoughts of pushing on to the lake were abandoned in favor of trying to return to the trailhead alive.

Once everyone was safely back to the cars, many of the survivors swore a Scout's oath they would never go back into the Alps again. Not me. I couldn't wait for summer and the chance to return. I had seen the elephant. I wanted to see more.

CANYON CREEK LAKE (UPPER)

Elevation 5,690 feet; 25 acres; 86 feet deep. A five-minute walk from the lower lake. Brook trout, rainbow and golden trout thrive. Upper Canyon Creek provides excellent angling for trout. The Canyon Creek lakes are popular and good campsites are nearby. **Canyon Creek Trailhead.**

In spite of the supermarket feeling of this area, there are some hidden aisles worth exploring in the Canyon Creek drainage.

The upper lake marks the end of about 90 percent of the crowds. Continue above the Upper Lake and you'll find a world-class waterfall, golden trout, and a series of high meadows overflowing with solitude.

From a campsite up here you are in a position to launch an attack on a superb ridge with killer peaks to the northwest and a challenging scramble to a small lake (Kalmia Lake) to the east. To the northwest is Wedding Cake Peak, 8,592 feet, and Thompson Peak, 9,002 feet, the highest point in the Alps. Aim for the gap between the two peaks. From there you can knock off both peaks in the same day.

Also from the gap between the two peaks there are excellent opportunities for cross country travel sans trails, the ultimate wilderness experience. Mike Butner, a friend from Germany, left this point and headed down into the Middle Fork of Rattlesnake Creek, where he found pristine wilderness, seeing no sign of people during the days he wandered the streambed, spooking a bear now and then. Eventually he came to the trail on Rattlesnake Creek and "signs of habitation", as he said.

Further down the ridge there is a double-humped mountain resembling a camel's back. Scramble around between these unnamed peaks, 8791 and 8913 feet, and you can drop in the back door to Papoose Lake. This is high country off-trail navigation and should be attempted only by properly prepared people. If it doesn't sound like your cup of tea, it isn't.

I've never done it, but it would probably be a good trip to bushwhack all the way down the East Fork of the North Fork of the Trinity River to the road at Todd Cabin. I'd almost bet that no living person has ever done that. Not on purpose anyway. It wouldn't be easy, but it would be all downhill and you'd be all alone.

Upper Canyon Creek Lake is the second floor of the already crowded supermarket found at the lower lake. Both upper and lower lakes harbor huge fish, but they are virtually uncatchable, lurking like submarines near the bottom. You can lie on your belly on the rocks and watch them for hours.

I saw Jim French one evening near the inlet to the Lower Lake make three casts on which he caught a fish on each cast. Surprisingly, each fish was a different species; brook, brown and rainbow trout. No lie.

Canyon Creek Trail

CANYON CREEK TRAILHEAD

Access: Turn north on Canyon Creek Road in Junction City on Highway 299. Follow paved road 13 miles to large, paved trailhead.

Ripstein Campground is a mile from the trailhead.

Trails: Trail 10W08 is probably the most heavily used in the Alps. It climbs moderately and steadily through an oak and conifer forest, breaking out into open granite slopes and meadows at the lower falls. Continues past waterfalls and beautiful views of high alpine scenery to Lower Canyon Creek Lake. Total length 7.3 miles. A spur trail (10W02) above the middle falls crosses Canyon Creek and winds through several small meadows before climbing steeply to level granite slabs opposite Canyon Creek Boulder Lakes. Total length 2.5 miles. A trailless scramble farther up the drainage leads to Forbidden Lake. Bear Creek Trail (10W06) leaves the trailhead and zigzags steeply over the divide to Stuart Fork. Total length 7.2 miles.

Destinations: Canyon Creek Lakes, Ell Lake, Boulder Lakes, Forbidden Lake, Smith Lake, Morris Lake, Kalmia Lake, Sawtooth Peak, many waterfalls and high peaks to climb.

Elevations/Difficulty: 2,600 feet at trailhead. Main trail to Canyon Creek Lakes is easy to moderate. Side trails to other lakes and peaks are difficult and strenuous.

Summary: This is the trailhead for the quintessential Alps hike.

EAST FORK OF THE NORTH FORK OF THE TRINITY RIVER

Todd Cabin Trailhead. No trail, no lakes, just a dozen miles of wilderness creekbed slashing through near vertical rockbound edges covered with impenetrable chinquapin, manzanita, and buck brush, that's what the East Fork of the North Fork of the Trinity offers. Very few people have found a reason to explore this stream, so very few have.

Gold can and has been found as far upstream as the East Branch (that's the East Branch of the East Fork of the North Fork of the Trinity River). You may visit two abandoned mines and sift through the remaining artifacts at the McClaron Mine 2.5 miles up the East Branch and the Alaska Mine 3.5 miles up Yellow Jacket Creek. I found the note found nailed to the wall inside an abandoned cabin at the McClaron Mine:

"Thunder last night. Kilt two rattlesnakes by cabin steps."

From Helena, County Road 421 follows the East Fork past a number of mining claims and mines and dead-ends at the site of the old gold mining town of Coleridge. An unmaintained trail follows the stream on up to Yellow Jacket Creek and the East Branch to the East Fork of the North Fork. There is enough water to support a small population of small trout.

To reach the upper East Fork of the North Fork, take County Road 421 north from Highway 299 at Helena five miles and go left on the Hobo Gulch Road 34N071 three miles and watch for a road to the right diving down into the canyon to the Todd Cabin site. The bridge will be washed out at the East Fork crossing before you get to the cabin site and can be difficult and dangerous to wade across during high water. Once on the east side of the creek, the road goes another mile before turning up and into a trail on the East Branch to the McClaron Mine.

The main creek continues without trail, without fire rings, deeper and higher into the wilderness to its source at the roof of the Alps on Mount Hilton. Few and hardy are the people who have ever visited the headwaters of the East Fork of the North Fork of the Trinity River.

EAST WEAVER LAKE

Elevation 6,350 feet; 1 acre; 12 feet deep. Take the Weaver Bally Lookout road out of Weaverville to the springs just below the lookout. From there it is just a short hike to the lake. Subject to fish mortality following severe winters. Contains both brook and rainbow trout. **Weaver Bally Lookout or East Weaver Trailhead.**

The trailhead for East Weaver Lake has been moved from the springs to the saddle on Weaver Bally Lookout road. It is also possible to reach the lake on a four-mile-long trail which begins at roads end above East Weaver Campground.

I read an account in the local newspaper about a group of young people in the 1880s who climbed to East Weaver Lake and enjoyed an afternoon of ice skating. The story impressed me. The walk from Weaverville to the lake would be a formidable undertaking, to say the least. Perhaps they rode horses.

Fishing at East Weaver Lake

A few winters ago I decided to take a look at the lake one cold day before any significant snow had fallen. I came to the conclusion that those 19th century ice skaters knew what they were doing. Ice skating may be the best use of East Weaver Lake. It faces north, ensuring freezing conditions for long periods of time. From late October until Christmas, little snow falls during most winters, yet it remains cold enough to build up a good sheet of ice on the surface. Always check for at least several inches of clear ice and stay near shore.

The day I was there I beat a hole in the ice with the lug wrench I carried from my truck for that purpose. The ice was at least eight inches thick in most places. The water that gushed up through the hole quickly spread and refroze. Large areas of the ice were transparent, allowing views of the lake bottom 12 feet below.

I built a little fire there by a log, after the sun dropped and deep blue indigo shadows stole around the lake, where my little pinpoint of feeble warmth combined with the frozen lake made it seem as if it were 1880 once more.

EAST WEAVER TRAILHEAD

Access: Two miles north of Weaverville on Highway 3. Turn on East Weaver road and go two miles to end of road beyond **East Weaver Campground.**
Trails: Trail 9W23 follows the East Weaver Lake outlet to the divide and down into Bear Gulch on the Canyon Creek side, with a spur trail to East Weaver Lake.

Destinations: East Weaver Lake. Monument Peak, Rush Creek Lakes, Canyon Creek.

Elevation/Difficulty: 2,350 feet at trailhead. Moderate with a few steep pitches.

Summary: Seldom-used trail, as most people going to the destinations mentioned use the Weaver Bally Trailhead, which provides more initial elevation.

ELL LAKE

Elevation 6,530 feet; 2 acres; 29 feet deep. From Upper Canyon Creek Lake outlet a dim trail goes to the lake; a good hour-and-a-half climb. Brook trout do very well in this "L" shaped lake. **Canyon Creek Trailhead**.

Ell Lake occupies a narrow groove in a side canyon of Canyon Creek at the base of Sawtooth's north face. The geologic orchestra is here if we could only develop an ear for the music being played on a record rotating once every 10,000 years.

High above the lake, the north face of Sawtooth Peak (8,886 feet) is always in a blue haze of shadowed granite. The sun rarely shines on this side of the mountain.

A campsite at Ell Lake will spare you the crowds that clamor down at the Canyon Creek lakes. It will afford you a base camp for visits up on the divide for vistas into Stuart Fork. You can follow the ridge to the north of the lake and wonder about the fate of the rain that falls there. In the space of a few feet, it either gets to flow free to the sea, down Canyon Creek, or is shunted off to Southern California via the tunnels and dams of the Central Valley Project where it might wind up in someone's swimming pool in Manteca. Which way would you rather flow?

A hike along the ridge can lead to Mirror Lake or Kalmia Lake.

If you do venture onto the Stuart Fork side of the divide, be warned that nearly perpendicular snowbanks linger until late in the summer. Proceed with caution. There is no easy way down under the best of conditions; many of the couloirs end in blind cliffs and you'll have to retrace your steps to escape. Don't learn the hard way about how it is possible to climb up something you can't climb down. Rescue in this part of the Alps might take days.

Ell Lake is an excellent place to launch an assault on Sawtooth Peak. Plan about four hours from the lake to the summit. Once you get to the base of the summit block there are several good ways to scramble up to the top. It might take you a little while to figure where the actual summit is amongst the spires and gendarmes. Some climbers use ropes and technical gear for protection on this summit, but it's worth the effort. You will not be disappointed.

FORBIDDEN LAKE

Elevation 6,250 feet; 1.5 acres; 18 feet deep. These small lakes are at the headwaters behind a glacial moraine just above Canyon Creek Boulder Lake. Because of extremely heavy snowdrifts, some fish may not be able to survive severe winters. Stocked with brook trout. **Canyon Creek Trailhead.**

How can anyone resist a name like *Forbidden Lake*? The name is a lure to adventure, romance, forbidden things. What you'll find is a pretty slip of a lake tucked into a thin crease in the mountain above Canyon Creek Boulder Lake.

There are campsites that offer an eagle's eye view of upper Canyon Creek or are intimate against the lake. The sun comes up about noon and goes down at two o'clock, so narrow is the canyon.

This is a fine base camp on the edge of wilderness for the advanced adventurer only. The country to the west is trackless. Up the draw above the lake, notice the two low gaps. Get into the right gap and you'll have at your feet the headwaters of the East Fork of the North Fork of the Trinity River. This is untraveled, untrammeled country, unbelievable wilderness. Waterfalls, granite cliffs, miles to wander in if you're brave enough. There are no trails down there.

The left-hand gap will put you in touch with equally untouched country, the East Branch of the East Fork of the North Fork of the Trinity River. What a mouthful that name is. The terrain is as complex as the name.

You could head off downstream and won't hit a trail until you get to the McClaron Mine. It's a couple of miles from the mine to the Todd Cabin Trailhead.

The two branches of the East Fork mentioned in the description above contain the most rugged, inaccessible, least visited portion of the Trinity Alps. Nobody spends much time in this watershed. There are no lakes, few campsites, no trails, and probably little chance of rescue if you get into trouble. The valleys are very steep and deep, leaving only the stream beds for travel. The appeal of the area is its remoteness and untamed beauty.

HOBO GULCH TRAILHEAD (NORTH FORK TRINITY RIVER)

Access: Turn north immediately west of the Helena Bridge from Highway 299, 13 miles west of Weaverville. After about four miles, watch for the road sign 34N07YA to the left, which climbs up over Backbone Ridge and down into the **Hobo Gulch Campground** and the trailhead after 15.5 miles.

Trails: The main trail 12W01 contours through dense forest to the Backbone Creek crossing, then follows the North Fork of the Trinity all the way to Grizzly Creek, which it follows to Grizzly Meadow and peters out. From the meadow it's a scramble to Grizzly Lake. Total length 17.5 miles. Trail 11W07 follows Backbone Creek 3.0 miles to the Russell Cabin site. Trail 11W06 provides a steep 5.2-mile connection via Bear Wallow Meadows to Limestone Ridge. Trail 11W05 follows Rattlesnake Creek 9.3 miles to Papoose Lake. Trail 11W03, 4.2 miles, connects Rattlesnake Creek with Grizzly Creek via Bob's Farm. Trail 11W04 at Morrison Gulch leads in 3.2 steep miles to Limestone Ridge. Trail 11W02 is a steep 5.1-mile climb up past Cold Spring and the Cecil Lake Trailhead. Trail 11W08 connects with the China Creek Trailhead 3.1 miles away and is the shortest approach to Grizzly Lake.

Destinations: Papoose Lake, Browns Mine, Jorstad Cabin, Limestone Ridge, Thurston Peaks, Cabin Peak, Grizzly Meadow, Thompson Peak, high challenging peaks around Papoose Lake, riverside camping and fishing.

Elevation/Difficulty: 3,100 feet at trailhead. Easy trail along North Fork. Trails leaving main canyon are steep and difficult.

Summary: Big wilderness in a major canyon. Gold mining relics. Good stream fishing.

KALMIA LAKE

Elevation 7,500 feet; 1 acre; 13 feet deep. Named for the "mountain laurel" that grows along its shore. Situated north of Upper Canyon Creek Lake near the top of the mountain. Hike up toward Ell Lake, then through the timber to the gap between Canyon Creek and Stuart Fork, then work around in a westerly direction on the Canyon Creek side to the lake. Stocked with brook trout. **Canyon Creek Trailhead.**

This pristine niche would have been a magnificent ringside seat during the late Jurassic ice flow that came crunching and grinding past at the rate of a few inches per for year for thousands of years.

The western edge of the lake is still a magnificent ringside seat. The river of ice is gone, but the huge U-shaped valley of the Canyon Creek pluton stretches off to the south, a reminder and a vivid example of the stunning forces that shaped this part of the Alps. Geologists think the sheets of ice were two to three hundred feet thick.

Kalmia will often have ice on the surface until July.

Being almost on top of the ridge gives the Kalmia camper outstanding views in all directions. A short walk to the east opens the upper Stuart Fork drainage for your viewing pleasure. Mirror Lake appears to be only a few stone throws away. Emerald and Sapphire Lakes glimmer like the jewels they are in their granite setting. To the northwest is a head-on look at Thompson Peak (9,002 feet) and Wedding Cake Peak (8,592 feet). Less than an as-the-crow-flies mile away, they are visually overpowering. Let your eyes scale them.

The conventional way to reach Kalmia is to go up to Ell Lake, struggle through the brush to the low gap on the divide, and then roughly contour west-northwest above some interesting rock formations that might remind you of those statues on Easter Island. A more direct, but more difficult, approach is to stay in Canyon Creek until you figure you are underneath the lake and find one of several steep ravines to scramble up. Not only is it steep, but you are looking at climbing about 1500 vertical feet, the key word being *vertical*. Only recommended for experienced climbers.

Kalmia Lake is about as deep into the Alps you can go. If you go much farther, you'll come out the other side. Even when the trailhead parking lot is overflowing with cars and the Canyon Creek trail is dusty thick with people, you can be pretty sure you'll find privacy and solitude at Kalmia.

LITTLE GRANITE PEAK

(8,043 feet) Bear Creek Trail from Canyon Creek Trailhead. Don't be fooled by the word "little" in Little Granite Peak. It's only 48 feet lower than its namesake across the canyon, Granite Peak. From Alpine Lake it's a scramble of a couple of hours up through the brush and granite slabs to the summit. There is an unmaintained trail between Bear Creek on Canyon Creek and Boulder Creek on Stuart Fork that leads to a high pass south of Little Granite. The most direct route is on this trail from the Canyon Creek trailhead on

Bear Creek Trail (10W06), turning northward at the pass and following the ridge to the summit.

The easier way is to camp at Alpine and spend a few days climbing not only Little Granite, but also the other two major peaks in the area. A little route-finding will get you to the summit of the first peak (8,073 feet) to the west of the lake, which has no name . It's a little higher than Little Granite and yields spectacular views of the upper Canyon Creek drainage with Hilton, Wedding Cake, and Thompson in the background.

North of Alpine Lake is another unnamed peak (8,203 feet). At one time there was a suggestion to call it Trinity Journal Mountain, but the name didn't catch on. Some people who want to add a little zest to the hike between Smith and Alpine Lakes take a side trip to this summit en route.

MANZANITA RIDGE TRAILHEAD

Access: From **Big Flat Campground** 19 miles west of Weaverville on Highway 299, drive through the campground and follow steep and winding road 33N46 to the trailhead. Locked gate October 30 to May 1.

Trails: Trail 12W15, once a road, dips and climbs along the ridgetop where it joins trail 11W13 above Mosquito Hollow, which runs east and west from Big French Creek to Hobo Gulch Road.

Destinations: Twin Sisters Mountain, North Fork of Trinity River, Upper Waldorff Ranch, and Big French Creek.

Elevation/Difficulty: 3,600 feet at trailhead to almost 6,000 feet on Twin Sisters. Moderate hiking, unless you leave the ridgetop going down to North Fork or Big French Creek, and then it becomes a strenuous hike back up.

Summary: Snow leaves early, thus a good choice for hiking or running when the rest of the Alps are still snowbound. From high on the ridge, good place to watch birds of prey in action. Possible loop with car shuttle to Treloar Ridge Trailhead.

MIRROR LAKE

Elevation 7,400 feet; 14 acres; 25 feet deep. Seventeen miles of trail up the Stuart Fork of the Trinity River brings one to the lower end of Sapphire Lake, from where a foot trail leads to the upper end of Sapphire Lake. From there it is necessary to climb up to Mirror Lake. It takes nearly one and three-quarters hours of foot work. Both brookies and rainbow are found here; the rainbows are reported to reach greater than average size. **Stuart Fork Trailhead.**

Reflect on the name of this lake for a moment. What would you expect of a lake with the name of Mirror?

This lake is at the very heart of the Alps. No, not geographically, but spiritually. You can't go much further up Stuart Fork than Mirror. You can't go deeper into the Alps than Mirror. Just over the ridge is Canyon Creek, or Grizzly Lake, or Little South Fork Lake. Caribou Basin is not far. Thompson Peak and Sawtooth Peak stab the nearby sky. Nope, you can't get much deeper into the Alps. You would expect a lake in this location to mirror the Alps. It does. After a 17-mile walk up Stuart Fork, you have arrived at the heart of it all.

Those snowbanks up above the lake never melt. The peak you have to crank your head all the way back to look at is so wild and free that it has no name. The peak is only 36 feet shorter than Thompson and two feet higher than Mount Hilton, making it the second highest peak in the Alps. Ironically, at 8,966 feet, it is not officially named.

There have been attempts to pin a name on this peak over the years, but none have stuck. A recent map calls it "T2 Peak," for some unknown reason. The most common unofficial name is Mount Caesar.

There's a long tradition among mountain climbers to leave some kind of record on the summits of their conquests. Often it is no more than a pile of rocks, called a *cairn*. Others carry a small aspirin bottle and leave a note with name and address inside. For many years it was common to find notes left in tobacco tins, but rust and weather have just about taken care of any that might remain. Upon arrival at the summit of a remote or unnamed peak, the first order of business is to search about for evidence of previous visitors. There's perhaps a book waiting to be written compiling the notes left on wilderness summits. The code of the mountain climber demands that all notes and artifacts found are to be left as they are or given even better protection for preservation.

Mirror Lake campsites put the mountaineer in the throne room of the mountain gods. Nobody can bother you up in this granite vault.

Of late, more and more people have discovered that it is a bit shorter, albeit rougher, to approach Mirror Lake from Canyon Creek via Ell Lake. I got the idea from Dick Everest, who told me he had done it in a single day. I gave it a try. It makes for a very long day. It's a hard hike, it's a hard hike, it's a very hard hike.

Morris Lake

MORRIS LAKE
Elevation 7,300 feet; 3.5 acres; 31 feet deep. It is a very difficult task to reach this lake, and there is no trail. Five to six hours of hard climbing are required to cover less than two miles from Morris Meadow on the Stuart Fork to the lake. It may be an easier climb from Canyon Creek. The first fish planted in this lake were Eastern brook in 1951. **Canyon Creek Trailhead.**

There is only one decent way to go to Morris Lake: up Canyon Creek. The old *Know-It-All Guide* started the rumor about going up Bear Gulch from Morris Meadow. Many people have cussed at themselves (and the author) all the way home for taking that advice. The failure rate of those who start up Bear Gulch and never get to the lake is very high.

First of all, Morris Meadow is ten miles from the trailhead, then it is a three-hour bushwhacking, nerve-wracking, eye-poking, skin-scraping, shin- busting, rattlesnake-dodging, sweat-and-blood struggle to the lake.

On the other hand, you could walk for and hour and half up Canyon Creek, hang a right turn at the first major gulch past the upper meadows and you'll be at Morris Lake hours before those fools down in Bear Gulch doing hand-to-hand combat with the rattlesnakes and buck brush.

Actually, you shouldn't go exactly up the gulch out of Canyon Creek. Stay on the south edge (right-hand side) of the gulch and head for the big boulder field that leads to the flat, but tilted, granite slabs. Contour gradually to your left and gain enough altitude to hit the low gap on the divide. Use Sawtooth Peak to beam in on, using the low gap like a gunsight.

Morris Lake is a nice little penthouse above Smith Lake. Can't say much for the fishing. There was an attempt to get a population of golden trout started in the lake years ago, but it seems to have failed.

The view of the south side of Sawtooth is uncluttered. As you gaze upward, ask yourself whether it is possible that someone has climbed that face, or better still, ask yourself if anyone ever will.

From Morris Lake you can take the tourist route to Sawtooth's 8,886-foot summit by circling around to the east and then up.

Regarding alternative approaches to Morris Lake: late in the season it is possible to find a fairly brush-free route from Canyon Creek by staying right in the stream bed rather than working up high and to the right as mentioned above. You still have to gain just as much altitude to reach the gap into the Stuart Fork drainage, and you'll still have some hands-and-knees work to get through the brush.

I know of one couple who prefer the steep chimney another half a mile up the Canyon Creek trail. There is no brush to negotiate; it's direct, dumping you almost right on the shores of Morris Lake. I will stress, however, that it is as steep as an elevator shaft, and you give up some hard-earned elevation when you drop several hundred feet down to lakeside.

If you are tempted to climb the south face of Sawtooth Peak, keep in mind that this is a mountain that means business. It is much easier to climb up places than to climb down. Major accidents often happen while down-climbing. Getting stranded on a pinnacle or ledge is always a possibility.

That said, reaching the summit of Sawtooth Peak is an exhilarating experience that you'll treasure the rest of you life.

MOUNT HILTON

(8,964 feet) Canyon Creek Trailhead. My guess the name came from James Hilton, author of *Lost Horizon.* His response to the question, "Where did you get the idea for the setting (Shangri-La) of your novel?" was quoted as, "Weaverville, a little town in northern California." That's the only possible link to Hilton that I know of.

Mount Hilton is the third highest peak in the Trinity Alps, giving up second place by a mere two feet to an unnamed peak (8,966 feet, often called Mount Caesar), and is only 38 feet lower than the highest, Thompson Peak (9,002 feet).

It's a fairly easy, though time-consuming, climb from Canyon Creek Boulder Lake. Head for the skyline rocks that look like a castle wall to the east of the summit.

As with many summit experiences, you come quite suddenly and unexpectedly to the top. After hours of short oxygen-starved steps, sweat- stung eyes focused on the ground, and lactic acid turning muscles to mush, you find yourself standing on the granite edge of time. The world falls away from beneath your feet in all directions on an inassimilable scale, deep, silent, distant, and timeless.

Looking back down the route, you'll see the irregular blue eyes of the C.C. Boulder Lakes lying on their back gazing quietly at the sky. The sky is a great blue cup inverted overhead, its apex directly over Mount Hilton, its rim just touching the distant, minuscule horizon. A faint breeze born out of infinity carries the distant sound of falling water.

Gaze in all magnificent directions; there's Thompson Peak, Mount Caesar, Sawtooth Peak, Gibson Peak, Monument Peak, Weaver Bally in the foreground, Mount Shasta, Mount Lassen, Shasta Bally, the Sacramento Valley, Bully Choop, Black Rock, and South Fork Mountain in the distance. It is a solid immensity, a feeling of penetrating openness.

Views from mountaintops, and Mount Hilton is no exception, combine immensity, openness, silence, and timelessness to put the rest of the world into its proper infinitesimal perspective.

Upon your descent, in mid-to-late summer, you won't find a better place to take a swim after a climb than in the sun-warmed waters of Canyon Creek Boulder Lake.

NORTH FORK TRINITY RIVER

Hobo Gulch Trailhead. A mile north of Highway 299 at Helena, the road bids adieu to the North Fork of the Trinity River and doesn't get back to it until Hobo Gulch Campground. Left alone, the river loses itself in a magnificent canyon sans road or trail, the domain of rattlesnakes, red-tailed hawks and river otters. The crazy few who kayak from Hobo Gulch to Helena know that once they shove off, there's no way out, except at Raymond Flat and Waldorf Crossing many miles downstream.

At the bridge a mile north of Highway 299, on the west side of the canyon, you can pick up an old mining ditch and follow it for a couple of miles upstream, and then fish your way back downstream.

I was on this lower stretch of the North Fork of the Trinity one afternoon in late October dragging a gold Mepps spinner through the shadows of the somber underwater bedrock ledges. It had rained the night before, leaving the water dark and a touch murky. Suddenly my line stopped dead. I yanked, hoping to avoid losing my lure on a snag. The biggest fish I had ever seen in these mountains erupted from the water, wiggled violently a few times, and fell back with a startling splash.

I feverishly reeled in line until I could feel the pulsing steelhead searching for escape downstream. Keeping the line tight, I followed the fish downstream, stumbling over rocks and slipping on wet weeds, the brush flapping me in the face. After about three or four pools and a hundred yards downstream, the fish stopped. Carefully I reeled in more line and inched my way closer. I could see it, three feet of dark shiny back and brilliant silver and red sides, violently thrashing between two submerged boulders.

I kept the tension on the line, not sure what to do next. My thought was that as long as the fish was moving, it was getting tired. When it was tired enough, I'd be able to skid it up on to shore. I waited and watched for ten or fifteen minutes.

I chose my spot for landing, a sandbar sloping gently into the water.

I began backing up away from the water while pulling steadily on the line. The fish stopped thrashing and I was able to pull it closer to the sandbar. Its deep green back came out of the water when it reached the shallows and I felt it was time to heave the behemoth onto shore. It skidded up onto the sand, clear of the water, and I pounced. The fish reacted violently by flipping all over the place. The hook fell out of its mouth. Throwing down my fishing rod, I grasped for the writhing body and grabbed air. The powerful convulsions, aided by the slope of the shoreline, inched the fish toward the water. I dove headlong belly first after the rapidly fading fish. My hands clutched the head and tail, but the head was too large to get a grip and my other hand slipped from the tail.

I lay prone on the sand, my face at the edge of the water, and watched as the huge steelhead trout sank deeper into the water and began slowly undulating its muscular body on a course taking it deeper and deeper into the gathering gloom of a watery evening. I watched as trickles of sand washed off the silvery scales of its magnificent body and drifted in slow motion to the bottom of the stream.

But you don't *have* to fish to enjoy this river.

The trail follows the North Fork of the Trinity River from Hobo Gulch eight miles to Grizzly Creek, where it departs and heads for Grizzly Lake. The river is accessible at any point along the trail for aquatic activities. A plethora of streamside campsites among huge old-growth Douglas-fir are available. Jorstad Cabin is a significant landmark.

"Saunter" was one of John Muir's favorite words. He used it in place of "hiking" which he considered a vile word. Muir told this story to a group of returning climbers.

"You know, when pilgrims were going from England to the Holy Land, the French would ask them 'Where are you going?,' and they did not speak French very well, but they would say 'Sante Terre' (Holy Land). That is where we get our word 'Saunter' and you should saunter through the Sierra because this is a Holy Land, if there ever was one."

"Sauntering in any wilderness is delightful."

–John Muir

There are miles of sauntering to be done along the North Fork of the Trinity between Whites Creek and Grizzly Creek. Backbone Creek, the first tributary you come to after leaving the Hobo Gulch Trailhead, makes an ideal day hike along a waterfall laced wilderness-stream. Once the trail leaves for Grizzly Lake, the North Fork of the Trinity becomes a mere trickle, spidering into tributaries high up on the Salmon Divide. (See Grizzly Lake and Papoose Lake for more information on the North Fork country.)

PAPOOSE LAKE

Elevation 6,663 feet; 28 acres; 70 feet deep. Fat, scrappy, trout 16 inches and larger have been caught here. From Hobo Gulch it's about 14 miles up the North Fork of the Trinity River and Rattlesnake Creek to Bear Valley Meadow. The trail crosses to the south of Enos Cabin and switches up to the lake outlet. **Hobo Gulch Trailhead.**

Papoose Lake is what Grizzly Lake used to be like 20 years ago–wild, isolated, a chance to see a bear up close and personal.

Turn off the well-traveled trail that runs up the North Fork of the Trinity River. Take the Rattlesnake Creek exit and step back in time. Isaac Cox reports a store, butcher shop, and blacksmith shop along with a population of 60 men, no women, in 1856. You can still see the rocks they moved for several miles as you walk the trail. Here they turned the land upside down searching for gold. You have to wonder how much they actually found and whether any remains.

As you walk and wonder, remember this isn't called Rattlesnake Creek for nothing. Stumbling across a snake in the trail can rudely snap you out of a daydream, pronto.

But it wasn't a rattlesnake that gave me my biggest adrenaline rush on this trail. Early one evening I was alone running down the canyon. It was August and the air was warm and balmy. Insects buzzed in front of my face while the sunlight cut sharp angled shafts through the dense forest, backlighting cobwebs and highlighting the mossy green velvet tree trunks. My feet were on autopilot, my mind a zillion miles away on a long solitary run of its own.

Coming around a tight blind turn in the trail just below the Brown Mine, I glanced up and, seeing a crouched figure next to the trickle of water that crosses the trail there, I thought to myself, *Why is that guy wearing a fur coat on such a warm evening?* The thought had no sooner formed and passed on to a more conscious area than I realized it wasn't a guy wearing a fur coat, but a bear! I could have reached out and touched it, but instead I hit the ground like a baseball player sliding into third base. My yell shattered the silence and the bear, until then unaware of my presence, shot straight up in the air about four feet. He hit the ground at a full run and bolted up the hill away from me. Adrenaline surged through my bloodstream and my heartbeat felt like a Richter 8.5 in my ears.

Lying in the trail, panting and sweating from excitement, I listened to the bear crash and snort its way through the underbrush and timber. Eventually my thumping heartbeat dropped below 200 and I continued on down the trail. I heard the bear for some time afterward and looked over my shoulder every so often to make sure I wasn't being stalked.

It was dark long before I got back to my car that evening. Several times I heard noises that I thought were probably other bears that had been alerted through the bear grapevine to find me and get even.

It's a long pull up to Enni Camp. It might not seem as long if you camped at Mill Creek and broke the trip into two days to reach the lake. The trailhead to Papoose takes seven hours of steady, serious walking.

Above Enni Camp you pretty much follow the outlet to the lake. Stay to the right of the huge gorge that develops below the lake. You may see rock ducks marking the way.

Knock them down if you believe the wilderness should stay as undisturbed as possible.

Spend some time at Papoose Lake. After you leave, you'll wish to return soon. Get up on the divide between you and Canyon Creek and enjoy that fabulous skyscraping spine of granite and snow. Take a dip in the lake and numb your body with the snow melt from those unnamed peaks surrounding the lake. Stay up late and count stars.

Evidence of mining along Rattlesnake is impressive. A solitary hiker can only imagine what this canyon was like when machinery and men chewed away at the hillsides and creek bottoms looking for that elusive metal: the sound of metal clanking against rock, roaring streams of water caving the creek banks into thick cocoa-colored torrents, and tattered, unshaven men shouting expletives upon picking up a gleaming nugget of gold.

George Jorstad, who lived on the North Fork of the Trinity River at Pfeiffer Flat from the 1930s to the 1980s, recalled:

Bob's Farm, a landmark in the Rattlesnake drainage for many years, was the name given to a locality high on the ridge once held down by a fellow called Bob. There was mining there, but also this Bob (what other name he had isn't known) had a garden on a hillside that was irrigated by a flow of water out of a grassy slope that grew hay. The story is that this fellow didn't care much about mining; growing things appealed to him more. There was a demand for vegetables in the nearby camps, and also there was a need for hay. Hence, somewhat fallaciously the place was called Bob's Farm, and the name persists to this day.

The mining was all hard rock, and so needed milling, which led to the building of a ball mill on Mill Creek at its juncture with Rattlesnake Creek. The ore was tumbled down or pushed down a very steep incline from the mines above to the mill site, and there crushed up, and the ground up rock sluiced for the gold in it. How successful the venture was, of course, isn't known. When I came to the country (1937) the mill was roofless, and much of it fallen in, but its frame was still intact. A man by the name of Chandler owned claims above, and there were tunnels, some 30 to 40 feet in length.

Danny O'Shay had a cabin in the same general locality as the Chandler cabin, but his mine, a chloride mine, was his own. Danny became well-known to me and visited me on Pfeiffer Flat several times. He was Dublin Irish and spoke the language so fast and furious that we had trouble following him. He always carried samples of ore with him, it seemed, that had been assayed or were about to be assayed, and was proud in telling us that it was worth $5,000 or $15,000 a ton. The trouble was that mining engineers investigating these sites were never able to find bodies of these ores extensive enough to warrant financing their mining. The gold ran in seams and stringers and never widened out enough to form a lode, as often happened in the Mother Lode country. It was this same tendency with hard rock mines throughout Trinity county. They might be very rich in spots, but that is all. A rich streak and then nothing. Very frustrating for the miner.

Jorstad on the Brown Mine on Rattlesnake Creek:

This hydraulic operation (also known as the King Mine and Corbett's Rattlesnake Digs) was probably the most successful venture of any in the whole North Fork District. It was not a big placer, probably only a single monitor was used, but it must have been very rich, and although the first old-timers had gone over the creek from end to end, and no doubt did very well, King with his giant, took out $50,000 in the space of *only a few years. Then he sold it to a man named Brown and it became the Brown Mine. This man did little with it. A caretaker, who did all the assessment work on the claims, held it down for another five or ten years, after which time it was allowed to lapse.*

Next, a man by the name of Mel Corbett from Los Angeles, a band leader, claimed it, and a new era in mining dawned on the Rattlesnake. He and his wife Faye and their two four-year-old daughters, Arlene and Darlene, were to bring not only a touch of Hollywood to the Trinity backwoods but also methods of extracting the precious metal from the sands that had never been attempted before. Machinery was the key, big machinery, bulldozers, backhoes, trummels and tools such as welding machines to keep the equipment in repair. Big trucks were also needed for the transport of oils and gasoline to fuel the machinery and bring in other supplies. This meant a road into the property had to be built. In order to build the road, permission from the Forest Service, the nominal custodians of the region, had to be obtained. This was accomplished, and for the next 20 years Corbett & Company held sway in the doings on the upper North Fork.

After Mel had done his bit and retired back to his old haunts in Los Angeles, one of his associates took over the operation, having first, however, married the daughter Darlene. But the associate didn't last long. A few years later it was Darlene herself, "Darlin' Darlene" as she came to be known, who had taken over the mining enterprise.

A huge forest fire in the 1980s charred much of the North Fork and Rattlesnake countryside. Inside the Wilderness Area, it was never logged. You can see for yourself how the land recovers from fire when left alone. Fire has been a natural force in the wilderness for thousands of years. None of those ancient fires were suppressed. Suppression of natural wilderness fires remains a questionable expense of money and time.

PONY MOUNTAIN

(7,478 feet) Hobo Gulch Trailhead Jim Jam Ridge Trailhead, or Green Mountain Trailhead. Not to be confused with Pony Buttes, several miles to the north, this prominent point on Limestone Ridge promises and delivers sensational views; a limestone watchtower with ringside seats, perfect for extended observation of the Alps, a sea of mountains in all directions.

The most direct route is from Hobo Gulch Trailhead via Bear Wallow Meadows and Hunters Camp. From a base camp at Whites Creek Lake, you can scramble to the summit in a couple of hours.

RAYMOND FLAT TRAILHEAD (BLUE RIDGE)

Access: Drive 13 miles north from Highway 299 on Hobo Gulch Campground road. Watch for large level flat on left. **Hobo Gulch Campground** is less than 3 miles on up the road.

Trails: Trail 11W12 stays high above the North Fork of the Trinity River for the six miles to Waldorff Crossing. Spur trail at 3 miles leads down to a private residence on the stream.

Destinations: Access to a roadless stretch of the North Fork of the Trinity River.

Elevation/Difficulty: 3,800 feet at trailhead. Easy hiking downstream, moderate going upstream or hiking out of the canyon

Summary: Trail never does get close to river below. Game trails and scrambling are your choices for river access. Loop hike with car shuttle between Blue Ridge and Waldorff Crossing possible.

Frozen Sapphire Lake

SAPPHIRE LAKE

Elevation 6,100 feet; 43 acres; over 200 feet deep. A long lake situated in a deep cut valley; 17 miles by trail up Stuart Fork from the end of the road. Has brook and rainbow trout. A few large brown trout also reported. Brook trout most numerous. **Stuart Fork Trailhead.**

There might be some places in this world too beautiful to describe. Places to be experienced and tucked away in the mind for later dispensing to our senses.

Years ago, under the golden haze of a late afternoon in summer, Sapphire Lake was our Valhalla. We were Viking gods and warriors riding our ships of granite boulders up the fjord. We stood on the prow of our rock boats and shouted praises to Odin.

The sky turned a deep turquoise blue, the lake was a piece of the sky, and as stars marked the limits of our visual universe we built huge pyres and feasted on spaghetti and applesauce; swaggered faux drunk on Wyler's lemonade. The thoughts of future conquests and blonde Nordic encounters briefly troubled our sleep.

Sapphire Lake gives the impression of being in a fjord. The Vikings of 1958 are long gone, but the granite walls still leap upward, gracefully skyward, for thousands of feet. Even now, if you camp on the shores of Sapphire on a summer's eve and don't build a fire, the quietness will stun you. Listen closely enough and you'll hear faint echoes, voices calling, "Oooooodinnnnn."

Sapphire Lake appears bottomless. Actually, the *Know-It-All Guide* didn't really call Sapphire Lake bottomless, but reported its depth at over 200 feet. Technically, if you can't measure the depth of a lake it could be called bottomless, since the bottom has not been found. There's a list of bottomless lakes published in some almanacs. It's interesting to note that the shallowest bottomless lake was in Russia which, when finally measured, was found to be 16 feet deep.

Near the summit of Sawtooth Peak

SAWTOOTH MOUNTAIN

(8,886 feet) Canyon Creek Trailhead, Stuart Fork Trailhead. This is one of the finest hike/climbs in the Trinity Alps. Sawtooth Mountain can be seen from almost any place in the Alps. Likewise, from the top of Sawtooth, a major portion of the Wilderness Area is visible. But the peak experience here is more than just climbing to the top of an 8,000-foot mountain–the approaches lead you through some of the best country the Alps have to offer. By the time you reach the summit, some gorgeous real estate has passed beneath your boot heels.

Coming up Canyon Creek, bushwhacking to Smith or Morris Lake, spending the night and summiting as the sun rises over Gibson Peak to the east may have been your choice. Spectacular is a word that may have crossed your mind. This is the shortest approach. Study the face of Sawtooth from the lake; there are several possible ways to attack. The easiest way is to get up on the east ridge and follow it on the north side to the summit block. Don't be tempted by the narrow couloir that appears to lead to the summit. It's jammed by a couple of imposing monster boulders. Even if you do manage to bypass them, loose rock could turn it into a lethal bowling alley. Avoid the couloir and walk on up to the divide and look down into Ell Lake. At this point, begin the scramble to the summit block. It takes a little route-finding and some folks opt for technical gear for this summit, but the view is spectacular.

The summit is a jagged splintered collection of granite spires. The north is a bit lower than the south. Both wear brass caps from the U.S. Geological Survey. The summit register is on the slightly higher south peak. As recently as October 1995, there were only a dozen names in the summit register for the season. Such a spectacular peak and so little traffic.

It's a little longer hike, but the approach is brush-free from Ell Lake. Starting at the lake, it is clear and clean boulder-hopping to the north summit. Pick your route.

Perhaps the worst way to tackle Sawtooth Mountain is from Morris Meadow on Stuart Fork. It is possible to get to Smith Lake via Bear Gulch, but involves several hours of nerve-racking bushwhacking. Descending Bear Gulch is reasonable.

If you are going to climb only one peak in the Alps, Sawtooth is the one.

SMITH LAKE

Elevation 6,950 feet; 24 acres; 167 feet deep. If it is possible to say that one of these glacial lakes is more spectacularly beautiful than the others, this one would be it. No trail. From Morris Meadow on the Stuart Fork it takes four to five hours to climb the granite mountainside to the lake. And it's about the same time and terrain by leaving the Canyon Creek trail near the mouth of Boulder Creek. The few adventurous anglers who visit this lake report the rainbows and brook trout are very lively. Usually free of ice by July 1. **Canyon Creek Trailhead.**

What lake is the most beautiful in the Trinity Alps? You may as well ask who is the most beautiful woman in the world. A task only to be undertaken by a fool. Alps lake beauty, like people, is in the eye of the beholder. It's only skin deep, and depends on how far away you are. All wilderness lakes, like all women, are beautiful when viewed from the right distance under the right light. You could better spend your time contemplating the number of angels able to dance on the head of a pin.

Smith Lake is in the Stuart Fork drainage, but don't be deceived. The only way to get there is via Canyon Creek (see comments under Morris Lake).

The place to camp is above the lake, on the inlet, so the granite cliff overhanging the lake becomes your balcony. There you can sit or stroll morning and evening and keep tabs on the heavens and mountains around you. Here's an entry from my journal:

Smith Lake

Wednesday, August 22, 1979–*Nighttime, Smith Lake. I've sat and stared into a lot of campfires, but none as soft and quiet as this one. My own thoughts are as still as the glowing embers, pulsating with the heat, burning and consuming themselves as the darkness closes in around me and my fire at Smith Lake.*

Once your campfire goes out, you rest your neck on a log. Your head goes back. Then you can see only the sky. No mountains, no campfire, no lake. Just sky. The stars are campfires of a million other hikers very far away. Ancient hunters thought that perhaps the night is a great black animal skin thrown over the sky. There are holes in the skin. We look through the holes and see flame. These ancient hunters thought that there was flame not just in a few places where we see stars; they thought there was flame everywhere. That flame covers the whole sky. But the skin hides the flame. Except where there are holes.

Sometimes it seems you might fall up into the sky. If the stars are campfires of other wanderers, I'd like to visit them. But if the stars are holes in a skin–no thank you.

There was a time when the lack of a trail discouraged all but the most aggressive hikers to this lake. Now the word is out, and probably too many people visit Smith Lake. Publicity has spoiled more than one beautiful place, so please take care that no one knows that you've come and gone.

A few years ago a helicopter had to be used to rescue folks from the snow fields above the Canyon Creek approach. They were packing in a boat and supplies to cache until summer. A boat at Smith Lake is not necessary.

THOMPSON PEAK

(9,002 feet) Canyon Creek Trailhead, China Gulch Trailhead. Of course everyone wants to climb Thompson Peak. Peakbaggers have to climb the highest peak if they climb any at all. The summit doesn't feel much higher than the surrounding peaks, some of which appear to be higher but aren't. The north and east faces are vertically challenging, but the long, sloping west ridge is a walk up. There are fire rings along the west ridge, evidence that people have camped there to catch a full moon, or perhaps to gain a ringside seat during a lunar eclipse.

The large snow field on the north side above Grizzly Lake has been called a glacier. Maybe. Depends on your definition of glacier. Most maps refer to it as a perpetual snow field or never-melting snow bank. There's another glacier, perpetual snow field, never-melting snow bank, to the east of Thompson Peak on the north side of what is coming to be called Mount Caesar.

The view from the highest point in the Trinity Alps is superb. Canyon Creek Lakes and the gnarled, twisted unnamed peaks to the south, Grizzly Lake to the north, and the long landscape in all directions is a banquet to the eyes of the mountaineer.

And the geologist. From this vantage point, the buckling and shifting of the earth's crust is apparent. It's as if the skin covering the Earth, ultra-thin at best, diminishes as altitude increases until there is a point on high mountains when there is no longer any Earth skin and the bare bones of the planet are exposed.

No one has yet found a rock as old as the Earth. The oldest known are found in Labrador. The greenstone from there is 3.8 billion years old. The age of the earth has been pegged at 4.8 billion years, give or take a day or two. The rock you touch on Thompson Peak is scar tissue from an unfathomable 140 million years ago. Adolescent in geologic time.

When ready to tackle Thompson Peak from Grizzly Lake, start up the ridge toward Lois Lake until the divide. From there it is a stroll to the summit, staying on the south side of the ridge.

From Canyon Creek, you'll want to hike almost to the base of the cliffs on

Thompson's east side and then make for the gap between it and Wedding Cake. From there, angle to the ridge and follow it to the summit.

Thompson Peak (right) from Canyon Creek Lakes

THURSTON PEAKS

(7,161 7,591 and 7,309 feet) Hobo Gulch Trailhead, Green Mountain Trailhead. While not particularly high, this trilogy of silver-colored peaks are dramatic the way they tower a thousand feet over the dusky green of this densely forested area of the Alps. Thurston Peaks are limestone bumps on the spine of Limestone Ridge, which has been judged by some to be the finest example of karst topography in the United States.

Limestone Ridge is a twenty-mile-long sub-range from the Trinity County line on the north to Twin Sisters on the south. A trail meanders along most of this ridge, dividing the North Fork of the Trinity River and the New River.

The peaks are fairly easy to climb from several directions.

The shortest and most direct is from Hobo Gulch on the North Fork of the Trinity, following the Bear Wallows Meadow trail to Hunter's Camp, where it intersects the New River Divide Trail on Limestone Ridge. Take the trail south past Pony Mountain and Pony Camp. When the trail crosses the headwaters of Devil's Canyon, make a break for the summits.

A less strenuous approach than Hobo Gulch is from the Green Mountain Trailhead, which can be found at the end of the road up Big French Creek. Big French Creek is halfway between Willow Creek and Weaverville on Highway 299. Turn north and follow USFS roads 5N13 and 6N04 about 13 miles. The trail takes off toward Brushy Mountain, which can be reached by a spur to the left. The trail, which once was a firebreak, dips and weaves its way past Panther Camp, Stove Camp, and another spur to the top of Green Mountain. Once past the fork diving down into Devil's Canyon, start thinking about heading for the Thurston summits. The easiest route is up the ridge just after the trail intersection. The gradual spur ends just south of peak 7591, the highest. The rock is pretty rotten, requiring some caution.

Point 7309 offers a view to knock your socks off. Pick out Thompson, Wedding Cake, and Mount Hilton to the east, Pony Mountain to the north, the blue-green tangle of the upper New River drainage overflowing with silence, and below, to the west, the splendid wilderness of Devil's Canyon.

Speaking of Devil's Canyon, it's a tough but alluring approach to the Thurston Peaks. From the trailhead a few miles past Denny, the first problem is to cross New River. After midsummer it's wadeable. If the water is high, consider using the road bridge farther upstream and work back down river to the trail, which is sometimes difficult to find. Hiking up Devil's Canyon, walk right in the streambed if the water isn't too high. The lush understory of moss-covered rocks and oak trees belies its devil name.

It's about ten miles of hiking in the canyon to gain 2,000 feet of elevation, but once the trail decides to leave the canyon and head for the divide, it means business, climbing another 2,000 feet in about a mile. A quarter of a mile shy of the ridge is Ladder Camp (maybe a hint at how steep the trail is?). Once on the ridge, keep climbing north to any of the Thurston summits.

TODD CABIN TRAILHEAD

Access: From Highway 299 at Helena, drive north 8.5 miles on the road to Hobo Gulch Campground. Watch for unsigned road to the right. Road drops quickly down to the East Fork of the North Fork, ending at washed-out bridge.

Trails: No official trail numbers, but there are two enjoyable trails: one to the Alaska Mine on Yellowjacket Creek, the other up the East Branch of the East Fork of the North Fork of the Trinity River to the McClaron Mine. A faint trail follows the East Fork downstream to end of road 421 at Coleridge town site.

Destinations: The McClaron and Alaska Mines, the trackless wilderness beyond.

Elevation/Difficulty: 2,100 feet at trailhead to 3,300 feet at the mine sites. Easy streamside hiking to the mines, unless you go beyond trail's end, where there is strenuous first-class bushwhacking to the top of a 7,000-foot ridge.

Summary: Little known or used area of the Alps, with easy day hikes to old mining cabins. Fishing for bait snatcher-sized rainbows in the East Fork, with the possibility of hooking a summer steelhead.

TRELOAR RIDGE TRAILHEAD

Access: Trailhead is behind the Big Bar Ranger Station 22 miles west of Weaverville on Highway 299. **Big Flat Campground** is 2 miles east on the highway and **Big Bar Campground** is just across the river from the ranger station. Park at the ranger station, walk through the rangers' housing area, past the corrals, following the stream on your left, and watch for the trail heading up the ridge to your right.

Trails: Trail 12W17 means business from beginning to end, as it tracks the top of the ridge on a steady climb of over 3,500 feet in five miles to join trail 11W13, the east/west trail from Big French Creek to Hobo Gulch Road.

Destinations: Upper Waldorff Ranch, Twin Sisters Mountain.

Elevation/Difficulty: 1,275 feet at trailhead to almost 6,000 feet on Twin Sisters. Difficult to strenuous depending on how far you hike.

Summary: Not much reason to use this trail, except for exercise, although bird watchers can see a lot of birds of prey from high on the ridge. Upper Waldorff Ranch from Big French Creek and Twin Sisters Mountain from Manzanita Ridge are easier approaches.

TWIN SISTERS MOUNTAIN

(5,932 feet) Manzanita Ridge Trailhead. Treloar Ridge Trailhead. Here's a cure for cabin fever. Early in the spring, while the high country of the Alps is still snowbound, you can day hike Twin Sisters, or do an overnighter, get the cobwebs out of the old backpacking gear, and get a start on the body conditioning needed for more serious hiking later on in the summer. Snow is usually gone from the ridge trail and summit in March. Unfortunately, the U.S. Forest Service, in its infinite wisdom, keeps the Manzanita Ridge Trailhead behind a locked gate until May first. Prior to that date, you have to use the Treloar Ridge approach, which starts at less than 2,000 feet, creating a stiff climb to the summit.

Sisters they might be, but twins they aren't. The southern summit is obviously much higher than the northern.

A loop with car shuttle between Manzanita and Treloar ridges is possible. A car shuttle between the Manzanita Trailhead and Hobo Gulch Road is also possible, but inquire locally about the water conditions at the North Fork of the Trinity at Waldorff Crossing. It may be impossible to cross safely, making retracing your steps back up 4,000 vertical feet a major bummer.

From the trailhead on Manzanita Ridge, the trail follows an old firebreak along the ridgetop, with just enough ups and downs to provide a full body workout. The views down both sides of the ridge, while interesting, promise something even better on the summit, about five miles from the trailhead.

The panorama north to Thurston Peaks is foreshortened, making them appear closer and higher than they really are. Along both approach ridgetops, birds of prey ride the thermals.

Can't wait for summer to do a mountain power run? Twin Sisters is the answer. The two thousand foot elevation gain in five miles is reasonable for a conditioned runner. You might find yourself walking the steeper uphill pulls, but you can kick into overdrive on the downhill stretches and carry enough speed to get well up the next incline before gravity and lactic acid dictate walking for a while. Carry water whether running or walking. No water anywhere on the trail.

WALDORFF CROSSING TRAILHEAD

Access: Turn north immediately west of the Helena Bridge on Highway 299. After about four miles, watch for a sign and road 34N07YA to the left. A little over two miles on 34N07YA is a sign and roadside parking. **Hobo Gulch Campground** is up the road another 7 miles.

Trails: Trail 11W13 climbs up and over the ridge and descends, past a junction with the Raymond Flat Trail (11W12), to the North Fork of the Trinity River. The stream crossing can be deadly during high water. It then climbs steeply up and around to Mosquito Hollow to the Manzanita Ridge Trail (12W15), climbs and contours along the ridge before dropping down to the Treloar Ridge Trail (12W17), and finally ends up at Upper Waldorff Ranch. Total length 16.3 miles.

Destinations: Offers access to the wilderness gorge of the North Fork of the Trinity River, designated a Wild and Scenic River. A tough approach to the Twin Sisters Peaks. Raymond Flat Trail (11W12) undulates upstream, staying well above the stream, to the Hobo Gulch Road at Blue Ridge.

Elevation/Difficulty: 2,350 feet at trailhead. Tough and vague in spots.

Summary: Remote and rugged river canyon with good stream fishing, including steelhead. Private residents have lived at Raymond Flat for many years.

Valley Fog from Weaver Bally

WEAVER BALLY TRAILHEAD

Access: Take the Weaver Bally Lookout Road 33N38 from Weaverville for 9 miles to the saddle just before the lookout. **East Weaver Campground** is three miles north of Weaverville off Hwy. 3.

Trails: Trail 10W11 climbs easily for a mile to the top of the ridge and drops sharply to East Weaver lake.

Destinations: East Weaver Lake, Monument Peak, Rush Creek Lakes.

Elevation/Difficulty: 6,600 feet at trailhead. Easy with one moderately steep section to East Weaver Lake. Strenuous to Rush Creek Lakes.

Summary: Brief, short hike to East Weaver Lake with spectacular views. Cross-country route to Rush Creek Lakes via Monument Peak for experienced hikers.

WEDDING CAKE

(8,592 feet) Canyon Creek Trailhead. I suppose it got its name because that's what it looks like from some angles–well, maybe not a whole wedding cake, just a slice. There might be a better story out there, but I've yet to hear it.

This is a nice peak to knock off on the same day you do Thompson. Its not much of a walk across the saddle between the two. It's best to come at it from the west. The east side below the summit is steeper than a cow's face.

South of Wedding Cake are three prominent peaks with no names: **8,791** and

8,913 sometimes called the Camel's Hump, a name you'll understand when you see them, and **8,911** directly west of Papoose Lake. One early climber called **8,911** the most inaccessible peak in the Trinity Alps. That's challenge enough to make a person want to go climb it.

WHITES CREEK LAKE

Elevation 5,400 feet; .5 acres; 3 feet deep. A little over five miles from Hobo Gulch at the headwaters of Whites Creek, a tributary of the North Fork of the Trinity River. **Hobo Gulch Trailhead.**

A nearly treeless bowl carved from the side of Pony Mountain cradles this fishless pond. The reason for a trip to Whites Creek Lake is not to fish, but to hike, camp and climb Pony Mountain (7,478 feet). Only during hunting season do you run the risk of having company in this off-the-beaten-path basin.

There may be no fish in the lake, but it makes an excellent mirror to capture reflections on film. Reflection shots dominate every hiker/photographer picture collection I've seen. The goal is to take a picture where it is impossible to tell whether you are looking at it upside down or not. Or, a reflection picture that actually looks better if it is viewed upside down.

Sleeping among the pine trees near Whites Creek Lake nearly four decades ago, something woke me in the predawn hours. Unable to go back to sleep, I watched the dark, bulky outline of Pony Mountain against a splendid star-studded night sky. To the east, ragged peaks along the North Fork/Canyon Creek divide lifted themselves out of ebony silence toward a sliver of a moon.

Time passed, the sky paled, and puffy clouds with flat bottoms cruised in from the north and spread from horizon to zenith. Their tops were slate gray, but their undersides began to catch fire with a brilliant exploding flame orange. The orange was reflected in the lake, out of focus and dancing as a breeze chopped the surface.

The lake reflection made two skies. Floating between the two skies, the dark hulks of Thompson Peak, Wedding Cake, and Mount Hilton rose beyond the blacker shapes of trees. The water doubled everything. The twinned mountains and the twinned trees seemed paper-thin and nearly transparent. It was a scene full of suspended, pure light. Like all perfect things, it was transitory. In a moment, the colors shifted and faded, and the flaming clouds dissolved into a gloomy gray soup that began to lower the ceiling overhead. The sun never did clear the horizon, and before noon it was drizzling.

Thoughts of the dawn spectacle warmed my mind on the soggy, chilled return to the Hobo Gulch Trailhead.

Chapter Ten

THE SOUTHWESTERN ALPS

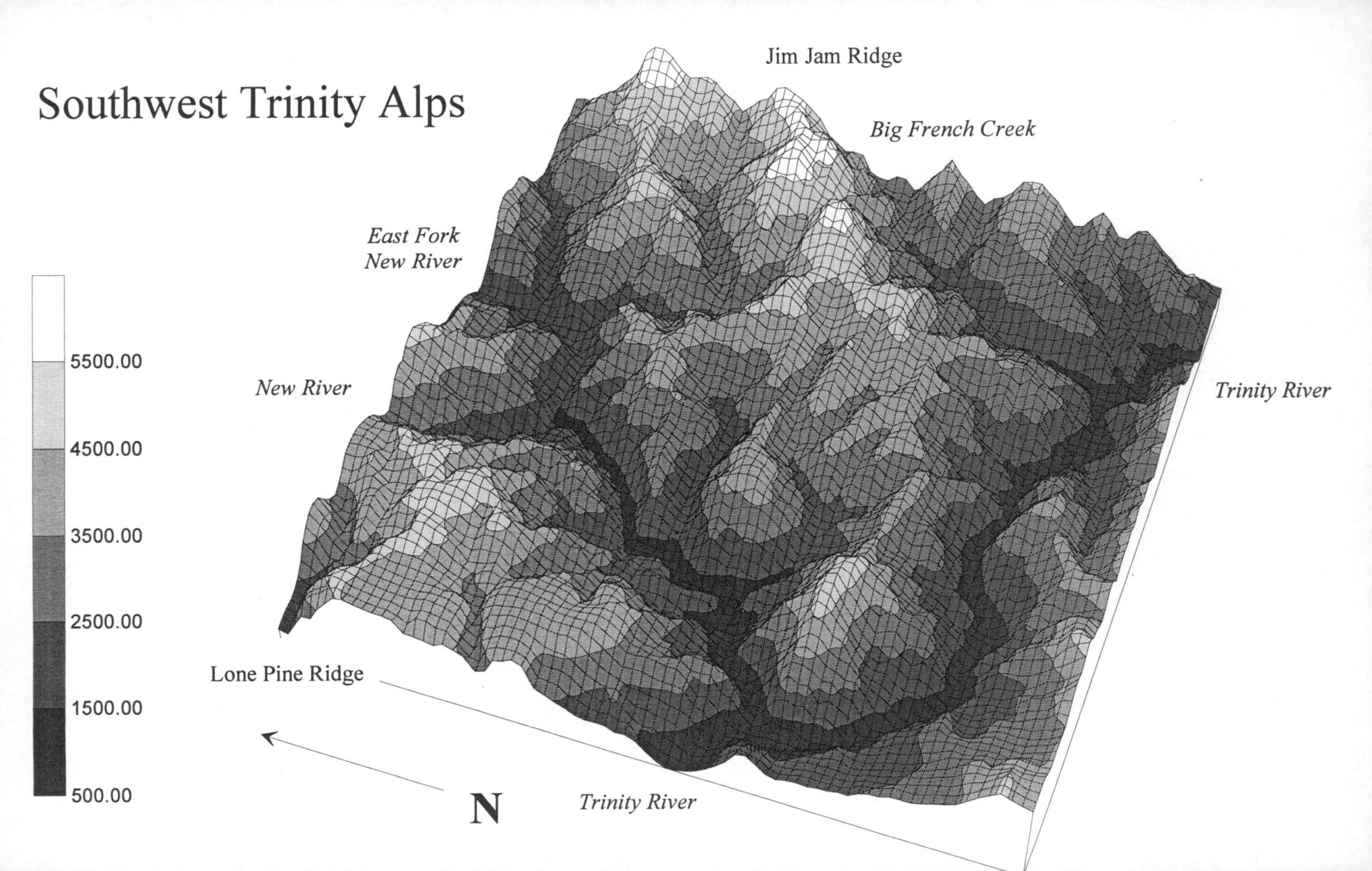
Southwest Trinity Alps
Jim Jam Ridge
Big French Creek
East Fork
New River
New River
Trinity River
Lone Pine Ridge
Trinity River
N
5500.00
4500.00
3500.00
2500.00
1500.00
500.00

Southwest Trinity Alps

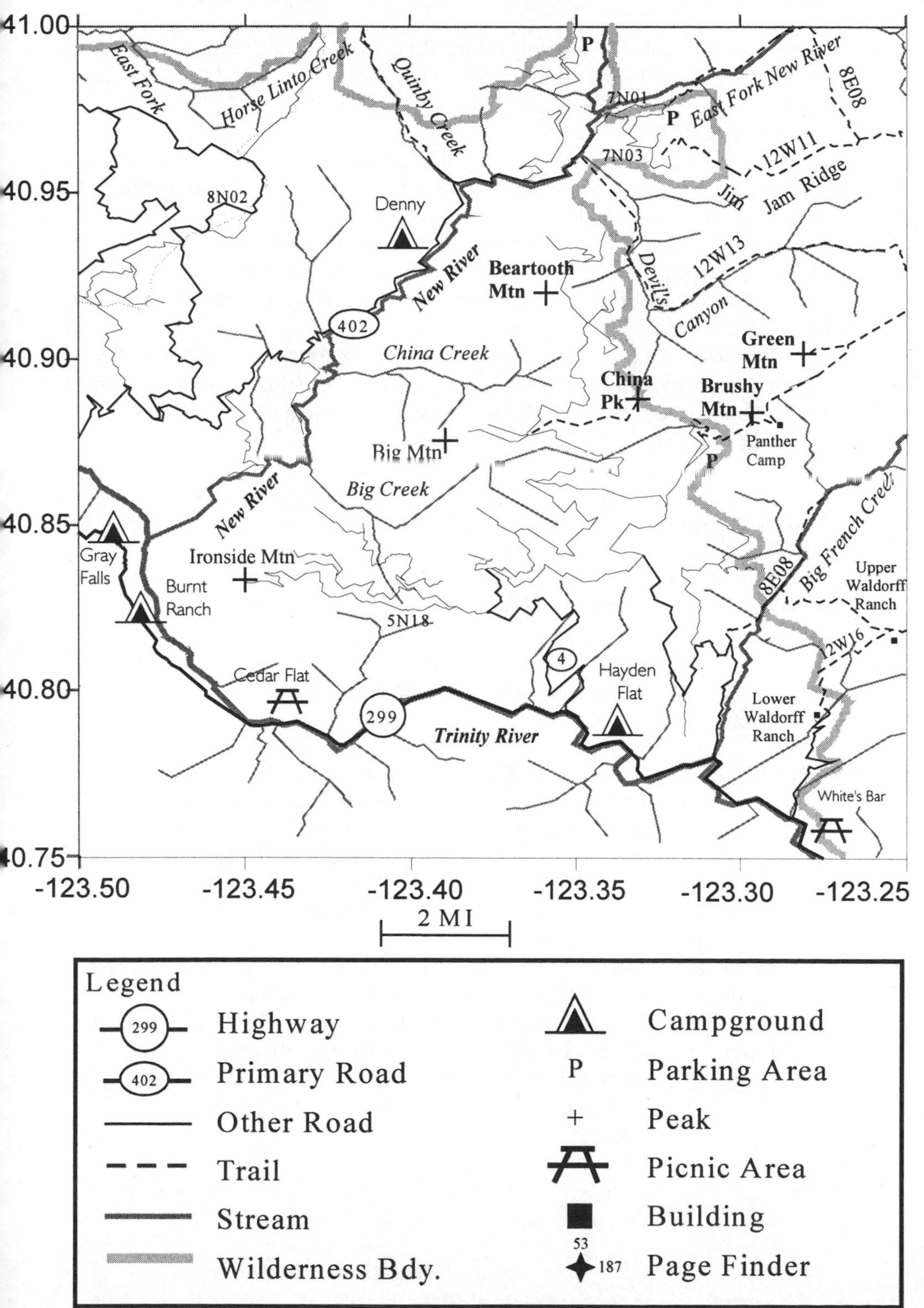

Well, here's the problem with imposing straight lines on the folded velvet tapestry of the Trinity Alps–there is only one major creek and no lakes in this region!

BIG FRENCH CREEK

Big French Creek Trailhead. This may be the least-known, least-visited stream in the Trinity Alps, running rambunctious and wild from the Thurston Peaks and touched by the trail only now and then. Hidden by a thick jungle of dark shady moss-covered oak, madrone, and dogwood, the hiker gets only glimpses of the deep pools, gravel bars and riffles of Big French Creek. Indian rhubarb, with leaves two feet in diameter in the autumn, can be more than five feet tall. These large leaves provide shade for trout during the hot dry months. Poison oak is prolific.

To reach the trailhead, drive 28 miles west of Weaverville on Highway 299 and take the road just across the bridge, marked *Big French Creek Road.* Three miles up the road, start looking for the trail at a wide turnout just before a hairpin turn in the road. There is usually a sign. Two miles of trail hiking brings you to Cherry Flat, where old orchard trees mark what was once an old homestead. The trail continues up the creek another 3 or 4 miles before dwindling into wilderness. Push beyond the last remnants of trail and you'll be in the beautiful remote valley of a wilderness stream. You'll probably be alone.

There are rumors of hikers following the stream all the way to the top of the Thurston Peaks, a major feat indeed. But a trip up Big French Creek that ends short of the headwaters is still very worthwhile.

From Oak Flat a steep 2-mile trail takes you to what remains of the historic Upper Waldorff Ranch. It's a worthwhile day hike, but the ranch is private property and should be respected accordingly.

BIG FRENCH CREEK TRAILHEAD

Access: Three miles from Highway 299 on Forest Service Road 5N13. Roadside parking. **Hayden Flat Campground** nearby on Highway 299.

Trails: Trail 8E08 drops down to Big French Creek at Oak Flat and Cherry Flat and continues for 5.8 miles before dwindling out near the East Fork of Big French Creek. Intersects trail 11W13 at Oak Flat, which goes to Upper Waldorff Ranch and Twin Sisters Mountain.

Destinations: Oak Flat and Cherry Flat. Rugged and challenging cross-country approach to Thurston Peaks. Historic Upper Waldorff Ranch.

Elevation/Difficulty: 2,140 feet at trailhead to over 7,000 feet on Thurston Peaks. Easy trail first few miles. Strenuous once the trail ends.

Summary: Trail is seldom used. Plenty of poison oak and ticks.

Devil's Canyon

DEVIL'S CANYON TRAILHEAD

Access: Turn north from Highway 299 at Hawkins Bar and drive 19 miles on County Road 402 to town of Denny (no services). Continue another three miles, staying right at all forks until opposite Devil's Canyon. Watch for canyon on opposite shore just before New River Bridge. Mile marker 22 marks the spot. Roadside parking. **Denny Campground** nearby.

Trails: Trail 12W13 is not maintained and may be impassable in places. First, it may be impossible to safely cross New River to reach the trail. The trail follows the creek through forest and heavy brush before finally switchbacking steeply up to Ladder Camp, where it joins the Green Mountain Trail. Total length 10.9 miles.

Destinations: Beautiful remote rugged canyon. Thurston Peaks. Limestone Ridge.

Elevation/Difficulty: 2,100 feet at trailhead to over 7,000 feet. Strenuous.

Summary: Devil's Canyon is seldom-visited wilderness offering an experience hard to match.

EAST FORK OF NEW RIVER TRAILHEAD (PONY BUTTES)

Access: Twenty-four miles north of Highway 299 (Hawkins Bar) on the Denny Road (402). Trailhead is at road's end. **Denny Campground** nearby.

Trails: Follows East Fork for three miles, then forks right on trail 12W08 to Rattlesnake Lake and Limestone Ridge ten miles from trailhead. Forks left on trail 12W07 to Lake City (site), where trail 8E16 goes over Bake Oven Ridge to Slide Creek, and 12W07 climbs ridge and eventually reaches the Siskiyou/Trinity county line at Election Camp.

Destinations: Lake City (site), Rattlesnake Lake, Cabin Peak, Pony Lake, Pony Buttes, Mullan Corral, Election Camp, Salmon Divide, Limestone Ridge.

Elevation/Difficulty: 2,300 feet at trailhead to 6,000 feet on ridgetops. Easy for the first few miles, difficult as the distance from trailhead increases after that.

Summary: Deep, narrow canyon hiking. Stream fishing good. Chances of seeing other people are slim to none. Historic mining area.

GREEN MOUNTAIN TRAILHEAD (LIMESTONE RIDGE)

Access: Twenty-eight miles west of Weaverville, turn north on USFS 5N13 at Big French Creek and then watch for 6N04 after 9 miles, then another 4 miles. **Hayden Flat Campground** is on the Trinity River on Highway 299 about three miles west of the Big French Creek turnoff to the trailhead.

Trails: Trail 12W09 undulates along what used to be a road around Brushy Mountain and Green Mountain to Ladder Camp and joins the Devil's Canyon Trail. It then climbs up to the ridge below Pony Mountain, passes Pony Camp and drops down to Whites Creek Lake and joins the Jim Jam Ridge Trail. It then contours through brush and forest over to Hunter's Camp past the junction with the Whites Creek Lake Trail. From here it climbs and drops steeply to Marble Springs before contouring around Cabin Peak to the Morrison Gulch Trail and follows the crest of Limestone Ridge, passing Rattlesnake Lake, and the East Fork of New River Trail junction. From here the trail climbs to the Salmon Summit Trail. Total length is 20.4 miles.

Destinations: This trail bisects the Trinity Alps from south to north providing stunning vistas and access to the North Fork of the Trinity River and East Fork of New River areas. The Limestone Ridge section has been called the best example of karst topography in the United States. Good approach to climb Thurston Peaks.

Elevation/Difficulty: 5,100 feet at trailhead. Moderately difficult, mainly due to lack of water and good campsites. Not a good choice for a midsummer hike.

Summary: Low-use trail except during hunting season, offering ridgetop rambling and solitude. Area north of Rattlesnake Lake and Limestone Ridge still shows damage from the 1987 forest fires.

JIM JAM RIDGE TRAILHEAD

Access: Twenty-three miles north of Highway 299 (Hawkins Bar), on the Denny Road (402), turn right at signed intersection and climb another steep 4 miles to an overgrown logging landing and start looking for the trailhead. **Denny Campground** nearby.

Trails: The trail (12W11) can be difficult to locate. It follows rugged Jim Jam Ridge up and onto Limestone Ridge, where it joins trail 12W09.

Destinations: Jakes Hunting Ground, Jakes Upper Camp, Whites Creek Lake, Pony Mountain.

Elevation/Difficulty: 3,800 feet climbing to 7,478 feet at Pony Mountain. Moderate to difficult.

Summary: Shortest route to summit of Pony Mountain. Jakes Camp and Jakes Hunting Grounds named for Jake Hersberger, resident of the area in the 1860s. An expert shot, he killed deer to supply winter meat for the miners along the East Fork, Pony Creek, and at Lake City. When he disappeared in July 1900 without a trace, it was believed at the time that he might have been murdered for his gold. A large A-frame shake cabin with a large fireplace at one end was built by Jake and still stands.

LIMESTONE RIDGE TRAILHEAD (see Green Mountain Trailhead)

PONY BUTTES TRAILHEAD (see East Fork of New River Trailhead)

WALDORFF RANCH TRAILHEAD

Both the Lower and Upper Waldorff Ranch are private inholdings and public access is denied by a locked gate on the road up Prairie Creek off Highway 299. You may visit what remains of the Upper Waldorff Ranch by using the trail from Oak Flat on Big French Creek.

Chapter Eleven

FINIS

Stones and trees speak very slowly. Sometimes it takes a full week before they say one sentence. Few people have the patience to wait for an answer from an oak.

–Garrison Keillor

So here it is, the culmination of a love affair I've had with the Alps. It started out with innocent flirtations 25 years ago and ended up an all-consuming mistress that demanded all the time and energy I could muster over the years. The passion was to visit very lake, to climb every mountain. Now it's done. The book has been written, or so I thought when I wrote those words in 1981.

Now another 15 years have passed and the end of the affair is not in sight. The things we love become part of us. Perhaps it is not in the best interest of wilderness to publicize the place. Perhaps a Wilderness Area is doomed from the day it is defined as wilderness.

Wilderness has a deceptive concreteness. The difficulty with a definition of wilderness is that while the word is a noun, it acts like an adjective. The term designates a quality that produces a certain mood or feeling in a given individual and, as a consequence, may be assigned by a person to a specific place.

But there is no material that is wilderness. It exists as an idea, and an elusive one at that. One person's wilderness may be another's picnic ground. The Yukon trapper would consider a trip to northern Minnesota a return to civilization, while the person from Chicago would think a trip there would be to a frightening wilderness.

Likewise, the streets of Chicago would prove to be an incomprehensible wilderness to the native from the Brazilian rain forest plucked from his brush hut and placed in The Loop.

Time further complicates the definition. Consider that people take ski vacations on the very slopes in California where desperate pioneers resorted to cannibalism while attempting to survive in their wilderness.

A workable definition of wilderness might be this: a wilderness condition exists when a person cannot readily get the things needed, especially those needed to survive, such as food, water, shelter, oxygen, information.

William Ashworth offers an intriguing three-phase concept to explain what happens when individuals come in contact with wilderness: 1) conquer and subdue; 2) learn and understand; and 3) peace and sense of place.

My first encounters with the Trinity Alps brought out the urge to conquer, to subdue, to vanquish the wilderness. I think this was quite natural for me, seeing my life as but an extension of an immense background of collective experience of incomprehensible millennia that went before. It was in my genes.

The earliest primates, among other attributes, developed a remarkable visual ability. Sight and open panorama meant security. My earliest ancestors developed a liking for open environments where vision could assist their brains in the struggle for security and survival. In forest or jungle good eyesight didn't help much. In those places the winners were good smellers, hearers, and physically stronger animals, and humans didn't rank very high in those categories.

Once my ancestors escaped their wilderness, they hated to return to a place that neutralized their visual advantage. In fact, they burned forests whenever possible to convert them to open grassland.

Fear of night may have developed from a wilderness fear or bias. Early people could not see once the sun went down. Their visual advantage was neutralized. The discovery and use of fire was not only a breakthrough for warmth and cooking, but provided some measure of sight security as well. It's probably not possible for 20th-century people to imagine how utterly black the nights were for most of the people who have lived on this Earth. Nomads, natives, castle dwellers, even a town the size of Boston in the 1630s, had no street lights, no store lights, no automobile lights. Any light there was came from a flicker of flame.

Relying for thousands of years on vision for the survival struggle stamped a lasting bias against wilderness on the minds of my ancestors which was passed on down to me in the microscopic threads of genetic molecules. There's a living piece shared by every human being, like the starter of sourdough pancake mix that never dies and is passed along generation after generation. I share the biases of ancient ancestors just as I share a bite of pancake containing a speck of the ones eaten by my great- great-grandparents.

This ancient association between security and sight might account for the removal of trees, the clearing of land, to bring light into the dark thickets and forests. Certainly there were economic motives as well, but the wilderness, basically, was dark, gloomy, nightmarish. A person still often feels uneasy in a thick forest. Consider why even today ridgetop houses, those with the best view, command the highest real estate prices. Remnants of the primordial dread of wilderness put medieval castles on high ground.

Ashworth's concept demonstrates that if a person can get through the conquer-and-destroy aspects of phase one, they readily pass into the second phase, the learning phase. If a person stays in the wilderness long enough, they will begin to use it like a classroom, a great outdoor laboratory. They begin to live with the land as ally and not enemy.

Over the years I have found the deepest and most profound essence of the wilderness experience can be savored only when it's just me, by myself.

I was approaching middle age before I dared take to the wilderness by myself. There was always the fear of "what if." What if I got hurt, sick, snakebitten, lost, frozen, ambushed, poisoned, avalanched, mauled by a bear, burned, maimed, shot, and/or robbed? Then what would I do? Who would help me? What if I got lonesome? Besides, if I was to conquer and subdue the wilderness, there was strength in numbers.

The truth of the matter, the great "ah-ha!", came to me one morning while camped at Papoose Lake. It was one of those seemingly insignificant events in my life that upon examination and over time proved to be a revelation of the first magnitude.

There I was at Papoose Lake, cooking some scrambled eggs laced with chunks of corned beef hash on my gas stove. Fourteen miles from the trailhead, I had not seen another person in two days. I was enjoying the warmth of the rising sun on my back, the zestful smell of my breakfast sizzling in the pan, and watching the cobalt blue mirrored lake when it happened. I turned to pick up the spatula on the rock behind me. There it was! *The spatula was right where I had left it the night before.*

The realization came in a flash. I was alone. When you are alone things stay right where you put them. It couldn't have been a more powerful message if it had come from a burning bush.

When you are alone you are responsible for everything. No one moves anything unless you do. Walking alone, you don't have to explain your decisions to anyone. A fork in the trail? Take the one you want. No debate except with yourself. Where to pitch camp? Wherever you decide. When to go to sleep? When you feel like it. When to get up in the morning? Your choice. To build a fire or not? No discussion. No need to clear it with anyone but yourself.

Time spent in the wilderness is a diversion from the normal routines of your life. Spend that time alone in the wilderness and you're free from even normal social routines.

You'll see more wildlife when you are alone, hear soft and subtle sounds available only to the hiker unfettered by the noise that comes with companions. You'll cover more ground and see more details around you since your concentration is unbroken by others.

A common phenomenon reported by solo hikers is hearing human voices when there is no possibility of anyone around. I've heard them in the Alps many times. Drowsing away the afternoon in the shade or walking along the trail I swear I hear voices, but when I stop and focus they are gone. One explanation is that the water running over rocks buffeted by the wind gives the impression of babbling voices. I've never heard complete words or anything, just a conversation I can't quite make out. I've listened to the voices, but nobody ever shows up. Must be the water.

I'm reminded of the note Lewis and Clark made in their journals when they were coming up the Missouri River in 1804. They reported a booming sound, like cannons being fired far away. There was not a cloud in sight, ruling out lightning and thunder. Couldn't have been distant guns, because they were in the middle of Montana in 1804. They were as puzzled then as I am now with the voices. Seems logical that the sounds I've heard are from moving water. Big guns in the distance? Your guess is as good as anyone's.

Perhaps it's from being alone and because our brains are programmed from habit to hear familiar sounds, like voices, from random sounds. When I've been alone for a period of time in the mountains, hearing natural sounds such as insects chirping, wind in the trees, my own voice when I say something out loud, is startling in its volume. Hearing what sounded like heavy artillery in the distance may have been simply the ears of the Lewis and Clark expedition yearning for sounds familiar to their minds.

What about the safety factor of not having a companion or two while in the wilderness? Examining the records for the last twenty years of the Trinity County Sheriff's Search and Rescue Team and those of the U.S. Forest Service might surprise you. Far more people who are traveling in groups seem to get in trouble than those who are alone. In fact, all the fatalities in the last twenty years have happened to people while in a group. Perhaps it's because people alone are extra cautious, knowing they have no one to rely on should they make a mistake.

Of course, if you do choose to go it alone, safety must always be present in your mind. And the obvious rules such as leaving your plan with someone back home still apply.

Traveling with a group does not ensure your safety, either. Often it is the group mentality that forces someone to take a chance or to extend themselves beyond their ability, to do things they would never attempt if they were alone. The result has been fatal for some.

There was the young boy who died from heat exhaustion on Sawtooth Ridge. He would have never been on that trail in that condition had he been alone. And the group he was with was no help to him, since they left him alongside the trail and continued their hike, not reporting their desertion of him until more than a day later.

A young man crossing the outlet stream below Canyon Creek Lake slipped into the churning water, frigid from snow melt, and drowned when he and his pack became wedged in rocks under the surface. Most likely he would never have tried to cross the stream at that point had he been alone. And what good did the group he was with do him? It was several weeks before rescue teams were able to recover his body.

There is great satisfaction in knowing that you can take care of yourself in the wilderness. The lessons the wilderness has to teach seem endless, and probably are.

But there's still that third and final stage, the one Ashworth calls a state of peace and acceptance. The sources of energy that drive a person from wilderness conqueror to wilderness student will, given a chance, all come together in some kind of harmony.

When I climbed Sawtooth Peak in 1959, it was with an aggressive haste and wild abandon. I had "powered" up the mountain like it was a demon I needed to trample into submission. I returned 35 years later and my steps were more cautious. I realized how much more philosophical I had become. My stamina was as good as it ever was, but age had taken the aggression, replaced it with control and tempered my thoughts. There was still a thrill in the adult climb, but the reckless, hell-bent need to race to the summit had gone.

Near the summit of Sawtooth Peak

The day I climbed Sawtooth Peak as a man, all the sensations of the earlier climb returned to me. It was if I were 16 years old again. I scrambled up over the last ledge and it seemed like I had been there just a few days before.

Sitting on top of the sharp granite pinnacle, looking to the west, I saw the wild panorama of the Alps: jagged snow-streaked peaks, mountainsides of evergreens like green folded velvet dissolving into the milky softness of the late afternoon sun. There was no wind, only a deep and total silence that I've come to be quite comfortable with.

I wondered what other people had thought as they sat on this mountaintop. I wondered whether they felt as good about being here as I did. I wondered if they sensed the subtle and invisible spirit that inhabits high places.

People have taken John Muir's advice and gone to the mountains to receive their "good tidings." Returning to the wilderness has not diminished the experience.

A wind started up and chilled me in my sweat-soaked shirt. I took a last look from Sawtooth and left. I wanted to be over the boulder field before the sun went down.

I cleared the last boulders as the sun dipped behind Mount Hilton. Stars appeared. I walked into the dark forest.

We could pity the generations that will have no wilderness to experience. Or we can help make sure they do.

Appendix A

Summer 1959

FOR DIXON DOUGLAS JONES

1942-1977

"...wilder and wilder
I sang
and my loins wrinkled
like the forehead of a sage."

FIRE DANGER CRITICAL IN TRINITY *Thursday, July 23, 1959...with the fire danger on the Trinity Forest at a critical point, Fire Control Officers on the various districts are taking every precaution in case of emergency.* (The Weekly Trinity Journal)

It was the biggest fire anyone could remember in northern California. The monstrous pyrostorm smoldered and seethed for five days rendering 10,000 acres of wilderness an immediate candidate for what might be labeled Charcoal National Park.

The drift smoke filled valleys and blotted out the sun for hundreds of miles in all directions. Moving at as much as seventy miles per hour, flames evaporated hillsides and leaped across even the largest streams effortlessly. Extreme heat and gigantic masses of burning gases created whirlwinds that tore up and leveled 200-foot Douglas firs like toothpicks. Often the entire mountainside of trees spontaneously burst into flame far in advance of the actual fire. Crown fires raced through the treetops high above the ground roaring like the gears of the hubs of hell. Those who saw it would never forget the Ramshorn Fire of 1959.

The fire is burning in an area about seven miles long and three wide, moving in a south-southwest direction. Coffee Creek village was in serious danger at 5:45 p.m. Tuesday when the fire jumped the Trinity River and headed toward the community...(The Weekly Trinity Journal)

Mick looked up from a campsite miles away and saw the smoke mushrooming upwards Vesuvius-like and remarked to his buddy, Bobcat, "Geez, check it out! Looks like that picture of the H-bomb on the cover of Life."

Mick and Bobcat were camped at the edge of Little Boulder Lake fifteen miles from the nearest road and perhaps ten miles from the Ramshorn Fire battleground. Having walked and run through the previous night to be here now, they were taking it easy by the lake. Clothed only by sunshine, an inflamed July sun poured down like honey on their goose-pimpled nakedness as the boys shivered warmth back into bodies draped on solar-heated granite slabs. The swim had been frigid; the water better suited for trout than humans.

"It really was a sight to see," said one seasoned smoke-eater at the base camp Tuesday night, "the flames were whipped up on the ridge so that from here they looked a mile high! When the fire had burned over the whole mountain, the embers left lighted up at night like the lights of San Francisco..." (The Weekly Trinity Journal)

On the map it was labeled Trinity Alps Wilderness Area. No motorized vehicles allowed. There appeared to be more land and space than two boys could hope to see in a lifetime. Primitive Area. There it was, beckoning, just outside the schoolroom window where Mick and Bobcat bred visions of being wild and free Alpsmen, but were, in fact, strapped to a bewildering world of English, social studies and geometry.

"Math is a waste of time for Alpsmen," said Mick.

These two wannabe Alspmen didn't know it then, but not only was it the end of the 1950's; the summer of '59 would be the last summer in the wilderness for these two young men with uncertain fires of the future yet to burn. Just outside of town was a lusty rich, forested country with brawling rivers and tough two-fisted peaks drilling ten-thousand foot granite holes into a flawless blue sky. The boys had the dream of the mountains and they had time for the task of dreaming if only for one precious summer. The magic was still in the mountains in nineteen fifty-nine.

FOREST FIRE CHARS 10,000 ACRES *Thursday, July 30, 1959. Crews battled the blaze Saturday, Sunday and Monday with the fireline just about circling the area. Then the wind spotted the fire across Ramshorn Creek to the south and raged out of control. So far, a total of 10,000 acres have been destroyed according to the USFS headquarters. 1,180 men have been assigned to the fire working in two shifts...*(The Weekly Trinity Journal)

Plans to explore, chart, and tame the Trinity Alps fermented in the boredom of high school geometry class for the two boys. The litany of high country names crept into their speech and became household words as the theorems and axioms of ancient math were tucked away into forgotten recesses of their minds. Permutations, polyhedra, probability, and parabola were slowly squeezed out of memory by Siligo Peak, Stonehouse, Sapphire Lake, and Sawtooth Ridge.

"We'll need Spam, rice, spaghetti, Kool-Aid, Fig Newtons, pancake flour, coffee, jelly, crackers, salami, salt, bacon, matches, and our fishin' gear," said Mick.

The food went into the packs just as it came from the grocery store shelf; jelly in jars, meat in waxed paper, coffee in cans. Freeze-dried, dehydrated food was buried in the future with video games, Mastercharge, cable tv, ATMs, Velcro, email and other wonders of ages yet unknown to mid-twentieth century civilization.

"Pussies need not apply to this expedition," was Bobcat's comment as he approved the food list.

Holo-fil, goose down, Thinsulate, Ultrex, and Gor-Tex were not yet ready for humankind in 1959; nor were waterbeds, pantyhose, Monday Night Football, blow dryers, or 4X4 mini-trucks. It was still a time when a trip to the wilderness required a person to borrow equipment from a world ignorant of the special demands of unsettled lands.

"Geez, check it out! I got this six-pound kapok sleeping bag from the army-navy store for less than fifteen bucks and there ain't no bullet holes in it." Mick was showing off his score from the local surplus store, the backpacking equipment purveyor of choice in the '50s. Much of the merchandise from these stores still showed signs of the previous owners outdoor experiences in the Big One, WWII; small arms fire or deep jungle corrosion on metal parts. But Mick's sleeping bag was top-of-the-line in 1959; flannel lining featuring bears and deer leaping about in autumnal splendor, the seams bulging with the mysterious wonder material, kapok.

"Yeah, the worth of a good sleeping bag is equal to its weight," said Bobcat, hardly looking up as he rubbed industrial strength oil into the canvas of his olive-drab pup tent. "This baby'll shed water in a monsoon long as nobody touches the sidewalls during a storm."

"Whatcha doin' fer shoes?" asked Mick.

"Iron Maidens," said Bobcat, pointing to his high-top black engineer boots with the leather strap across the instep.

Mick would wear his black Red Ball tennis shoes because of their lightweight and speed. The cotton construction offered little in the way of venomous snake protection, stayed soggy wet for miles after creek crossings, acted like ice skates on high angle snow banks, but closely resembled in comfort and feel of Alpsman moccasins.

"How 'bout guns?" A real Alpsman should have a Hawken rifle like the ones that commanded a price of at least 15 plews at the trapper's annual rendezvous a century and a half earlier.

"I figure we'll take a .22 single shot rifle for the "big stuff" and for casual camp use, my Colt double action pellet pistol." Mick was not one to take the Trinity wilderness lightly.

The weeks of spring 1959 crept agonizingly toward summer. The days seemed to just dribble by. School for the boys became an ugly beast that had to be slain daily. The redbud bloomed, awed the tourists, and faded as April slowly merged into May. In geometry class Mick and Bobcat rehearsed their coming itinerary.

"Once the snow clears, we can camp in Bear Basin and then angle right up over Sawtooth Ridge and drop down Lightning Gulch until we hit Deer Creek and follow it to Mumford Meadows."

"Or we could work our way over into Elderberry Duff, Bear Wallow and the into Bear Basin. Maybe knock off Deadman's Peak, get into the meadows the second day, and ding some brook trout before dark.

Finally, just at the point when it seemed the movement of time had ceased and world no longer turned, the last school bell of the year rang. Moments later, Mick's '50 black Chevy Deluxe Coup, bloated with camping gear and soaring adolescent expectations, plowed up the dirt road to the trailhead on Ramshorn Creek. Dust billowed off the bald tires. The days of summer stretched out ahead of them in miles of unfulfilled promises. The air was hot.

"...for five days, it's been a losing battle against the blaze which exploded Saturday on the powder-dry Coffee Creek Ranger District of the Shasta-Trinity National Forest. Power in the area has been out since Sunday when the lines were destroyed. (The Weekly Trinity Journal)

"Geez! What was that?"

“Muffler fell off again," said Bobcat. The Chevy's muffler retrieved from the roadway, tossed into the back seat where it rode the rest of the way to the trailhead scorching the upholstery and filling the car interior with acrid smoke. All signs pointed to a season of fires.

Engulfed in smoke from the campfire that evening, coughing, eyes burning, stinging, Mick wheezed, "Isn't this even better than we thought it would be?"

Bobcat, shoveling in the last of his semi-cooked noodles crowned with cold tomato sauce, pine needles, fire ash, and few dead mosquitoes, nodded in agreement.

"...an hour later the fire had jumped the road twice near Coffee Creek bridge but was stopped as men poured into the area and threw up a suppression line to keep the fire from moving into the town of Coffee Creek. Residents in homes along the road were evacuated Tuesday afternoon. (The Weekly Trinity Journal)

After a sleepless night of quivering and chattering on the cold ground in his six-pound kapok sleeping bag, Mick rolled over to watch the sun creep down the tree tops, needle by needle, to the ground. The smell of warm pine needles can charge the human spirit and inspire it to great deeds. This particular morning was charged with doughballs masquerading as pancakes. Old Log Cabin syrup, poured from a metal can shaped as a replica of a log cabin, slathered the amoeba-like objects from the frying pan. The syrup exited out the chimney of the cabin-shaped container.

"Wash 'em down with coffee and Kool-Aid," suggested Mick.

"Time to kill some fish," said Bobcat as soon as what passed as breakfast was over. "Those little eight inch brookies are the best eating. You begin to taste 'em as quick as they hit the frying pan and go into their curl. Once they're crispy brown eat 'em with your fingers like corn on the cob."

The method for catching fish in a remote high mountain lake, like all rewards in the wilderness, is simple and direct.

"If ya wanna nail big brookies, ya sink and egg to the bottom and bring'er up slowly."

Mick watched as Bobcat took a single, pale yellow salmon egg from the Tyee bottle and impaled it on a gold barbed hook. Extreme care as taken not to puncture the "eye" of the salmon egg. About eighteen inches above the hook he pinched on a double spitshot sinker. Tossing it all out into the lake in a single smooth heave, he settled himself down on a rock projection next to the water and waited.

"Do it this way or you don't catch fish in the Trinity Alps," he said.

"You got the bottle. Where do I carry the salmon eggs?" asked Mick.

"Take a few and hold'em in yer mouth, right between your cheek and gum. Be careful not to mash'em, they're kinda salty tastin'."

The salmon eggs in Mick's mouth were not unpleasant tasting. He wondered if they tasted the same to the fish. The Tyee brand of salmon eggs, at 59 cents a bottle, were the best money could buy and well worth it.

Summer days slipped through the boys' hands and passed beneath their feet as they walked the trails. The horizon receded. They counted 57 lakes on their map and were determined to touch each one. July was almost over before the mountains began to feel a little more friendly, the valleys less mysterious and dark. Nights became a less lonely and a little less cold. The wilderness started to feel, as Bobcat put it, "like home."

"We have no idea how many men are on the fire", said McCaffery, Tuesday afternoon. "We still have lumber crews from Covington Mill, Trinity Lakes Mill, Fall River Mill, 200 Zuni Indians from New Mexico, (hired by the Forest Service as professional firefighters), volunteers and recruits coming in by bus and plane, convicts from Soledad, San Quentin, and Folsom...We've been working around the clock and are getting down to a two shift deal now." (The Weekly Trinity Journal)

It was a warm evening, almost dark, when the boys reached the upper meadow along Ramshorn Creek. They prepared a camp back among the aspen trees a hundred yards or so from the stream.

"Won't be able to sleep if we're too close to that noisy creek," was Bobcat's thought.

They built a fire ring of rocks and lit a small cooking fire.

"We need to get over to the creek and get some water before it gets any darker," said Mick.

The small fire was left alone; a solitary flicker obscured by trees in the gathering gloom of evening.

There was some horseplay at the creek; small sticks thrown into the current became battleships to be blown out of the water with shots from the .22 rifles. A few rocks were heaved into a swampy area with effect of absolute silence for a moment followed by a gradual increase in the decibel level of the tens of thousands frogs gathered together for an evening of croaking.

"Everyday, it's a gettin' closer, going faster than a roller coaster.."

Singing, the boys returned to the campsite twenty minutes later, laden with filled water containers. It was Mick who first noticed the orange glow beyond the ridge.

"Looks like maybe a UFO has landed up there."

Curious, they scrambled up to a rock outcropping for a better view of the mysterious light. Finally able to see over the ridge, what they saw was stunning. They were in the wilderness and the canyons were on fire!

As the boys watched, a tossing, blinding tempest of flame surged up the adjacent hillside, surmounted it, and momentarily disappeared in the canyon beyond before bursting into view again on a farther hillside higher and farther up the canyon. Crimson spirals of sparks swirled erratically in all directions starting new webs of red lava-like streams climbing the side draws. Away across the canyon the granite crags were lit in a ruddy glare, and the night sky above was a reflected blast furnace. There was no time to think, barely time to run.

"Grab what you can," shouted Mick, "we gotta get outta here...fast!"

The two Alpsmen flew down the canyon, seeming to only touch the ground every few strides. It was totally dark by now. Bathed in sweat and panic, the two struggled up a side canyon bent on getting across the divide into another drainage as quickly as possible. Once when they stopped, panting and dropping to their knees, they could hear a low roaring hum back from the way they had come. Glancing in that direction, a crimson glow could be seen back down Ramshorn Creek. Even in the cooling darkness of night the fire was gaining momentum.

Kneeling in the blackness to catch his breath, sweat dripped from his nose to his chin, Mick felt his heart pounding inside his chest. The night air stung his nostrils as he sucked in air.

"We get over to Little Boulder Lake, we'll be o.k.," said Mick.

"We thought we had it until the hard wind hit Monday night, actually early Tuesday morning. It really blew up. Control is rough in a country where cats can hardly be worked." (The Weekly Trinity Journal)

It was midmorning the next day when they saw the mushroom shaped cloud of smoke from several miles away. A sinister wind had sprung up in the predawn hours as they staggered down to the shore of Little Boulder Lake. They had stumbled and struggled all night long to get as far away from Ramshorn Creek as possible. Now, as the day warmed, the fire was ripping in a dozens of canyons and ridges. It was "starting to cook", as firefighters say.

The two Alpsmen shivered as much from the chill from their swim in the lake as from the thrill of excitement seeing the enormous, destructive force of a major forest fire from their secure perch on the lakeshore boulders. Security was a wilderness lake in 1959. The fire would rage for many days.

Bobcat and Mick were not nearly as secure as they thought. Never again in their lives would they be granted an entire summer to roam carefree and explore the world at will. There was no way of knowing it then, but soon their campsites would be in the wilderness of Southeast Asia. M-l rifles would replace their fishing poles; combat boots instead of Red Ball tennis shoes.

Even if it would have been possible to have another summer in the wilderness of the Trinity Alps, it would never the same. The fire damage would scar the land for decades.

"Damages to virgin timber in the Ramshorn Burn is estimated at $1,900,000 in timber and "future growth loss." Cost of fighting the fire has been $200,000 and total cost will probably add up to $350,000 according to the USFS. The fire was started by a smoker, presumed a fisherman or camper on Ramshorn Creek. 'A lot of money for one cigarette tossed away,' said one ranger." (The Weekly Trinity Journal)

In the end it was not the fire that directly destroyed the wilderness. Fire is a natural force that wilderness can recover from. The forest can handle fire. What it couldn't handle was the roads probing deeper and deeper into the interior. “Salvage” logging and clear cuts snuffed out any chance the forest would recover.

Mick died suddenly while jogging years later and never did get back to the Alps. Sometimes Bobcat wished he hadn't. Once he stopped at a new store that had popped up near the old trailhead where he had begun so many wilderness trips years before. He asked the old man by the cash register if there might be some decent fishing along Ramshorn Creek.

"You kiddin? They've logged the shit out of that place since 1959!"

Later that same day, Bobcat noticed that the trailhead didn't look a lot different. He hiked alone up toward Little Boulder Lake. Coming into the basin holding the lake, he had no trouble picturing the thin blue smoke of the campfire curling up in a flat ribbon through the trees over three decades ago. Walking a few miles without a trail, he stopped on a low outcropping of rock and paused.

The air was very still. There came a sound of labored breathing down the canyon and the clatter of loose rock underfoot. Bobcat was a little surprised to see two ragged kids sweating and straining under homemade pack frames toiling up the creekbed. They were talking and laughing. One boy was wearing black Red Ball tennis shoes and briefly made eye contact with him. There seemed to be a flicker of recognition, but they quickly passed on up the creek and out of sight. Both seemed so young and unconcerned.

BIBLIOGRAPHY

Bernstein, Art, 1993, *Best Hikes of the Trinity Alps*, Mountain N'Air, La Crescenta, CA 92124.

Cox, Issac, 1858, *The annals of Trinity County*, reprinted by John Henry Nash, University of Oregon, Eugene, Oregon, 1940.

Diller, J.S., 1902, *Topographic Development of the Klamath Mountains,* U.S. Geological Survey Bulletin #196.

Eastwood, Alice, 1902, *From Redding to the Snowclad Peaks of Trinity County,* Sierra Club Bulletin 4:39-58.

Ferlatte, W.J., *A Flora of the Trinity Alps of Northern California*, 1974, University of California Press.

Gass, C.L., 1976, *Regulation of Food Supply by Feeding Territoriality in the Rufous Hummingbird*, Canadian Journal of Zoology, V.54, 12:2046-2054.

Hershey, O.H., *Ancient Alpine Glaciers of the Sierra Costa Mountains in California,* Journal of Geology, 1900, V.8:42-57.

Hershey, O.H., *Some Evidence of Two Glacial Stages in the Klamath Mountains of California,* 1903, V.9:155-165.

Hinds, N.E.A., *Geologic Formations of the Redding-Weaverville District, Northern California,* California Journal of Mines and Geology, 1933: 76-122.

Jones, Alice Goen, *Flowers and Trees of the Trinity Alps*, 1986, Trinity County Historical Society, Weaverville, California.

Jorstad, W.O. "George", *Behind the Wild River.* 1995, Trinity, Lewiston, California.

Lipman, P.W., 1962, *Geology of the Southwestern Trinity Alps, Northern California*, Stanford University Ph.D. thesis, University Microfilms, Inc, Ann Arbor, Michigan.

Linkhart, Luther and White, Michael, *The Trinity Alps: A hiking and backpacking guide,* 1994, Wilderness Press, Berkeley, CA 94704.

Moss, Wayne F., *The Know-It-All Guide to the Trinity Alps,* 1981, Mossart, Weaverville, California.

Sharp, R.P., 1960, *Pleistocene Glaciation in the Trinity Alps of Northern California,* American Journal of Science, V. 258, #5:305-340.

Williamson, Frank A., 1933, *The Unknown Alps of the Salmon River*, Sierra Club Bulletin, #11.

Index

-V-

-W-

-X-

-Y-

-Z-

Notes

Notes

Trinity Alps Regions

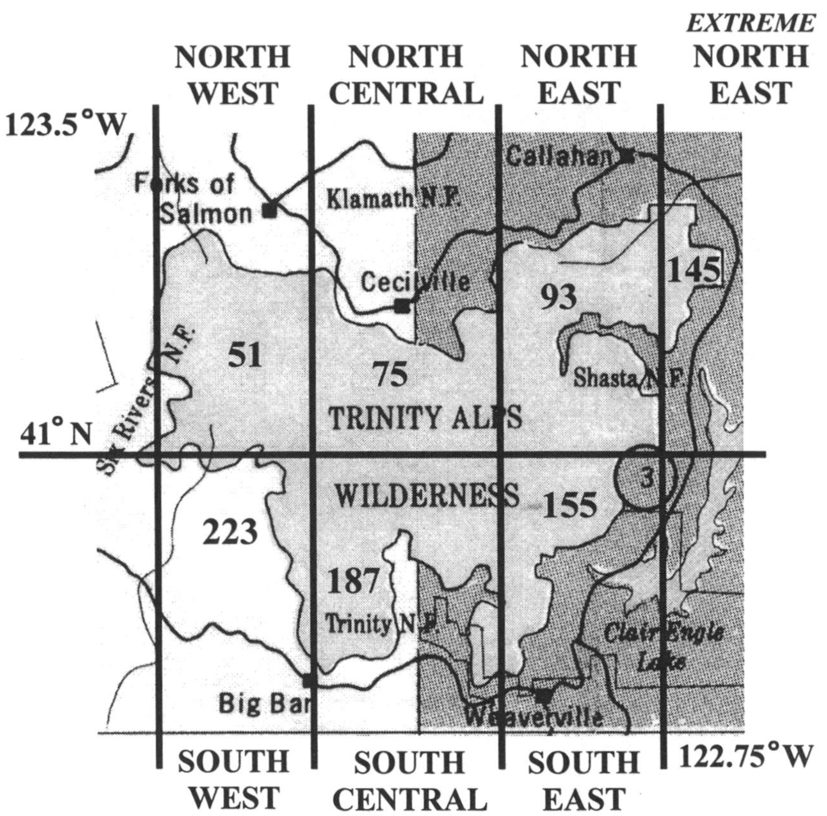

MAP PAGE NUMBER LISTED IN BOLD FOR EACH REGION